NEW WORLD NEW MIND

NEW WORLD

MOVING
TOWARD
CONSCIOUS
EVOLUTION

NEW MIND

Robert Ornstein

Paul Ehrlich

Doubleday

NEW YORK LONDON TORONTO SYDNEY AUCKLAND

Published by Doubleday, a division of
Bantam Doubleday Dell Publishing Group, Inc.,
666 Fifth Avenue, New York, New York 10103

DOUBLEDAY and the portrayal of an anchor with a dolphin
are trademarks of Doubleday, a division of
Bantam Doubleday Dell Publishing Group, Inc.

Library of Congress Cataloging-in-Publication Data

Ehrlich, Paul R.
    New world new mind/Paul Ehrlich, Robert Ornstein.—1st ed.
       p.   cm.
    Bibliography: p.
    Includes index.
       1. Human ecology.   2. Environmental policy.   3. Human evolution.
I. Ornstein, Robert Evan.   II. Title.
GF50.E34   1989   87-36605
304.2—dc19

ISBN 0-385-23940-8

FOR SALLY AND ANNE

Acknowledgments

WE WOULD LIKE to thank Ginger Barber, D. Loy Bilder-back (Department of History, Fresno State University), Ann Bowcock (Department of Genetics, Stanford University Medical School), Brent Danninger (Legal Economic Evaluations), Jared M. Diamond (Department of Physiology, UCLA School of Medicine), John P. Holdren (Energy and Resources Group, University of California, Berkeley), Terry Leighton (Department of Microbiology, University of California, Berkeley), Christina Lepnis (Stanford University), Mary Ann Mason (Lone Mountain College), Evan Neilsen (Law Offices of George Nowell), David Widdicombe (Queens Counsel, London), and Darryl Wheye (Menlo Park, California) for reading and commenting on the manuscript.

Pat Brown, Shane DeHaven, Carol Holland, Pam Nakaso, and Steve Masley helped with various aspects of preparation of the manuscript. The staff of Stanford's Falconer Biology Library skill-fully tracked down several obscure references. Christina Lepnis contributed valuable research.

We are especially grateful to our wives, Anne Ehrlich and Sally Mallam, who not only worked diligently on the manuscript, but also supplied other assistance essential to maintaining our sanity while we completed it.

Contents

NEW WORLD NEW MIND

1

THE THREAT
WITHIN THE TRIUMPH

IT ALL SEEMS to be happening at once. A small group of terrorists murder a few Americans far away—and fear of getting murdered changes the traveling habits of millions. But Americans continue to slaughter more people *each day* with handguns than all the people the terrorists have killed up to the writing of this book. No one does anything about it.

People swamp AIDS testing centers, desperate and anxious to know if they are carrying the virus. If they have it, it will likely kill them. Can society even care for AIDS victims?

Meanwhile populations explode, stockpiles of nuclear weapons grow, budget deficits mount, our education becomes more and more obsolete, and the environment—on which our very existence depends—deteriorates. But most people's attention is fixed upon eye-catching "images," such as the taking of the Iran hostages, horrible murders, airplane crashes, changes in stock prices, and football scores. Cancer terrifies us, yet we keep on smoking. Oliver North testifies that he lied—yet his good looks and smooth talk lead many people to propose that he run for President.

And the President operates the same way. Ronald Reagan, by his own admission, perverted an important U.S. global policy because *his* mind was similarly fixed on another set of hostages. He said, "I let my preoccupation with the hostages intrude into areas where it didn't belong. *The image, the reality of Americans in chains, deprived of their freedom and families so far from home, burdened my thoughts.* And this was a mistake." [italics ours]

Why does the growing budget deficit attract relatively little attention while the comparatively meaningless stock market "crash" makes headlines? Why do many popular writers yearn for a return to an education suitable for Oxford men before World War I, when the world has changed in critical ways to a greater extent since World War II than it changed between the birth of Christ and that war? Why do the numbers of nuclear weapons expand astronomically but largely unheralded, while a small girl trapped in a well commands the front pages? Why do we collectively spend billions on medical care while neglecting the simple preventative actions that, if we took them, would save many times the lives?

We believe it is no accident.

All these things are happening now, and are happening all at once, in part because *the human mental system is failing to comprehend the modern world.* So events will, in our opinion, continue to be out of control until people realize how selectively the environment impresses the human mind and how our comprehension is determined by the biological and cultural history of humanity. These unnoticed yet fundamental connections to our past, and how we can retrain ourselves for a "new world" of the future, one filled with unprecedented threats, are what this book is about.

We don't perceive the world as it is, because our nervous system evolved to select only a small extract of reality and to ignore the rest. We never experience *exactly* the same situation twice, so it would be uneconomical to take in every occurrence. Instead of conveying everything about the world, our nervous system is "impressed" only by *dramatic changes*. This internal spotlight makes us sensitive to the beginnings and endings of almost every event more than the changes, whether gigantic or tiny, in the middle.

The perception of dramatic changes begins deep within the nervous system, amid simple sensing such as seeing light. Put a three-way bulb (50-100-150 watts) in a lamp in a dark room. Turn on the lamp: the difference between darkness and the 50-watt illumination is seen as great; but the increase from 50 to 100 and from 100 to 150 seems like almost nothing. Although the change in the physical stimulus is exactly the same, you notice it less and less as each 50 watts are added. Turn off the lamp, even from the 50-watt setting, however, and you feel it immediately! We notice the beginning and the end and overlook the greater changes in the middle.

You might be thinking that this analysis of lamps and sensing light is very far removed from the major dilemmas of our current world. But our point is that many of the predicaments of our society come about from the way people respond to, simplify, and, ultimately, "caricature" reality in their minds. Our caricature emphasizes the dramatic and distinctive features of events, in the same way as a cartoon caricature of a politician might exaggerate Lyndon Johnson's outsize ears, Richard Nixon's ski-jump nose, Mikhail Gorbachev's forehead birthmark.

This simplified focus on the dramatic is now out of date in complex modern life; the same routines of internal analysis that originally developed to signal abrupt physical changes in the old world are now pressed into service to perceive and decide about unprecedented dangers in the new. Scarce and unusual items, be they a headline news event, a one-day dress sale, or a chance for peace, come into the mind through the same old avenues and are filtered and judged in the same old way.

This mismatched judgment happens in the most basic as well as the most momentous situations. In psychology experiments, a word at the beginning of a list heard once is recalled 70 percent of the time, words in the middle less than 20 percent, and words at the end almost 100 percent. In 1980, presidential candidate Ronald Reagan illustrated these principles. He said: "Politics is just like show business. You need a big opening. Then you coast for a while. Then you need a big finish." Reagan is renowned for his political savvy.

The same sensitivity to sharp changes gets called into play in judging the most important, life-or-death essentials. Consider this: the first atomic bombs were kept secret and then were unveiled suddenly. The mushroom clouds over Hiroshima and Nagasaki, and the sudden vast destruction they caused signaled a sharp change in the world. The new threat was readily noticed and properly feared.

But two responses indicate that humanity did not perceive this important change in the world correctly. First, that atomic explosion on Hiroshima made a *far greater impression* than the much greater destruction and death visited upon Tokyo by conventional incendiary bombs, since burning cities seen from the air (in newsreels) had by then become routine and so were ignored.

And, second, since the first frightening explosions, nuclear weapons have accumulated gradually until they now number in the *tens of thousands,* and most of them are ten to a hundred times more powerful than those that devastated Hiroshima and Nagasaki. Our minds are inhibited in noticing the threat; the continuing accumulation of gigantic arsenals doesn't get the same attention as the first weapons. Only public relations events, new "beginnings" like the nuclear winter announcement, or the showing of the TV film *The Day After,* can reattract old minds—and then only temporarily until habituation sets in again.

The human nervous system, well matched to a world in which small, sharp changes were important but large gradual ones were not, is inadequate to keep attention focused on this most ominous nuclear trend. Our nervous system and our world are *mismatched* now. The original image of a single nuclear detonation signaled an awesome threat. Graphs and tables describing the sizes of arsenals fail to produce a comparably realistic understanding; occasional news events have only temporary effects on most people. Our response to nuclear armaments has followed the Reagan caricature. The big opening was Hiroshima; now we're coasting; with lots of luck we may avoid the big finish.

A set of hydrogen bombs joined to an intercontinental ballistic missile is one of the ultimate triumphs of biological and cultural evolution. Think of it: humanity, whose own origins were as a few relatively large molecules in a tiny droplet in a primitive sea, has now itself developed the power to annihilate much of life on Earth.

But why? Why have we done it? Why, on a planet that has an exploding population, a deteriorating environment, and massive social problems, has the only genuinely creative species invested so much time, energy, and genius in building arsenals that can only be used to destroy itself?

Why has humanity not redirected its efforts instead into seeking ways for people to live together without conflict and to limiting the size of its population so that everyone can lead a meaningful life? Why hasn't humanity tried vigorously to preserve the earth that people and all living species depend upon?

The answers to these kinds of questions are not simple. The dilemmas will not be "solved" by the next political campaign, government program, educational critique, or international conference. They are to no small degree problems of how we perceive our environment and ourselves.

The problem has much deeper roots than most people envision. To trace its history will take us into the world in which our species evolved, into the world that made us. That world has produced in us certain ways of interpreting our surroundings, ways that once enhanced our survival. But these "old ways" are not necessarily adaptive in a world that is utterly different from the one in which our ancestors lived.

Some scientists recognized our evolutionary mismatch decades ago, but their insight has had as yet little effect. On May 23, 1946, Albert Einstein sent a telegram to President Roosevelt on behalf of the Emergency Committee of Atomic Scientists saying, in reference to nuclear explosions, "The unleashed power of the atom has changed everything save our modes of thinking, and thus we drift towards unparalleled catastrophe." The power of human destructiveness is far greater forty years after the Hiroshima and Nagasaki explosions that prompted Einstein's statement, yet human thought processes still remain largely unchanged.

The weapons in the United States and Soviet strategic arsenals now contain enough explosive power that, if packaged as Hiroshima-sized bombs, they could blow up one Hiroshima *each hour* for more than a lifetime (seventy-eight years)!

To recognize how extraordinary human history is, we must reset our idea of time: in evolutionary time, a million years is not very much. Given the time scale of the history of the Earth, which condensed from cosmic gases and dust about 4.6 billion years ago, humanity has evolved and multiplied with unprecedented speed. In only a few million years human beings have spread from the African plains to inhabit every part of the planet. Humanity has grown from scattered groups of a few thousand to a mob of over 5 billion.

Suppose Earth's history were charted on a single year's calendar, with midnight January 1 representing the origin of the Earth and midnight December 31 the present. Then each day of Earth's "year" would represent 12 million years of actual history. On that scale, the first form of life, a simple bacterium, would arise sometime in February. More complex life-forms, however, come much later; the first fishes appear about November 20. The dinosaurs arrive around December 10 and disappear on Christmas Day. The first of our ancestors recognizable as human would not show up until the *afternoon of December 31*. *Homo sapiens*—our species—would emerge at about 11:45 P.M. All that has happened in recorded history would occur in the final *minute* of the year.

It's been a long evolutionary climb, one taking several billion years, from our evolutionary origins in the sea to our ability to make and deliver hydrogen bombs.

The mental machinery of human beings developed almost entirely before that fateful final "minute." And that, we maintain, is what makes it extremely difficult for us to diagnose our major problems, let alone to solve them. It is still possible, however, to change the way we perceive the world, to change the way that humanity thinks, and thus to survive.

Hundreds of thousands or millions of years ago, our ancestors' survival depended in large part on the ability to respond quickly to threats that were immediate, personal, and palpable: threats like the sudden crack of a branch as it is about to give way or the roar of a flash flood racing down a narrow valley. Threats like the darkening of the entrance to the cavern as a giant cave bear enters. Threats like lightning, threats like a thrown spear.

Those are not threats generated by complex technological devices accumulated over decades by unknown people half a world away. Those are not threats like the slow atmospheric buildup of carbon dioxide from auto exhausts, power plants and deforestation; not threats like the gradual depletion of the ozone layer; not threats like the growing number of AIDS victims.

In this book we'll say a great deal about threats—the dangers to us, to our civilization, to the very capacity of the earth to support human life—that exist because we have changed the world so completely. We'll concentrate on the difficulties our minds have in interpreting and even perceiving the new kinds of threats and responding appropriately to them.

In our view, there are several parts to the human quandary:

• The world that made us is now gone, and the world we made is a new world, one that we have developed little capacity to comprehend.

The old world for which our perceptual systems were "designed" was one where the overall environment was a relatively stable, limited one in which threats were signaled by short-term changes and action was usually required immediately. Consider the branch-flood-bear kinds of threats that our human progenitors faced over

millions of years of evolutionary history. Apes, australopithecines
(our first upright ancestors), early human hunters and gatherers,
and the inhabitants of early civilizations, like other animals, had
evolved quick reflexes to deal adequately with such threats.

The benefits of having evolved "quick reflexes" also accrue today;
in modern life we also must often react quickly. On hearing a
cracking sound from our chair, we are instantaneously apprehensive
and ready to act. If a child lurches into the street ahead of our car,
we hit the brakes before even thinking about it. If we're not half-
witted, thunderclaps over the golf course tell us to put the clubs
away quickly and retreat to the clubhouse for a drink. An unexpected intruder into our home arouses an automatic series of responses that we interpret as fear and a physical necessity to fight or
flee. These are all reactions that would serve us well against bear,
burglar, breaking branch, or downpour.

· All nonhuman species evolved to fit into their physical habitats,
and people originally evolved to do this as well. Human beings,
however, have changed the world more in the last ten thousand
years than their ancestors did in the preceding 4 million. Much
more than any other species, we have turned the tables on the
physical environment and made it change to fit *us*. Clothing, fire,
dwellings, and agriculture all enabled people to live where none
could before. Modern human beings have left their evolutionary
home in subtropical Africa to live all over the earth, in the freezing
winters of Alaska as well as in the scorching deserts of the Middle
East. More importantly, human beings have built entirely *new environments:* farms, villages, towns, crowded cities, ocean liners, even
underwater dwellings, and more. Human beings can even live for
brief periods away from earth itself.

· The human experience has been one of expanding creations
and adaptations. This cyclic pattern spooled us, in an evolutionary
instant, from small groups of hunters and gatherers into a complex
civilization. Agriculture led to the construction of cities and the
population explosion. Cities led to epidemics of the diseases of
crowding and to large-scale warfare. Public health measures led to
further increases in population and then, by permitting people to

live longer, to an increase in cancer and heart diseases. Cities also led to universities and the uncovering of many secrets of the universe. And uncovering secrets of the universe led to Hiroshima and Chernobyl.

And the pace of change itself becomes ever faster. Next month the world population will *increase* by more than the number of human beings that lived on the planet 100,000 years ago, a time when evolution had already produced a human brain almost indistinguishable from today's model. In the next 4 years alone more people will be added to the Earth than made up the entire population living at the time of Christ. It is difficult to comprehend this kind of world, and most people, too many, have been unable to do so. Human inventiveness has created problems because *human judgment and humanity's ability to deal with the consequences of its creations lags behind its ability to create.*

· There is now a mismatch between the human mind and the world people inhabit. The mismatch interferes with the relationships of human beings with each other and with their environments. Our species did not evolve to comprehend the problems associated with gigantic numbers of people—yet 5 *billion* human beings now occupy the Earth.

Human beings, like all other organisms, have to adapt to the environments in which they live. For most of the history of life our ancestors evolved biologically, as do all living things. (Biological evolution consists of changes in the information encoded in our genes. It typically operates over thousands of generations.) Then, for the relatively brief period of human prehistory and history—a few million years—adaptation took place primarily by means of cultural change: the development of language and tools; the invention of agriculture, cities, industry, and high technology.

Cultural evolution can be much more rapid than biological, for it involves alterations of information stored in minds or in books, tools, art, and other artifacts of societies. Cultural evolution can make significant changes in a matter of decades or less. But the rapid changes human beings are making in the world now have made even the pace of most cultural evolution far too slow.

As a result we are losing control of our future. The serious and dangerous mismatch is this: civilization is threatened by changes taking place over years and decades, but changes over a few years or decades are too *slow* for us to perceive readily. That is a time scale too leisurely for a nervous system attuned to bears, branches, burglars, and downpours. At the same time the changes are much too *rapid* to allow biological or cultural evolutionary processes to adapt people to them. *We are out of joint with the times,* our times.

· The rate of change in the world around us is increasing. Humanity is refashioning the world so quickly now that each *decade's* environment differs dramatically from that of the last. Each triumph of technology contains new kinds of threats. With the advent of television and other modern communications, we can even feel threatened by events, such as terrorist acts, occurring thousands of miles away.

The physiological tendency is to respond to them immediately, as if they were local emergencies, while at the same time we ignore some occurrences such as the gradual increase in homeless people or thinning of the ozone layer, that really are serious threats to us or our neighbors. Thus our old mental system struggles and often fails to distinguish the relevant from the trivial, the local from the distant, just as the ability to make such distinctions is becoming increasingly crucial.

· The human mental "hardware"—our senses and brains—is effectively fixed. That hardware equips us with what we call the old mind. Although we are evolving, our mental machinery will not change biologically in time to help us solve our problems. *The same mental routines that originally signaled abrupt physical changes in the old world are now pressed into service to perceive and decide about unprecedented dangers in the new.*

In saying this we don't mean to downgrade our accomplishments; indeed it is human inventiveness that causes our major dilemma. Our minds now conquer challenges and tasks that appear to have no parallels in our evolutionary past; we read and write, learn more than one spoken language, use word processors, and design and fly aircraft. But none of these tasks represents a break with the standard animal pattern of planning to reach short-term goals. Many of our highest achievements represent, then, a *refinement* of the old mind, not a new kind of perception. They cause significant changes in our environment decade by decade, but they are generally responses to perceived immediate needs, not to changes happening over decades. We cleverly develop more fuel-efficient cars when gasoline prices suddenly rise. When they drop, we relax fuel-efficiency standards, even though careful analysis indicates that much higher gasoline prices are a near certainty in coming decades.

Like those of other animals, our brains evolved to understand only a small portion of the world, the portion that most affects our capacity to survive and reproduce. Each animal, whether a bee, butterfly, frog, chimp, or human being, lives within its own "small world," which is a mere caricature of the outside world. This simple caricature of the environment, as we shall see, sufficed for most organisms in most environments, for most people throughout history; and it still works for many people. But it is fatally obsolete in a world where much more explosive power can now be carried in *one* nuclear submarine than has been detonated in all wars so far.

To retrain ourselves requires a radical shift in our normal way of perceiving ourselves and our environment: we have to look at ourselves in the long view and understand an evolutionary history of millions of years rather than the fleeting "history" that is taught. We need to be "literate" in entirely new disciplines, such as probability theory and the structure of thought, rather than just learning more about the sequences of English monarchs.

We are writing this book in an effort to help decision makers, educators, physicians, businessmen, and concerned citizens to change their "minds"—not in the conventional sense, but rather to change the way they make decisions. We don't think there is any panacea for all the problems of society; nothing simple that we can do right now is guaranteed to prevent a nuclear war or avoid the next plague. Everything, unfortunately, cannot be solved by one book! But we do think that if people understood the fundamental roots of our many problems, they might begin to change in a direction that could secure the human future.

Today's situation is unprecedented, but the human situation has often been unprecedented. In part, successfully facing the unprecedented has distinguished human beings from other forms of life. Since they spread out of Africa, people have always created new environments for themselves; they have always had to adapt to new and unexplored territory.

There is a difference now, though. At no previous time have people had the capacity to destroy their civilization in a few hours and to ruin much of the planet's life-support systems in the process. And never before has a species been engaged, as are we, in the process of destroying those systems wholesale in a "gradual" manner that could complete the job in less than a century.

But fortunately there is still time to change. Scientific evidence developed over the past three decades illuminates many aspects of the nature of both the human mind and the human predicament, and points the way to the changes needed. This evidence is drawn from many disciplines, including evolutionary biology, neuroscience, cognitive science, climatology, and geochemistry.

We believe that the only permanent means of resolving the paradox that our minds are both our curse and our potential salvation is through conscious change. Our biological evolution, including the physical evolution of our brains, is much, much too slow to help. And the undirected evolution of our culture, in view of the demands being placed on it, is still too sluggish and often inappropriate. Both biological and cultural evolution are inadequate to adapt us to the environments we are creating.

The time has come to take our own evolution into our hands and create a *new* evolutionary process, a process of conscious evolution. The human predicament requires a different kind of education and training to detect threats that materialize not in instants but in years or decades—we need to develop "slow reflexes" to supplement the quick ones. We need to replace our old minds with new ones.

It will not be nearly as exciting as fighting a bear or running away, not a simple speedy solution that can be summed up in a slogan. The remedy will demand a sustained, persistent, and complex effort. We need to learn to perceive and respond to the slow changes in the size of human populations, the increasing extinction of other species, and the proliferation of nuclear weapons. These and other such gradual alterations of our world are threats much more dangerous than hostages, mass murderers, lightning bolts, and drunken drivers.

Section One

THE WORLD THAT MADE US AND THE WORLD WE MADE

2

THE WORLD THAT MADE US

IF WE WANT to understand the biological and cultural factors that shape the human worldview, we need to look backward in time and understand why evolution favored ancestors with limited perceptions and quick reflexes. Then we will see why it is vital now to expand our perceptions and add "slow reflexes" to our behavioral repertoire. Perhaps most difficult of all, we must learn when to call on the quick reflexes and when to rely on the slow ones.

Expanded perceptions and slow reflexes will have to be added to our brains, brains that are built on the basic ground plan of those found in other vertebrates (animals with backbones). That vertebrate brain and its attendant mental structure evolved to confront short-term phenomena.

The human brain's physical structure is based on that of early primates. In fact the entire brain of a modern tarsier—a large-eyed, insect-eating distant cousin of ours from the East Indies—is quite similar to the primitive brain centers of a human being. Fifty million years ago (four "days" in the past on our year-long time scale of Earth history), our tarsierlike ancestors had brain structures that were evolutionary modifications of those of lower vertebrates. The earliest fishes had (and modern fishes still have) a brain stem, limbic system, and cortex, as do human beings. All vertebrates, indeed all of our ancestors even back to very primitive single-celled animals, had sensory and coordinating systems tuned to react to the transitory.

That is what was necessary for survival. For those ancestors, the transitory was pretty much all there was, or at least it was all they could react to. A single-celled animal either bumps into its food or it doesn't; a fish detects the color pattern of a potential mate and approaches it or it doesn't reproduce; an ape hears or smells a leopard or it dies. Nonhuman animals today, for the most part, live for the moment or die in a moment. Their small worlds appear to them (as far as we can tell) as a series of caricatures. Each caricature replaces the one that preceded it.

A caricature simplifies reality so that much of the environment is not registered on the organism's sensory system. Like the political cartoonist's caricature of a president's face, only a few aspects of reality are emphasized. An amoeba can detect differences between light and dark and can tell from its touch and chemical senses when it has found a food particle. But it is not only utterly unaware of the microscope that makes it visible to a human observer, it is also unaware of that observer.

Evolution has not provided nonhuman animals with much of a capacity to contemplate past or future environments or to wonder about the completeness of their worldviews. Why should it, since neither activity could help in their main enterprises, survival and reproduction? Even our closest evolutionary relatives, the great apes, have no capacity to respond consciously to long-term trends.

Why should that matter? It matters because for billions of years of evolution, our ancestors were in situations in which extreme caricatures sufficed for survival. In order to understand our present limitations, we have to understand their origins. Evolution is frugal; it would never favor organisms that invested energy in sensory frills if that same energy could be used to enhance reproduction.

A limited ability to sense the environment has been built into all animals by eons of natural selection. *All* sensory systems filter information from the outside world, their environments—and the human sensory system is no exception. We, too, live in a world of caricatures. You, for example, are unable to see patterns of ultraviolet (UV) light that are quite visible to butterflies searching for nectar. You don't spend any time sipping nectar from flowers, so evolution has not provided you with the capacity to see the UV designs on petals that guide insects to that sugary delight. You cannot hear the sound of a dog whistle or, like a bloodhound, smell the scent of an escaping prisoner. And you can't perceive certain novel hazards that exist today. The radiation from Chernobyl is real enough to kill you, but you cannot sense it.

Nevertheless, biological evolution did its job well. It adapted our ancestors to their environments and, in that process, shaped us into rather special creatures. To understand our special physical and behavioral characteristics, let's take a brief look at the recent chapters in the story of human evolution.

Many of the most striking features of humanity seem to trace back to a period when our forebears lived in trees. Shocking as it may be to our sensibilities, that period was rather recent—it happened only about one hundredth of the way back to the origin of life.

Duke University primatologist Elwyn Simons discovered the fossil remains of small tree-dwelling primates, named *Aegyptopithecus zeuxis,* in northern Africa. Several well-preserved skulls of this creature, which was about the size of a house cat, have now been uncovered. Apparently this "Ape of Egypt," which lived some 32 million years ago, was an arboreal fruit eater. It dwelled in the relatively moist forests that once grew in what is now the Sahara Desert. It had a relatively large brain and, Simons conjectures, lived in male-dominated groups. And it appears to have been a direct ancestor of ours or at least a close cousin of our forebears.

About 20 million years ago (two days ago in Earth's "year"), another fruit-eating ancestor or near-ancestor, called *Proconsul,* was hanging around in the forests of East Africa. Although its feet and shoulders resembled a chimp's, its wrists resembled those of monkeys, and its lower back that of a gibbon. Whether either *Aegyptopithecus* or *Proconsul* was a direct ancestor of *Homo sapiens* is beside the point. Both typify the *kinds* of animals that were our ancestors in the middle years of the Age of Mammals. Our progenitors were almost certainly already swinging from limb to limb when the mammalian fauna of earth was taking on its modern form, 30 to 40 million years or so after the dinosaurs disappeared.

We can still see traces of our ancestors' sojourn in the trees. They lived high above the ground, and swinging and jumping from branch to branch is risky, especially for large animals. Unlike very small animals such as mice, large ones can be killed by long falls. There must have been substantial evolutionary pressure for developing good eyesight and excellent depth perception, and less for maintaining a superlative sense of smell. Odors disperse easily high in the treetops, and a thin branch tends to smell pretty much like a thick one (or the tree trunk). Therefore using smell to pinpoint a place to leap to when you are 100 feet off the ground is not a recipe for living to a ripe old age. "Branch sniffers" would not have had many of their genes represented in the next generation.

Successful reproduction, passing on one's own kind of genetic material, is what natural selection, the creative force in evolution, is all about. The genes of the next generation are of those individuals that survived and reproduced. That's why our ancestors' time in the trees is so consequential to our story today. Arboreal primates with good eyesight mated with each other and raised their young in the branches high above the shattered bodies of those who tried in vain to detect the next branch by smell.

Arboreal life probably also led to the eventual movement of human eyes, through a long process of evolution, to the front of the head, so that vision from the two eyes overlapped. That overlapping vision enabled our ancestors to judge the distance between branches and to spot tasty insects that could be snatched from twigs. This in turn could have led to a shorter snout and less extensive membranes in the nose for detecting odors. Tree-dwelling thus made it inevitable that human beings would become predominantly "sight animals" rather than "smell" or "taste" animals.

This sensory emphasis on sight has many consequences in today's world. We notice the "visual pollution" of litter much more readily than we do carcinogens in automobile exhausts, potentially deadly chemicals in drinking water, or toxic contaminants in cooking oil.

Good depth perception and grasping hands, which together now enable us to suture a slippery aorta to a transplanted heart or put a fine screw into the mount of a gyroscope in the inertial guidance system of an ICBM, may first have been evolved so that our ancestors could leap from branch to branch and snatch up bugs.

Not only can our good vision be traced to treetop life, so also, surprisingly, can our dextcrity and our use of language. All primates have developed varying degrees of fine motor control. The main mode of locomotion of nonhuman primates is swinging through trees, which requires the ability to grasp branches tightly. To do this, an animal must have extremely well-developed step-by-step motor control in the small muscles of the limbs.

A kind of "grammar" is necessary to know how to move from one place to another, which hand to use, where and how tightly to grasp. Anthropologist Gordon Gallup points out that those areas of the brain that control fine motor movements, and that became further developed in tool making, are the *same* ones that are involved in language. The increasing size of the cerebral cortex thus gave our ancestors great advantages, from control of delicate muscle move-

ments to the development of speech and, eventually, to written
language.

Yet, important as the arboreal portion of our evolutionary history
was, some of our most "human" characteristics arose after a return
to the ground. The hominoid fossil record for the critical period of
about 25 to 5 million years ago is incomplete, to say the least. It
consists primarily of fragments of skulls and jaws of several kinds of
creatures. Nonetheless it is clear that in that period, probably about
8 million years ago, a succession of events led to the divergence of
two primate groups: human beings and the African apes. Sometime
before 13 million years ago the forests of East Africa began to thin
out, forcing many of the tree-dwelling primates out of their homes,
challenging them to evolve life-styles suited to new ecological
niches in the expanding savannas.

Those that remained in the forest evolved into chimpanzees and
gorillas. Of those that were forced or attracted out, some did not
adapt and became extinct, whereas others succeeded in living on the
ground. They took up residence in the surrounding grasslands, survived, prospered, and evolved into prehuman beings, the first members of the hominid family. (Hominids include us and all our
humanlike ancestors.) The change from prehuman to human involved the development of four important hominid characteristics:
an upright stance, an increased use of tools, the enlargement of the
brain, and the emergence of a cooperative society.

By the time the first hominids, the australopithecines, appear in
the fossil record some 3 to 4 million years ago, members of our
ancestral lineage seem to have been fully terrestrial. The wonderful
fossil "Lucy" *(Australopithecus afarensis)*, a half-complete skeleton
discovered by anthropologist Donald Johanson and his colleagues in
the Hadar region of Ethiopia, dates from that approximate time.
Fossil finds by Johanson and others now include many specimens
from that general area and may represent more than one species.
Nonetheless Lucy and her contemporaries appear to have been able
to walk fully upright. Hominid footprints made almost 4 million
years ago in Tanzania at Laetoli also show upright, or "bipedal,"
walking.

If they had had the appropriate social organization and knowledge, our ancestors might have started farming right then—but that fateful development was still more than 3 million years in the future. For another 200,000 generations hominids lived much like modern-day baboons, feeding omnivorously on tubers, young birds and mammals, carrion, and so forth. It was a slow start for a creature that eventually would create missiles that could span half the planet in half an hour.

The next ancestor, *Homo habilis,* appeared about 2 million years ago. *Habilis* had a distinctly larger brain than the australopithecines and was probably the first to manufacture stone tools. Then came *Homo erectus,* who lived about 1.6 million years ago. *Homo erectus* had even larger brains, the biggest reaching 1,200 cubic centimeters (cc) in volume (about the size of a 4-inch cube), well within the normal range for modern human beings.

These people were the first to break out of humanity's home continent of Africa and spread over Eurasia. *Erectus* was probably the first hominid to control fire and the first to have to deal with dramatic seasonal changes as the species spread out of the relatively benign tropical climate of humanity's African birthplace. They probably looked much like us—a clean-shaven, well-dressed *Homo erectus* male might prompt little comment if he wandered down a busy street today.

Erectus ruled for more than a million years, and about 300,000 years ago it began evolving into early *Homo sapiens,* the boundary being quite imperceptible. Early *sapiens* was widespread and variable, and some of the varieties were quite different from us. A burly prehistoric one, known as Neanderthal (named after the Neander Valley in Germany, where its bones were first found) was widespread in Europe and western Asia. These people are believed to have had a "spiritual" or at least animistic sensibility, because fossils show they performed elaborate burials perhaps 100,000 years ago.

We don't need a fossil record, however, to tell us that there were no radical changes in the brain in the course of vertebrate, primate, and human evolution, because members of all groups of vertebrates show basic similarities of brain structure today. The main difference is that additional nerve cells and nerve circuits and new neurochemicals to help transmit more information were added to the basic structure. These additions provide the basis of new abilities, such as the use of language. To make room for them, our brain has become, in relation to body size, larger than that of any other vertebrate. Thus we carry the remains of our long history inside our own heads, but we have completely changed the environment in which those heads must function.

In most organisms evolution is almost exclusively genetic. The information contained in the cells and transmitted to offspring gradually changes as generations pass. That information is contained in the sequence of four building blocks of long molecules that have the shape of double-stranded spirals. These molecules go by the complicated name of deoxyribonucleic acid, abbreviated as DNA. The kind of DNA present in our branch-spotting ancestors became increasingly common, while that in the branch sniffers faded from the picture. "Survive and reproduce" is the law of natural selection. In the DNA bible that law might read, "Go forth and beget multitudes of your clan of DNA to the next generation."

Genetic information, remember, is not the only kind of information that can be passed to offspring or other individuals. In many birds and mammals a significant amount is transmitted from parents to young nongenetically and between individuals of the same generation. Wolves teach their cubs to hunt, and shorebirds called oyster-catchers teach their young to open oysters. Rats decide what is safe to eat, at least in part, by watching what other rats stuff themselves with. This kind of nongenetic information is part of the culture of these animals.

Cultural information can, of course, evolve just as can genetic information. Some British birds learned to open milk bottles on people's doorsteps in the 1920s. A few titmice discovered they could puncture the foil caps and drink the cream. First other titmice and then other species learned from the pioneers and perfected their own techniques. The behavior of the birds evolved culturally, so that by midcentury at least eleven species could pilfer milk from wagons and doorsteps. Such a rapid change is characteristic of cultural evolution. It does not suffer from the two major constraints on genetic evolution. In cultural evolution, change can spread *within* a generation, and the duration of a generation is not a critical factor.

Generation time *is* a critical factor in genetic evolution. Species with short generation times, such as gut bacteria and fruit flies, can change by genetic evolution much more rapidly than can species such as people and elephants, which have long generation times. That is because natural selection involves some individuals having more offspring than others—it operates from generation to generation. This is an important point, because substantial genetic changes, such as the creation of a new species, ordinarily take many thousands or millions of generations. But extraordinary cultural changes, like replacing the horse and buggy with the automobile, inventing spacecraft, and increasing by more than a hundredfold the speed at which human beings can travel, now take place within the lifetime of a single human being, or even within a generation (a human generation is about twenty-five years).

Evolution in human beings has thus acquired an entirely new characteristic—an ability to cause change at an unprecedented speed. Our species is unique in its development of an extremely large body of culture. This collection of information is now so enormous that its possession has made people different in character from all other species that possess culture. The millions of volumes in the Library of Congress and in other libraries represent but a fraction of the human cultural heritage; much other cultural information, embodied in art objects, oral histories, tapes of TV shows and computer codes controlling nuclear-tipped missiles, never makes it into libraries. Because of culture, human evolution over the past few million years has been an extraordinary and triumphant story.

The human brain has been one of the most rapidly expanding organs in the history of life. Its large size (rather than the development of unique structures) gives it the ability to store and manipulate a huge body of knowledge. In human history these two processes—the increase in brain size and the increase in the quantity and complexity of culture—were doubtless involved in what is known as a positive feedback loop, where each change in one characteristic encourages changes in another.

The more culture there was to manipulate, the more natural selection favored increased brain size. The larger people's brains were (and the more people there were), the more culture there could be. A more complex culture, in turn, favored those individuals with the mental equipment best suited to manipulate it.

Eventually human beings stopped evolving larger brains. At the moment we can only speculate about the reason our brains stopped growing. Perhaps the cause was the need for heads small enough to slip through the narrow birth canal, perhaps evolution found ways to cram more efficient mental processing into the same-sized brain, or maybe there was no longer any particular reproductive advantage in being able to manipulate more information. At any rate the positive feedback loop appears to have been broken—there is no sign now of evolutionary pressure to produce people with bigger heads, regardless of what science fiction writers might dream up.

But triumphant we are, even if our brains have stopped growing. *Homo sapiens* evolved language, a large brain, and hands that could fashion tools; it has created high society, art, religion, and science and has vaulted to domination of the earth.

Which brings us to a major mystery of the history of our species. On the road to heart transplants and thermonuclear weapons, there was an eternity of hunting and gathering in comparison with the time spent organizing cities and making war. During most of that hunting-gathering period the pace of cultural evolution seems to have been imperceptibly slow. Up to about 35,000 B.C., for a million or more years our ancestors were upright, relatively highly cultured primates whose impact on the planet differed little from that of baboons.

Indeed until hominids gained control of fire, their hunting and gathering activities would have been indistinguishable from those of other primates. Once fire was mastered, however, the human impact increased, as fires—sometimes quite large ones—were set to aid in hunting. But lightning ignites many fires naturally, so humanity was not making fundamental changes in the world, even as recently as ten thousand years ago, when it had occupied the entire planet except for the oceans, remote islands, and land in regions with the severest climates.

Farming was invented shortly after our ancestors' geographic expansion was essentially complete. Although it transformed the world, only some ten millennia have been spent practicing agriculture, and there has been just a relative instant of playing with high technology. Space vehicles, scanning electron microscopes, personal computers, and thermonuclear bombs were all developed in the last forty-five years—about one hundred-thousandth of the period since the first hominids walked upright.

What took so long? What vital catalyst was missing that kept people from breaking out of their cultural rut 500,000 years ago, inventing agriculture and moving on to remake the entire planet as they have now done? Was there some step in biological evolution that still had to precede a critical cultural advance? Was there some missing climatic factor, or were populations too small to pressure people to farm (which is certainly more trouble than hunting and gathering)? Or did some special situation have to evolve culturally before societies could start to change rapidly?

It was not biological evolution that caused us to remake the planet; indeed no sizable changes in the brain occurred during the expansion of humanity to the ends of the Earth. The place to look for answers would seem to be in recent prehistory, but so doing only emphasizes the mystery. Culture was almost static for a million and a half years before 35,000 years ago. Then in the late Stone Age, only about an Earth "hour" ago, there were spurts of cultural evolution every few thousand years, and human beings burst out of Eurasia to occupy Australia and the New World.

The people of that ice-age era had become very efficient hunters of large animals. Quite likely they used techniques similar to those of recent Eskimos, often herding game over cliffs or into lakes (where the animals could easily be speared from wood-framed skin boats). These hunters are suspected to be responsible (along with climatic change) for the extermination of the large animal species that once made much of the Northern Hemisphere look like an enhanced version of the Serengeti Plain in East Africa today. Huge herds of grazing and browsing animals roamed over Eurasia and North America, including forms such as mammoths, woolly rhinos, wild cattle, and giant ground sloths, which have been extinct for ten thousand years or more.

The ability of the peoples of the late ice ages to occupy new environments was amazing. The ancestors of American Indians spread across North America and down to Tierra del Fuego at the southern tip of South America in less than four thousand years. Those hunters and gatherers managed to travel on foot across ten thousand miles of tundra, mountains, coniferous and deciduous forests, deserts, jungles, and grasslands. They advanced at an average rate of two and a half miles per year into unexplored, hostile territory. Consider the problems of moving your family and shelter at that rate in a setting with no marked trails; only game, wild fruits, nuts and berries for food; many large and dangerous animals; and little or no protection against diseases.

The late Stone Age also brought the astonishing flowering of cave art. Caves in southern Europe and Asia were decorated with both naturalistic and abstract paintings, etchings, and sculpture. Polychrome renderings of bison, reindeer, horses, woolly rhinos, lions, and other animals show, even after thousands of years of deterioration, a magnificence that places them among the greatest artistic creations of our species. The simplicity of line, shading, and implied action all appeal to the modern eye. Many experts have concluded that the aesthetic senses of our Stone Age ancestors were virtually those of people today.

All this means, as we consider the human predicament today, we should keep a basic point in mind: while humanity has become the most successful animal on the planet, *almost all its biological evolution occurred long before it achieved such exalted status,* and it occurred in a very different environment. The world inhabited by a prehistoric human being, the world where natural selection was molding us into our present form, was much smaller than that of the average person today. It was a world of a few dozen miles rather than continental distances, and it included societies of perhaps fifty to five hundred individuals, who were rather isolated from other groups of similar size.

Prehistoric people did not know they were living on a planet containing several million human beings, and events of importance to one group had no impact on distant groups. Some of those early human beings led nomadic lives, but they moved in cycles through familiar landscapes containing many rapidly appearing opportunities and dangers.

Our "mental structure" evolved in large part to deal with those environmental opportunities and dangers. The human brain, like that of the crocodile and the tarsier, promotes the survival and reproduction of individuals, but it evolved to help individuals living in circumstances very different from ours today. Our evolutionary history equipped us to live with a handful of compatriots, in a stable environment, with many short-term challenges. Benefits had to be reaped fast if they were to be reaped at all. The lion had to be dodged before it ate you; the antelope speared before it escaped.

Thus the human mind evolved to register short-term changes, from moment to moment, day to day, and season to season, and to overlook the "backdrop" against which those took place. That backdrop only changed significantly on a time scale of centuries or longer. Not only did our evolutionary background predispose us to live in a world of caricatures and physically equip us to draw only part of the picture, it also predisposed us to focus on certain parts of the "image" and ignore others.

Such selectivity is a necessary heritage. If all sensory information that we *can* receive were treated as equal, we would concentrate as much on the stage setting as on the actors. We would be continually trying to memorize every detail of everything we saw, heard, smelled, touched, or perceived. All aspects of the world would demand our notice. The sound of the breeze in the trees would be given the same weight as the cracking of a branch or the footpads of a tiger, the temperature of your room and the press of your rump on a chair would be as attention-demanding as the words on this page. The selectivity of human perceptions was produced by both biological and cultural evolution. That selectivity is critical to survival, yet, in today's world, it threatens survival.

This extreme selectivity is found in the perceptual systems of all animals. If a male butterfly of a certain species is attracted to a female by a prominent white spot on the female's wing, it may be even more turned on by a model of the female with a "larger than life" white spot. The oversized spot is called a supernormal stimulus. Parallels can be found in Western society in everything from the size of noses in political cartoons and of breasts on the models in men's magazines to sweeter-than-nature candies and soft drinks, and in other societies in the exaggerated symbols of dance masks, totem poles, and the like.

What constitutes an attention-commanding stimulus varies greatly from culture to culture. A nude picture of Harrison Ford would probably bore a female Australian aborigine. Responses to some stimuli, however, such as a liking for sweet flavors or high-speed movement, are nearly universal. They may have been genetically programmed so that most people are susceptible to their "supernormalization." But the penchant for responding to superoptimal stimuli is a biologically evolved trait—and not a recently acquired one at that, if we can judge from Stone Age "Venuses," Earth-mother carvings with greatly exaggerated breasts and buttocks.

The pattern of selectivity programmed into human beings by the old world is now fatally obsolete in the new. We need a new basis for making selections. Our nervous systems are designed to make decisions based upon the presumption of a constant environmental framework. Early in a person's development certain perceptual rules, based on the stable environment of previous generations, are built in by genes and culture. Those rules help to shape the subjective world we inhabit.

It is hard for most of us to understand how much of our worldview is derived from our inheritance and early experience. One way of comprehending it is to consider the visual experience of a person who was born blind but was suddenly able to see. Psychologist Richard Gregory of Bristol University in England had the good fortune to analyze such a case. At fifty-two, a man blind from birth had a successful corneal transplant. When the bandages were removed, he heard the voice of the surgeon, turned to look at him, and saw nothing but a blur. He was immediately able to distinguish a figure from its background—he could see a black spot on a white piece of paper. Although he could not see the world as crisply as we do, he almost immediately was able to recognize objects for which he had previously developed an "internal picture" through touch. In a few days, however, he could walk around the hospital corridors without touching the walls and could tell time from a wall clock.

The man was surprised by the appearance of the moon. He could see and draw objects that he had known before by touch, but had difficulty with objects that he had not had the opportunity to touch while blind. His drawings of a London bus even a year after the operation omitted the front of the bus, which he had never touched. Windows and wheels, which he had touched, were drawn in pretty fair detail right from the beginning. When Gregory showed him a lathe, a tool this previously blind man was experienced in using, he had no idea what it was. Then the man was asked to touch the lathe; he closed his eyes, examined it thoroughly with his hand, and said, "Now that I have felt it, I can see."

Perceptual systems require rules; the rules are partly encoded in the genes and partly learned in the course of development. The rules of the newly sighted man were different from the rules of people who have been able to see from birth.

Some of the best evidence for the development of perceptual rules comes from studies of the susceptibility of people in different societies to optical illusions. Those who grow up in "carpentered" societies—with rectangular rooms constructed with straight lines and right angles—are more susceptible to the so-called Muller-Lyer illusion than people raised in round huts.

As with the once-blind man, the visual system of normal people in "right-angle" cultures develops so as to be able to interpret information in the local environment. In this case the left-hand set of lines is interpreted as a corner receding, and the right-hand set as one projecting toward the viewer. The visual system then immedi-

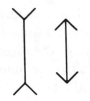

ately computes the left-hand vertical line to be farther away and longer. Similarly the Ponzo illusion, that one of two identical lines is longer if the pair is enclosed between two converging straight lines, is more powerful to those at home in wide-open spaces than to those who dwell in tropical forests. Presumably the converging perspective lines—much like those of a railroad track disappearing into the distance—supply size and distance cues to nervous systems trained to perceive them.

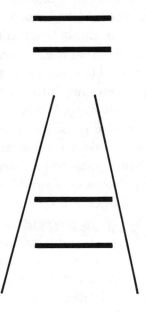

But if the world has shaped our perceptions in the same manner as it has shaped those of other animals, why has humanity been so much more successful than, say, lions or chimpanzees? Some scientists continue to seek answers to this riddle on the biological side, in the development of the human brain and its abilities. As we shall see, the human brain operates in the same general way as that of a frog, but frogs are a long way from building thermonuclear weapons. We may perceive the world much the same way as frogs do (if somewhat more completely), but we obviously do a lot more with our perceptions. Could it be that some biological change in the brain that increased "reasoning" ability explains humanity's dominant position on Earth?

Unfortunately for that thesis, studies of other primates almost always fail to show striking gaps between their reasoning abilities and those of people. Some chimpanzees score higher on certain reasoning tests than do many adult human beings. Among other abilities, chimps seem to be able to understand cause and effect. So it probably was not an increased ability to find solutions to everyday problems that caused our ancestors' evolutionary line to diverge from that leading to chimpanzees and other African great apes. Even pigeons can solve problems such as learning to press a button a certain number of times to get food.

Instead, it was, we suspect, the development of speech, rather than brute increases in reasoning power that moved humanity forward. Imagine trying to transmit without speech an idea as simple as, "Around the corner on the wall is a red button; if you push it three times, you will get food."

If so, the human success story doesn't trace to unique properties of our ancestors' nervous systems that made them better problem solvers than other contemporary large primates. Rather, the development of language gave a greater scope to problem solving, so natural selection favored speakers. Both language and problem-solving ability in turn, could have spurred cultural evolution. For a long time, perhaps millions of years, our ancestors evolved in a world of speech, changing themselves slowly but radically.

Several other qualities set human beings apart from other animals. While controversy remains about what preceded what in evolution, it is better to think of the process as a simultaneous development of several characteristics, in positive feedback loops. Large brains allowed for a more elaborate culture, which then increased the need for larger brains. Increased tool making encouraged more complex speech, which then allowed for the manufacture of more elaborate tools.

One of the most distinctive qualities of human beings, bipedality, preceded speech. Chimps and gorillas can stand upright at times, but when they move, they typically do so on all fours. Bipedal walking and running are surprisingly efficient. The great biologist J. B. S. Haldane pointed out that human beings can cover greater distances over time than any other animal. We are the only animals that can climb a tree, swim a mile-wide river, and run twenty miles all in three hours. Walking enabled our ancestors to travel into new and unexplored territory, which in turn led them into new and often dangerous situations, which they had to conquer. Almost all other animals live their entire lives within the environment in which they are born.

Get down on all fours and look around; the view is more limited than when you stand. That's why smell is important to four-legged animals. An animal on its hind legs can see farther than it can smell. Erect animals with good eyesight can detect approaching danger as well as opportunities farther away. Therefore a more sophisticated long-distance visual system, building on the improved sight acquired earlier in the treetops, probably evolved in human beings along with upright posture.

Standing on hind feet meant that hands, freed from weight-bearing responsibilities, could make tools and carry things. Erect posture also led to profound changes in human sexuality and social systems. Although we cannot be certain of it, this complex of factors surrounding bipedalism was probably our first adaptive advantage over other apes.

Bipedalism even affected family life through a long process of feedback. Although the front limbs were freed, the hind limbs had to bear the entire weight of the body. The human back was not originally "designed" to support upright posture (this is why back pains are common). To support the full weight, the human pelvis thickened, thereby reducing the size of the birth canal.

But while the birth canal was becoming smaller, the brain and head were growing larger. These two trends could not continue for long unless natural selection could find a solution. One solution was to have human babies born very early in their development. This immaturity of human babies at birth has great consequences for the brain and for the baby's family life.

Another important difference between us and apes is that we are sexy mammals. Female mammals, other than human beings, have an estrous cycle, which means that they ovulate only once or a few times a year. Copulation is performed mostly during these times.

Human beings are different. Females ovulate every month, and a woman is always (as male anthropologists are fond of saying) "sexually receptive." To put it a less potentially offensive way, sex is possible throughout the year, not just in a "mating season." Continuing sexual activity combined with the eye contact during intercourse related to bipedality, seem to form bonds based on sexual pleasure.

Bipedalism and the human system of sexuality laid the foundation for a stable society built on family units: fathers stay with, care for, and most often (compared with other animals) care about their families. A mother can care for several small children at home if the father brings home most of the food. In ideal circumstances a human female could produce and raise a child each year from the onset of menstruation to menopause—as many as thirty. In contrast a female chimpanzee takes about sixteen years to produce and raise two.

Bipedality and these unusual sexual habits are two key reasons that human beings dominate the planet. Early on, hominids descended from the trees, reared up on their hind legs, and in so doing developed this adaptive system. Millions of years ago they were able to leave the cover of the forest and to invade the more marginal, more seasonal habitats of forests mixed with grasslands that were then increasing in area.

Perhaps the close pair bonds among early hominids placed a high premium on communication. A female informed a male of her needs and those of their offspring; a male communicated his needs and plans as well. This may have pushed the transition from signals and grunts to true language. With that development much more abstract ideas could be transferred, such as, "I saw five men on the other side of the hill carrying rocks, and they looked dangerous."

The extensive use of tools is also a key to our planetary dominance. At first our ancestors probably used tools much as chimpanzees do today. Chimps will fish in crevices for termites, using a broken twig, or brandish a branch to threaten a leopard. But they don't routinely modify natural objects into more useful forms and then keep them around for future employment. The best chimps seem able to do is to strip a few leaves from a twig to make it a better termite probe or roll a leaf into a straw and suck water from a hole in a stump. However, unlike people, chimpanzees are in no way dependent on tool use for survival.

The first extensive tool use that was made possible by walking on the hind legs probably was not the wielding of clubs or rocks for hunting or warfare. Instead our ancestors are thought to have employed big leaves, hollow pieces of wood, poles, and so forth for *carrying*.

These tools (including weapons) were acquired gradually. The extensive use of wood and bone artifacts and unmodified rocks no doubt came first. Later, tools would have been modified in ways that permit archaeologists today to identify them with certainty as the product of human industry. Selecting as tools rocks of suitable shapes and hardness probably led to breaking up rock until a well-shaped stone tool was made. In addition, probably early in the process of acquiring tools, people began to master the uses of fire. It was a slow cultural, not a biological, process.

Recent history confirms that jumps in brain size did not necessarily precede great cultural advances. There is no sign of a significant physical difference between hunters and gatherers of fifteen thousand years ago and today's human beings. The agricultural revolution; the rise of cities and nations; the development of mathematics by the Arabs, which laid the foundations of modern science, industrialization, and high technology—all are the harvest of cultural evolution without a detectable corresponding physical evolution of the brain.

It would be preposterous to suppose that biological evolution could, in a mere thirty generations, convert the serf of the Dark Ages into the computer programmer of today. The cultural gap between serf and computer programmer is vast compared with the difference between our ancestors of 3 million and 2 million years ago. The latter stretch, in which there was little cultural change (but substantial biological change), spanned more than thirty *thousand* generations.

Within spans of many millennia, great cultural change does not necessarily imply great biological change, and vice versa. The Chinese had an advanced culture when Britons were still living in caves and painting themselves blue. Then, in only a few centuries, the British surpassed the Chinese in many areas of technology.

Also, conclusions about the capabilities of people based on the artifacts they leave behind may be very misleading. If an anthropologist a million years in the future compared the traces of a twentieth-century Eskimo camp with those of New York City, she might conclude that Eskimos were biologically a very inferior people compared with New Yorkers. Yet, almost any keen observer who has seen at first hand the intelligence, ingenuity, and creativity of Eskimos would dispute this.

Eskimos quickly learned how internal combustion engines worked; and many became skilled mechanics, often shaping spare parts for the engines of their boats from scrap steel and even bone. Their ivory and soapstone carvings and sealskin stencils are art forms in great demand throughout the Western world. There is no sign that New Yorkers would be able to adapt more rapidly to the Eskimos' environment than Eskimos would to New York.

Further, within the normal range of human brain size (1,250–2,000 cc), quite large differences among individuals are in no way related to mental performance. Scientists in the nineteenth century tried to show that the brain size of great novelists was larger than that of illiterate peasants, but to no avail. In short, although the human brain appears to have enlarged rapidly (in geological time) in response to the pressures of culture, it does not seem likely that the brain crossed any real physical threshold that suddenly permitted new kinds of cultural activities. The evidence available today is consistent with the idea that changes in social organization (as opposed to genetically programmed changes in brain and behavior) determined the course of cultural evolution. Meanwhile there was a gradual, genetically based, increase in the capacity to store and manipulate cultural information.

Most important to our thesis, our ancestors, from their days in the trees to their creating the art of the Lascaux cave, had little reason to evolve a capacity to perceive significant long-term, large-scale changes in their environment, changes that might have taken decades, centuries, even millennia, to develop.

When truly long-term changes occurred, early hominids could do little or nothing about it. They could respond to undesirable shifts in climate or to a gradual reduction in availability of game or fruit only by migrating or perishing. But such challenges were rare. The "environment," both natural and cultural, remained relatively constant for very long periods, hundreds of thousands of years in the case of early human beings. In the tropical forest homes of our distant ancestors, seasonal (and even daily) changes in temperature were minimal. Serious planning for a cold season was probably not necessary until the global climate began to cool less than 2 million years ago, and perhaps not until *Homo erectus* finally spread out of Africa around a million years ago.

Indeed since little or nothing adaptive could have been done by individuals about such long-term trends, perceptions of gradual long-term change may have been actively *suppressed* in the course of our evolution. Take a look at photographs of yourself or your friends a decade or more ago. One is almost invariably surprised at how different we (they) looked—the weird hairstyles, the strange clothes, and so on. Our perception ordinarily is that we, and those we see frequently, are unchanging. We almost have to force ourselves to recognize advancing age. Only when comparisons are produced artificially by photographs can we see the long-term changes.

The same applies to our physical environments; we rapidly incorporate dramatic changes into our "normal" world. The brand-new house or car is taken for granted in a few months. Security checks at

airports seem as though they've always been with us. Rush hour
starts earlier and ends later; highways expand to four, then six, then
eight lanes. Smog is incorporated into the weather reports and perceived as one of the normal, minor, daily perturbations in the environment.

Here also, photographs can produce a necessary antidote to the
automatic sensory adaptation. Ecologists studied changes in the vegetation of the Great Basin (the area of Utah, Nevada, and Oregon
that has no drainage to the sea) by taking photographs at precisely
the same localities where early photographers had taken theirs. The
seemingly unchanging landscape had actually undergone dramatic
changes in a few decades. Forests, brushlands, and grasslands
change composition and position in a stately botanic minuet.

In the world that made us there was no reason for people to
detect such changes. But in the world we have made, there are
many reasons why we *must* perceive them—and people have created devices such as cameras that can help us to do so.

Our species was shaped by an old world, but since the agricultural revolution, we have changed Earth into a new world. In so
doing, most of us fail to realize how the human outlook, designed
by our heritage, actually obstructs understanding of humanity's increasingly precarious situation. Let's now take a closer look at how
humanity's triumphant and dangerous transformation of Earth was
accomplished.

3

THE WORLD WE MADE

A T THE TIME of the Agricultural Revolution, the stable
world of hunter-gatherers began to change quickly. Fifteen thousand years (less than a thousand generations) in the past,
the entire human population consisted of perhaps 5 million souls
surviving by hunting and gathering. Then, about ten thousand years
ago, rather than search out food in the wild, people began to do-

mesticate both plants and animals. Farming settlements grew up on the flood plains of the Nile, in the Fertile Crescent of the Middle East, and around the Ganges and Hwang Ho (Yellow) river deltas in Asia.

Farming created an especially favorable environment for both rapid population growth and the rich elaboration of culture. Births could be spaced more closely when people settled down to farm. Women were then not limited to the number of infants they could carry at one time, and soft foods became available for early weaning. As a result birth rates began to creep upward.

Death rates may also have risen at the dawn of agriculture because of novel hazards associated with the new venture, such as susceptibility to crop failures. In addition, relatively unsanitary conditions in early permanent settlements may have increased the danger of epidemic diseases. But the rise in birth rates was greater than the rise in death rates most of the time, and eventually the latter decreased as agriculture became better established and the ability to store food against times of low yields improved. The result was the beginning of a human population explosion that continues to this day, because birth rates in most nations are still much higher than death rates.

It took a few thousand years for food production to become efficient enough for one farming family to provide reliable sustenance for more than itself. Surplus production by farmers freed part of the population from the several-million-year-old imperative for each family or clan to supply its own food. This opened the way to specialization of activities, cities, and civilization. To get food, people who were not farmers had to provide some product or service for food producers. At first, these specialists doubtless mostly provided services for farmers, perhaps helping to construct shelter, transporting food, or making and repairing tools and farm implements—or providing farm credit.

As numbers grew, so did opportunities. A village of five families could not provide a living for a shoemaker; a village of fifty families could. Occupations diversified; some people became merchants, some artisans, others organized financial institutions, others could

be full-time politicians. Religion, once the province of elders, shamans, and medicine men, could become controlled by priestly orga-
nizations.

In most hunter-gatherer societies all healthy adult males were
doubtless part-time warriors, for whom combat was almost a game
of honor. Gradually they were replaced in some societies by specialists, full-time professional soldiers whose interests naturally were
intertwined with the ambitions of the political leaders of emerging
states who paid for the soldiers' services. The great civilizations of
the historical era sprouted from the roots of the Agricultural
Revolution, and human cultures evolved rapidly as tribes became
nation-states, and states became empires.

With the development of states and empires a brand-new set of
ideas emerged and helped to drive cultural evolution—the belief
that people could conquer large numbers of other people, control
large swaths of territory, and even subjugate Mother Nature herself.

When people settled down to till the soil, they started on the
road to cities, wars, overpopulation, toxic air pollution, and nuclear
weapons. The trip down that road was slow at first. Even in the ten
thousand years from the Agricultural Revolution to the late Middle
Ages, there was no great alteration in the speed of change in the
lives of most human beings. The world was and would forever be
the same, and one had only to find one's place within that stable
world. Culture changed very little in the course of each individual's
lifetime; its evolution was not sensed by people then any more than
biological evolution is sensed by people today.

But, since farming began, cultural evolution has gradually transformed *Homo sapiens* from a species evolving in response to a
natural environment into one that is literally "making" the world in
which it lives. After many millions of years living in groups of
dozens or hundreds, in a mere ten millennia people have changed
the world so much that they now must adjust to living in a "group"
of 5 billion (since a global human community is emerging).

In our time tens of thousands of people are being crammed into
skyscrapers in Chicago, Singapore, Rio de Janeiro, and other me-
tropolises, producing population densities hundreds of thousands

times greater than that which existed in America before it was settled by Europeans. Before the Agricultural Revolution, historian V. Gordon Childe estimated, the carrying capacity (the number of people the land could support) of Middle America was less than one person for every ten square miles. Only on the coasts, where fishes were plentiful, were there as many as two people to a square mile. Now, in cities like Tokyo, Mexico City, and New York, there can be hundreds of thousands of people per square mile.

Our ancestors' early population growth reflected more the multiplication of settlements than any great change in the way people lived. The largest European settlement known before agriculture, Barkaer in Jutland (now a part of modern Denmark), fifteen thousand years ago encompassed only fifty-two small dwellings, while sixteen to thirty was the usual village size.

People, especially women, didn't live very long in early farming societies. Archaeological evidence from the seventy-six skeletons found in Europe and Asia from settlements of ten thousand years ago shows a shocking picture of life expectancies. Less than half were of people who had reached twenty-one, only 12 percent were over forty, and *not a single female had reached thirty*. Few realize how different that world was from ours.

Most of the momentous changes throughout the short (on the time-scale of biological evolution) period of recorded human history have involved cultural shifts, many taking less than one hundred years. Consider some of the shifts of the last five centuries: the Western Hemisphere was opened to European exploitation, mercantilism ended, the Industrial Revolution began, and communism became a global force. But although these changes occurred swiftly compared with prehistoric cultural change, *there is no longer sufficient time to rely on the normal pace of cultural evolution* to deal with today's dilemmas. We are facing problems of a scale and speed of change for which our biology and history have left us poorly prepared.

Human beings are quite rightly proud of their accomplishments. Our species has been more successful than any of the other billion or so animal species that have inhabited the Earth, not just by self-centered standards of our achievement self-awareness, moral and religious values, high culture, high technology, and so on, but by a purely biological standard.

The "biomass" (collective weight) of living human beings is probably greater than that of any other animal species. There are some 300 million tons of people. Only an animal dependent on humanity, cattle, is in the same weight league—and there are only about 1.3 billion cattle. No other large animal species has ever even approached a population size of 5 billion individuals—even the fabled bison, which blackened the American prairies, numbered only about 50 million.

Samuel Butler once quipped that a hen is just an egg's way of making another egg. Human beings might be considered just one more device invented by DNA for producing more DNA. Maybe—but we're one of the best devices DNA has yet invented for increasing itself.

Homo sapiens is also the first animal species to achieve anything remotely resembling the dominant position it now enjoys on the planet. Humanity now turns to its own use or destroys about 40 percent of the food that must supply all of the millions of species of land animals with which it shares the Earth. People now mine and move some mineral resources faster than those resources are normally freed from the Earth's surface by the action of wind and water.

People now construct their own environments; concrete and steel supersede dirt and trees. Heat-exchange devices warm where it is cold and cool where it is hot. We can make water flow in deserts and create breathable atmospheres in the vacuum of space. We influence the population sizes of many other creatures, such as cats, pigs, cheetahs, and parakeets, and now, with the size of our nuclear arsenals, the fate of most living things is in our power. Indeed, the scale of human activities is now large enough to change both local and planetary climates.

Increasing numbers is a "goal" of all organisms. But never before has there been an "outbreak" of a single species on such a global scale. Unfortunately it is not yet clear how enduring our unprecedented triumph will be, because it has created an unprecedented paradox: our triumphs can destroy us. As people strive to increase their dominance even further, they are now changing the earth into a planet that is inhospitable to civilization.

Considering how much better we now promote the survival of individuals to old age, we can believe some of the self-congratulatory rhetoric that our species has produced at least since it learned to write. Consider one critical change that has been occurring over the past few hundred years and has accelerated enormously over the past few decades. It is a change that has been filtered out of the perceptions of almost everyone, one best discussed in economic terms.

Humanity, until very recently, lived almost entirely on its "income"—on solar energy captured by green plants in fields, on farms and in forests by the process of photosynthesis. Now, thanks to cultural evolution, humanity is living largely on its "capital"—nonrenewable resources. *Homo sapiens* was the recipient of a one-time bonanza—whose use has shaped our societies and attitudes as nothing ever did before. The capital that we inherited included fossil fuels, high-grade mineral ores, rich agricultural soils, groundwater stored up during the ice ages, and above all, the millions of other species that inhabit the Earth along with us. Our total inheritance took billions of years to assemble; it is being squandered in decades.

We are acting in a way that was relatively harmless when humanity first began to spend some of its fortune, but in a way that is now lethally foolish. Using fossil fuels *ad lib* to improve the lot of the billion or so human beings that lived at the time of the Industrial Revolution made sense. But now there are more than 5 billion of us, and most of them are striving to *increase* their use of dwindling supplies of those energy resources. Humanity is rapidly and wastefully depleting fossil fuels before satisfactory substitute energy supplies have been developed and, in the process, seriously damaging its environment. Similarly our wealth of metals is being used so rapidly that more and more energy must be used to extract them from poorer and poorer ores. That use of energy contributes to, among other things, problems of air and water pollution.

In the rich nations, and to a growing extent in the poor nations as well, farming is becoming increasingly dependent on fossil fuels —so much so that modern, high-yield agriculture has been described as a process that turns calories of fossil fuel into calories of food. Modern agriculture also tends to use both soils and groundwater at rates very much higher than natural systems can replace them. And the accelerated clearing of land for agriculture is a major cause of the dwindling of that most precious and irreplaceable part of our inheritance, Earth's biological riches.

In short, humanity is doing what no sane family on your block would do if it could help it: living on its savings. We are a nouveau-riche species struggling to become "nouveau broke."

Until a few thousand years ago human beings could do nothing else but live on their income. Some of that solar income was acquired by people directly, when they ate the plants, while some was acquired indirectly, when they ate animals that had eaten the plants (or that had eaten plant eaters). Plant fibers and animal skins for clothes; wood for fires; gourds and leaves for carrying and cooking; wood, skins, poles, and fronds for shelter; herbs and poultices for medicines; flowers and feathers for decorations—all derived from the same source: solar income. With some minor exceptions, such as rocks for tools and weapons, clay for pots, and earth pigments for painting, what humanity needed was supplied continuously by a nuclear power station 93 million miles away.

There were fluctuations in the supply of that income, of course, due to drought, insect plagues, and other factors, but basically the income was always there, and usually abundant. Early human beings evolved in a situation where resources seemed infinite, where shortages were temporary, where overharvesting was rarely possible. Early hunters and gatherers probably led leisurely lives, often free from want. Their population sizes, limited by disease, predators, and the difficulties of caring for children in wandering communities, seldom grew large enough to put much of a dent in available food supplies.

The new world is not like that. The capital being squandered by modern *Homo sapiens* is not renewed daily as is sunlight. It was produced by thousands to billions of years of geological and biological evolution. Our inheritance accumulated over very long periods as geological events gradually converted the energy of sunlight stored in the remains of ancient plants into coal, petroleum, and natural gas. It accumulated as the slow grinding together of the drifting tectonic plates of Earth's crust concentrated minerals; as the action of wind, water, and living organisms gradually converted rocks into the complex ecological systems we call soils; as surface water from melting ice-age glaciers percolated into underground water-bearing rock formations; and as "speciation," the process that creates different kinds of animals, plants, and microbes, slowly increased the diversity of life-forms on the planet.

In most cases that capital cannot be replaced any faster than it was originally produced, and yet we are spending it in one tenth to one millionth of its production time. In one year the United States burns in its automobiles more petroleum than the Alaskan oil field accumulated in 100,000 years, more soil goes down Haitian rivers in a day than soil-building processes can replace in a year, and more species are exterminated in tropical forests annually than speciation could replace in a million years.

Think of what we've gained from the living part of our capital, the millions of other species of plants, animals, and microorganisms with which we share the Earth. For some 4 billion years species originated faster than they disappeared. Our dependence on the capital of other species that thus accumulated cannot be overestimated. Without the descendants of three species of wild grasses—plants we know as wheat, rice, and corn—most people would starve to death, and civilization would disappear. Without many crucial medicines and industrial materials that have also been drawn from the library of other living beings that evolved along with us we would be much less healthy and prosperous. The potential of that library has barely been tapped, but *Homo sapiens* is rapidly destroying it.

All organisms of our planet are working parts of Earth's natural ecosystems. They help to ameliorate the climate and to supply us with fresh water. Those systems generate and maintain the soils that are essential to forestry and agriculture, dispose of human wastes, and recycle nutrients. Without the latter service life would gradually grind to a halt. Natural ecosystems also control the vast majority of potential pests of agricultural crops and organisms that can carry disease to human beings. Agriculture has often suffered when misuse of pesticides has disrupted nature's free pest controls. Human beings have repeatedly suffered when changes in natural systems have made them more vulnerable to diseases, including malaria, yellow fever, bilharzia, and possibly even AIDS.

Overspraying of pesticides usually has a greater impact on the insect enemies of plant-eating insects than on the plant eaters themselves. The enemies usually have both smaller populations and less natural resistance to the sprays. Thus, using pesticides often leads both to a greater abundance of the pests the spray is intended to kill and to the appearance of new agricultural pests—pests that were once controlled gratis by predators in natural ecosystems.

It is bad enough that humanity is rapidly spending its capital, but in the process our species is also destroying the very systems that make usable the solar income that people will be forced to live on once our inheritance is used up. The increasingly rapid destruction of Earth's capital of organic diversity (more than half of it may well be gone by A.D. 2025) is gutting the very ecosystems that support the human economy and thus hold the key to the human future.

Cultural evolution, by giving us the ability to live on capital, has made biological evolution completely inadequate as a way for human beings to adapt to their environments. Time is too short: even a "rapid" change through biological evolution ordinarily takes hundreds of generations; a major change, such as the evolution of mammals from reptiles, ordinarily takes millions of generations. We are less than ten generations from the time that human beings began, through the Industrial Revolution, to create the new world. We are only a few hundred generations away from the Agricultural Revolution, and but two thousand generations from the days of the Neanderthals. The human gene pool cannot change fast enough to make a creature originally suited for dodging spears suddenly suited to dodging thermonuclear warheads.

Cultural evolution, in only a few generations, has made the size of the human population a threat to the survival of civilization. The gene pool cannot respond to that threat at all; for individuals to lower their reproductive output goes against the basic rules of biological evolution. Natural selection has engraved one fundamental message on the genes of all organisms over billions of years: *reproduction of your own kind is your reason for existence.* That message, by definition, cannot be erased by natural selection, because natural selection operates through some individuals reproducing more than others. Biologically we are the same old *Homo sapiens* that the world once made—and therein lies the rub. A modification of the message to "reproduce to the maximum" must be accomplished by another kind of evolution, and cultural evolution has not been up to the task.

The triumph of humanity has not been in adapting to or understanding the natural world, but in transforming that world to make it a more hospitable place for more human beings. That triumph clearly had roots in the invention of agriculture. From the start, people modified entire landscapes to serve their own needs, gradually changing nearly all land surfaces. Because of agriculture, where once there were only prairies and forests, now farms and factories operate; where once only plains and deserts existed, now livestock graze and weapons laboratories and ICBM silos have been built. Most importantly, from our viewpoint, agriculture marks the point at which human beings became able to change their environment rapidly and drastically. That revolution inexorably led to the need for an ability to perceive relatively long-term trends, trends that people must redirect if their civilizations are to survive.

A few thousand years after the invention of farming in the Middle East, humanity began to fashion a world in which "slow reflexes" were first needed. The Mesopotamian "hydraulic civilization" was the first known example. It developed around 5000 to 4000 B.C. in the Tigris and Euphrates valleys of what is now Iraq. A

dominant theme of Mesopotamian mythology was that the chaos of
nature could be converted into a human-divine order. For a while, it
must have seemed that the Mesopotamians could pull it off. As the
term "hydraulic" implies, that civilization was dependent upon the
first major engineering modification of the natural world by *Homo
sapiens:* a system of irrigation canals that distributed water from the
rivers to nearby farmlands.

The human brain made the desert bloom; it allowed the Mesopotamians to shape their land as no animal had done before. But
that brain was still the old brain. It lacked the habit of projecting
and interpreting long-term trends. Irrigation is normally a temporary enterprise. Silt gradually tends to fill in canals, so they must be
dredged or their banks raised to keep the water flowing. Irrigation
water, unlike rainwater, is not salt-free; so when irrigation water
evaporates from the fields, salt accumulates in the soil, slowly but
surely destroying its fertility. In the Tigris and Euphrates valleys
these factors (along with the destruction wrought by invading armies) eventually brought down the irrigation system and the Mesopotamian civilization with it.

At the time, of course, the Mesopotamians struggled against the
day-to-day, short-term symptoms. Some individuals may even have
been able to perceive where the long-range trend was heading. But
we can imagine that Mesopotamian leaders labeled the farsighted
people doomsayers and ignored their advice. Mesopotamian decision
makers continued to try to solve the problems with short-term measures. Levees were raised along the canals until those waterways
were actually elevated many feet above the surrounding plain, making the nearby land subject to flooding if the levees were breached
by natural catastrophes or enemies. At that time, however, Mesopotamians had neither the social organization nor the technological
ability to solve the long-term problem of irrigation, even if it had
been recognized.

The opportunities for specialization that were opened up by agriculture were amplified by the rise of cities. They, in turn, led quite
gradually to the technological and organizational innovations that
would eventually produce the triumphal rise of *Homo sapiens* to

global dominance. In that enterprise the Earth was extremely cooperative. In southwestern Asia, even before they used metals, people learned that fire was an extremely useful tool for modifying materials that composed the planet's surface into more useful forms: ceramics, plasters, glazes, bricks, and glass.

Fortuitously, high-grade copper ore was lying around on the surface, and gradually, through accident and design, people learned to produce temperatures high enough to separate that metal from its ore. Copper dominated the metallurgical scene for more than 5,000 years—from approximately 7000 to 1500 B.C. It first was used unprocessed, as decorative iridescent blue and green stones, and after about 4000 B.C. as a metal to work. Copper was tougher and lighter than stone and quickly replaced it as the main material in tools and weapons. People soon learned to alloy it with tin to make bronze, which was stronger still and would hold a sharp edge.

Then, a couple of millennia before Christ, the Hittites in northern Syria and Asia Minor learned to win iron from its ore. Things would never be the same again. Iron, properly processed and alloyed with other metals, has a strength and range of uses far beyond those of copper and bronze. Its properties made it ideal for fabricating everything from knives and guns to steam engines, automobiles, and skyscrapers.

Learning to use metals was very nearly as important a step in humanity's shaping of the Earth as was discovering how to till the soil. It is almost impossible to envision a technological civilization developing without metals. Even in today's world of "space age" nonmetallic materials of great strength and durability, metals play key roles for which no suitable substitutes have been found. The use of metals paved the way for the introduction of plastics, fiberglass, and more exotic composites and are still necessary in their production and in the fabrication of items made from them. If copper had not been lying around on the Earth's surface, more or less waiting to be picked up, it is possible that *Homo sapiens* would still be largely restricted to small mud and brick towns and subsistence farms.

Metals, along with salt and timber, became important commodities in the regional trade that gradually encompassed the Mediterranean basin and by about 1500 B.C. extended as far as England (where tin was extracted from mines in Cornwall). Technological advances affected social organization; social organization, in turn, promoted technological advances. The movement of metals and other materials meant that wealth could be accumulated by successful traders. Traders had to know what and how much was moving where, what they owed to whom, and who owed them. Social niches opened up for bankers, accountants, entrepreneurs, merchants, shippers, highwaymen, and so on.

In the beginning, it seems, there was the bottom line. Commodities led to commerce, and commerce appears to have led to writing. The very first known examples of writing, incised on small clay tablets in Mesopotamia around 3500 B.C., were accounting records.

Writing (both words and numbers) was obviously a precondition for the advance of civilization. Without it, records of transactions and inventories could not be kept, land could not be surveyed, banking (and credit) could not have progressed past the most primitive stages, and well-organized economic systems could hardly have developed. Such systems generated incentives for invention, division of labor, and economies of scale. Without those organized systems the technologies that created the modern world would never have been developed.

Another crucial invention was Arabic (more accurately Hindu-Arabic) numerals, which came into use in India around 300 B.C. Try to multiply MCMXVIII by CXXXI. No one who has ever attempted to do arithmetic with Roman numerals will underestimate the importance of the invention of Arabic numerals. Science is completely dependent upon quantification—the ability to express complex relationships in a form much more compact than any other language. Arabic numerals provided a basis for that capacity and led to Newton, Einstein, and the explosive release of the technological genie out of the bottle in this century.

Of course, many other giant steps occurred in the rise of technology: the printing press; coal burning; the use of clover to restore soil fertility on farms; the invention of the steam engine, then the inter-

nal combustion engine and the airplane; the development of telephones, radio, and television; the discovery and release of the energy
in atomic nuclei; and the rise of computers, to name just a few. All
of these advances destabilized the environment; they contributed to
making the static everyday world much more dynamic and to increasing the need for humanity to perceive changes occurring on a
scale of decades and centuries.

But these technological developments would not have occurred
without the series of social and organizational inventions that set
the stage for them. Cities, states, empires, laws, slavery, organized
religion, monotheism, political parties, mercantilism, democracy,
and capitalism, to mention some key innovations, all played their
roles in pushing humanity toward dominance of the planet.

The invention of monotheism by an Egyptian pharaoh, Ikhnaton,
and its establishment among the Jews, was a major step in distanc-
ing people from nature. Early religions had evolved from the rites
that hunter-gatherers had invented as they attempted to "control"
the impersonal ecosystems that ruled their lives. In those days human beings feared not only death, loneliness, hunger, and violent
storms, as we do, but also wild beasts, ghosts, witches, and the
spirits of slain enemies and game animals, as well as many other
inanimate and animate features of the natural world.

Gradually gods were invented who could better hear and answer
the pleadings of fearful people than could the spirits of the dead,
but these were very humanlike gods, superpeople like the gods of
ancient Greece and Rome, who were assigned human emotions and
frailties. In Mesopotamia, however, the gods were stripped of many
of their human qualities and granted near-omnipotence. They were
identified with the planets—too far removed from mere mortals to
be pressured by magical rites. People were not expected to understand the motives or actions of the gods; one simply submitted to
them. Submission might or might not result in an earthly reward. A
fatalism thus was injected into cultural evolution that made the
detection, let alone the manipulation, of long-term secular trends
even less likely than it had been before.

For a while the Egyptians retained polytheism, but amplified an element that traces to prehistory and is still seen in major religions today: belief in an afterlife. Indeed, as the pyramids attest, that belief was an obsession for the Egyptians. However, later, Ikhnaton conceived of the sun as a single nonanthropomorphic god with a personal relationship to the pharaoh.

The priests of the old religion are thought, however, to have brought about a return to polytheism, and the idea of a single god only reemerged with the Jews. The Jews went further than Ikhnaton and invented a god that offered them a personal covenant to be the bearers of his religion. They imagined a god with no connection to physical things but rather one who had created all things. Their god had an ethical character and a concern for individual moral behavior (including behavior toward the world environment, although this point has been lost on some modern theologians). All of history was associated with the purpose of this god of the Hebrews, who was thought to be establishing his hegemony over all people.

Thus, according to the Jews, secular trends were thought to be under divine control, moving in ways that were often mysterious to mere mortals. Such notions were and are congenial to leaders wishing to quell unrest in a people living in poverty and desperation; they led to Marx's famous aphorism that religion "is the opium of the people." To this day some powerful monotheistic religions invoke God as an excuse for not facing and doing something about the changes that human beings have brought to the planet. Thousands of years after the pharaohs the concept of an afterlife still helps to slow the recognition of dangerously changing environments. It focuses the minds of the faithful on the fate of individuals in another world rather than on the fate of the life-support systems (and therefore of societies) in this one.

Over these millennia not all people failed to perceive long-term change and its consequences. Greek philosophers attempted to understand the environment rationally as well as mythically. Aristotle's student Theophrastus was not satisfied with a fatalistic acceptance of god-devised purposes for natural events. Instead he wished to determine the natural causes of such phenomena.

Theophrastus' contemporary, Plato, was very much aware of the drying up of springs and soil erosion resulting from the deforestation of his homeland. He wrote of Attica that "what now remains compared with what then existed is like the skeleton of a sick man, all the fat and soft earth having wasted away, and only the bare framework of the land being left." The Greek legend of the Golden Age, in which the Earth gave forth her bounties without the need for human labor, is thought by historian J. Donald Hughes to have promoted both a consciousness of change and a suspicion of it.

Writers in the large cities of the Hellenistic age placed a great emphasis on the virtues of the earlier agricultural period—much as there is an emphasis on old-fashioned virtues among conservatives in the United States today. Overall, however, the Greeks and Romans saw the world not as progressing but as going through endless cycles of "ages," whereas Christians saw it as a "fall" from the perfection created in the Garden of Eden as a result of intervention from the supernatural.

In practical terms, though, the average person in the Greek and Roman eras, and in the Dark Ages to follow, viewed the world as static. The idea of "progress" did not exist. There was little or no conception that human beings were permanently transforming the planet, because the pace of change was much too slow. People expected to live in the same kind of world as their grandparents had, and their grandchildren to live in one like theirs. In the Middle Ages artisans willingly participated in the building of cathedrals that would take several lifetimes to complete, presumably never doubting that such edifices would be used and appreciated by their great-grandchildren when construction was complete.

Imagine the reactions of an American today if asked to contribute to a building project that would take 150 years to finish: "We don't want to tie up our capital in something with no return for a hundred and fifty years!" "Don't you think we'll have robots to construct it long before then?" "Won't a new design and construction process make this one obsolete long before it's finished?" "Maybe it won't be needed then, so shouldn't we spend the money on projects that will benefit the poor right now?" The questions, attacks, and comments would be legion, and they would all have the same underlying theme: technology is changing too fast to make projects taking more than a century sensible.

Americans are aware of some kinds of rapid technological change because the change comes to them in discrete packages and is pounded at them by advertising. One year there were only analog watches, whereas the next year digitals seemed to flood the market. First everyone had to have a small black-and-white TV set, then a large screen, then color, then a VCR, then a Dolby stereo sound system, then a VCR with a Dolby stereo sound system. Soon anyone who can't download any of 514 European, Asian, and cable television channels into his TV's quadraplexed digital memory over the cellular modem in his moving car, transmit it to his home while moving, and play it back for his kids later that night will probably feel deprived.

Each year people are bombarded with propaganda about how the latest model of automobile will make their sex lives even better. Ads for ever more powerful home computers fill magazines and are trumpeted on the Super Bowl TV broadcast—in a world where home computers did not exist a decade before. People do not have to "detect" some technological trends—they are thrust upon them in ways cleverly designed to attract the attention of old minds.

Advertisers do not, however, treat us to fifty beautifully produced television commercials a day saying, "The arms race is becoming more and more unstable; you and your children are increasingly likely to be slaughtered." Ads do not continually announce, "The carbon dioxide buildup continues; more than a billion people may die in a few decades because of it, including you. Get out and do something." The tried-and-true techniques of advertising are rarely applied to helping people see the connections between their future well-being and gradual changes in the physical and sociopolitical environments.

Billions of dollars are spent on television to use sex to sell various products to Americans, but, until recently, not a nickel was allowed to be spent on network television ads to advertise condoms. Ads berate us day and night to cure our halitosis, hemorrhoids, and diarrhea, but none urge us to do anything at all to halt the explosive growth of the human population—which, next to the increase in numbers and explosive power of nuclear weapons, is the most dangerous trend ever faced by human beings.

So cultural evolution has produced awareness of some trends, especially those associated with "progress" and those whose promotion can be the basis for making money for the promoters. This awareness of progress has come in a relatively short time. It was not until the eighteenth century, with the revolutionary overthrow of the old order in France and North America, that a systematic idea of progress appeared.

Although at the time of those revolutions people had the urge to demolish the old order, they also felt the need to rebuild. People in the West began to believe that the present was better than the past and that the future would be better yet. They began to imagine that modern society could transcend the achievements of the ancients, that *Homo sapiens* had possibilities as yet unrealized.

Edward Gibbon, author of *The Decline and Fall of the Roman Empire,* declared in 1787, "Every age of the world has increased, and still increases, the real wealth, the happiness, the knowledge, and perhaps the virtue of the Human Race." The age of exploration produced the beginnings of an understanding of the geography of our globe, and the scientific advances of Newton, Galileo, Pascal, Boyle, Descartes, and others in the seventeenth century had sparked the Enlightenment. Those achievements, combined with the first stirrings of the Industrial Revolution, convinced educated people in Europe and North America that humanity would progress continually onward and upward.

Between 1492 and 1800 the new world started to emerge. When the possibility of change began to make inroads into human consciousness, it was a possibility of people fashioning a better world for themselves. The world began to stretch beyond the village (or nation) to far horizons. Frontiers existed to be conquered, to be colonized, and to supply previously undreamed-of wealth.

After Columbus "discovered" the Western Hemisphere and gold and other precious materials began to flow toward Europe, the feudal system was breaking down, and the economic system of the West began to assume its modern form. The old system, based on payment in kind—direct exchange of goods, labor, produce, and so on—was giving way to one bound together by money. A way of life developed in which trade (as opposed to war, religion, or politics) became the major focus of everyday life. At first, attempts were made both to encourage and to closely regulate this expanding economic activity, producing the period of "mercantilism."

In the mid–eighteenth century, however, the Industrial Revolution ended the last vestiges of feudalism and led to the replacement of mercantilism with a market, or "laissez-faire," economy and the establishment of a capitalist society. Scientific and technological advances merged with this new form of social organization in the nineteenth century. This interplay led to dizzying material and economic advances, rapid urbanization, and an unprecedented interconnection between individuals, regions, and nations. Steam engines installed in factories, locomotives, and steamships made capitalists wealthy, carried travelers and goods rapidly from place to place, and made it easier for armies and navies to kill people who lived great distances away.

In ways that are not fully understood, the *idea* of progress stimulated advances in science and technology, which greatly accelerated humanity's power to alter the planet and, in the process, to increase its own population size. The human population doubled between 1600 and 1850 from 500 million to a billion people, so not only were vast new horizons opened for each individual in this period, but the numbers of those individuals increased dramatically as well. By 1850 people in western Europe and America had made a new world, one as different from the world of feudalism as that world was from the world of hunter-gatherers.

There still, however, was little or no perception of, or thought about, the alterations in the physical, social, and political environments that human advances were generating. Most of humanity's great social and organizational innovations—cities, organized religion, democracy, and so on—came early. The explosion of technology in the last couple of centuries has not been followed by further social changes to meet the challenges it has created. Cultural evolution continued to create caricatures that biased people in such a way that they perceived in "progress," changes that would be individually beneficial in the near term, yet filtered out cues that indicated less desirable long-term trends. Clear advantages could accrue to those who promoted the good things progress would supply; more often than not, only disadvantages were the lot of those who perceived and pointed out the backside of progress.

This failure of cultural evolution to focus more attention on long-term changes is a major reason why an understanding of the human predicament lags far behind the transformations we make in the world. Cultures did not spontaneously develop the ability to deal with long-term trends because they had no need to until very recently.

The short-term view was characteristic of people like the Aivilikmiut Eskimos, with whom one of us lived on Southampton Island in northern Hudson Bay in 1952. In their extremely harsh environment, this group of walrus-hunting Eskimos, like other Eskimo groups, had developed a fatalistic philosophy. The spirits controlled everything, and there was little the Inuit ("the people," as the Eskimos called themselves) could do about it. Life was lived from day to day, with little thought of the future.

It was exceptionally difficult to teach the concept of conservation to the Eskimos. In the early 1950s their hunting activities were decimating local populations of seals, on which the Aivilikmiut depended heavily for food and skins. High prices for white-fox pelts had brought temporary prosperity to the group, prosperity that soon disappeared as fox coats went out of fashion with the women of the Kabloonak ("big eyebrows"—the Eskimo name for Europeans). With cash to spend, Eskimo hunters bought high-powered rifles, with which they took potshots at the seals from the decks of the Peterhead motorized fishing boats they purchased from Scotland.

Unfortunately much of the seal hunting was done in the spring, when a layer of fresh water floated atop the salt water of Hudson Bay. Something on the order of twenty seals killed by rifle fire sank out of reach in the fresh water for every one that was retrieved.

With the old method of hunting seals, using a harpoon equipped with a line affixed to a detachable point, virtually all animals killed were recovered. The pressure of Eskimos' hunting on the seals increased many-fold, but the Aivilikmiut did not connect the growing scarcity of seals with their own activities—because they believed the spirits controlled the supply of game.

Similarly the Aivilikmiut had inherited their own little stock of fossil fuel "capital" after World War II. An airstrip had been built on the island to be used as a staging point for wounded soldiers being flown home from Europe, but the war had ended before it went into service. The project was abandoned, and thousands of fifty-gallon drums of aviation gasoline had been left sitting on the tundra. In those days of cheap oil, the cost of shipping it south was greater than the fuel was worth. A few years later when one of us visited, the supply was well on its way to being exhausted. An Eskimo desiring fuel for his outboard motor or Peterhead would simply drive an ax into a drum, collect a bucketful of the gasoline that poured out, and leave the rest gushing out on the tundra. The spirits had caused the Kabloonak to bring the supply; the spirits would repeat the act if they felt like it.

The fatalism of the Eskimos was exemplified by one of the commonest words in their vocabulary: *ayornamut*. The word is difficult to translate into English, but it more or less means "that's the way the ball bounces" or "it couldn't be helped." The seals are disappearing—*ayornamut*. The gasoline is running out—*ayornamut*. The storm caught the hunting party in open boats, and they all drowned—*ayornamut*.

Eskimos control their immediate environment with a brilliance that elicits great admiration in any sensitive outsider; they know just what to do when a polar bear attacks or a dogsled slips off an ice pan into the water, and they have quickly adapted to dealing with many of the mechanical devices of Kabloonak society. But long-term planning is even more foreign to Eskimo culture than it is to ours. Differences between today and tomorrow are seen as chance differences, controlled by the spirits and not amenable to intervention.

Like other peoples living close to nature today, and like our ancestors for millions of years, the Eskimos' culture was designed to focus the skills of individuals on the immediate problems of sustaining life and the social group. There was nothing lacking in their reasoning power—it just wasn't adaptive for them to spend a lot of effort reasoning about an uncontrollable future, so their biological and cultural evolution did not prepare them to do so.

A similar lack of readiness to register change is widespread in modern society. Leaders of many states still view international relations in much the same way as Assyrian leaders did in Ninevah seven centuries before Christ. They act as if nothing has changed, even though chariots, spears, and bows and arrows have been replaced by tanks, machine guns, and ICBMs carrying multiple nuclear warheads. Nation states attempt to subjugate their fellow human beings in large numbers and to secure and hold as territories large portions of the Earth's surface (including chunks of ocean).

Increased military power, of course, is just one of the critical changes wrought so rapidly by cultural evolution after its agricultural triumph. The astonishing increase in the size of the human population is another. The basics of our culture developed when we were animals living in small groups, where everybody knew every member of the group and his or her relationships to the others. And those basics were the possession of all members of the group. The shaman may have had some secret rituals, the scrapers made by a master stonesmith could not be duplicated by many, and men and women led very different lives, but everyone knew basically the same things.

And everybody could keep track of all, or almost all, of the relationships among the people in their tribe. In a society of one hundred people, typical of communities before the Agricultural Revolution, about five thousand relationships are possible between the different individuals.*

---

* In a group of 4 individuals (ABCD), 6 different two-person relationships (AB, AC, AD, BC, BD, CD) are possible—assuming that A's relation to B is the same as B's to A, something that is not always true. Among 10 individuals there are potentially 45 different

This number is large, but possible to comprehend. One hundred people is probably close to the "designed limit" for human acquaintance—the maximum number of individuals with whom a human being can reasonably interact at more than a superficial level.

Today things are very different. Even small societies are usually composed of hundreds of thousands or millions of people. In a nation like the United States, a city dweller might see about 1,000 people in a single day, many more than hunter-gatherers would see in a lifetime. Moreover the number of potential relationships increases much more quickly than does the number of people one person might encounter. It is impossible for one person to keep track of the 12 million possible relationships between 5,000 people —but many high schools in large cities have that many students. A small town of only 15,000 people has *112 million* possible relationships. Understanding that many is simply inconceivable, yet much of humanity lives in cities of ten times that population or more.

It is interesting to note that most people have regular relationships approximately as large as our "design limit." The total number of one's friends and relatives rarely is more than the population of a prehistoric village—about 100 to 200 individuals.

---

relationships, and among 30 there are 435. An individual can keep something like that number of relationships in mind, but if the group size increases even to 1,000 (almost 500,000 relationships), the task becomes impossible. In modern societies no individual can grasp all the relationships among the members of the society—since the number of relationships is roughly half of the *square* of the number of individuals. The actual formula is $n(n-1)/2$, where n is the number of individuals; some results of using the formula are given below:

PEOPLE	POSSIBLE RELATIONSHIPS
10	45
20	190
100	4,950
1000	499,500
5000	12,497,500
15,000	112,492,500

As the number of people increases from 10 to 15,000 (not beyond the number of people in a large city with whom a person may interact in some way), the number of possible relationships increases by 2.5 million times!

If the increase in numbers of people has accelerated enormously
in the last century, then so has other cultural change. Think about
the rate at which we have entered this "new world" in the twentieth
century. Many people who are alive today were born when the
automobile was a curiosity and there were no freeways, airplanes,
radios, refrigerators, dryers, paperback books, frozen dinners, tape
recorders, TVs, VCRs, compact disc players, computers, antibiotics,
credit cards, lasers, satellites, or nuclear weapons.

Anyone who is over fifty years old today was born into a world
where a majority of the countries that are presently in the United
Nations did not even exist. At the time of the birth of those who are
now over seventy-five, there had never been a world war, electricity
and pasteurization were rarities, and one in three babies died in
infancy. In 1945 only half as many people lived on earth as there are
in 1988; at the end of World War II, the gigantic nuclear arsenal
that now threatens the population was nonexistent.

Many of us remember the enormous computers of the late 1950s
behind glass walls in colleges and in banks, processing "IBM cards"
for registration and accounting. In computing power we are more
separated from the world of the 1950s than the 1950s was from the
accountants of Hammurabi. Those "mainframe" computers that
housed school and other records in the 1960s could perform fewer
calculations per second than the average AT-class machine of today,
now available for under two thousand dollars.

There was a famous advertisement for IBM in Britain in the early
1980s that said (to translate into dollars), "A Rolls-Royce for $55? A
custom-tailored suit for 19 cents? These would be the prices today if
cars and suits had followed the same cost trends as computers." A
new computer down the road from us at NASA Ames can calculate
250 billion times per second, more calculating power than existed in
toto in 1960.

But the trends in most of the rest of our life are not so benign,
although they may be just as startling if we learn ways of perceiving
them. And the situation they have created is unprecedented in our
history. There has never before been a time when we have dramati-

cally overpopulated the Earth and have the ability to alter the ecological systems of the entire planet in a few days.

The overload of information in modern society means that even the most brilliant and well-informed members can store only a small portion of the society's culture. It has been said that John Stuart Mill was the last man to know everything. This may or may not be true in detail, but, as we have just seen, the complexity of our culture has multiplied astronomically in the past hundred years.

This lack of familiarity of people with their culture can be a fatal flaw. Politicians often make critical decisions about issues ranging from the proliferation of nuclear missiles to AIDS in nearly total ignorance of the technical aspects of the problems involved. At the same time the scientists and technologists that politicians need to rely on for technical advice frequently have little grasp of the manifold social and political consequences of their discoveries.

Unconscious cultural evolution developed in small-group, short time-horizon animals in full possession of their culture. It is inadequate to deal with a world overpopulated with individuals who are only partially in contact with their own cultures yet who must make critical decisions about the medium and long term.

Unconscious cultural evolution has not led people to pay explicit attention to their biological or cultural evolutionary heritage. Cultural evolution has not compensated for the baggage of an outdated human perceptual system. It has not, for example, invented a cultural "time lapse" system for perceiving the gradual changes that human biological systems are incapable of sensing. It has not led school curricula to convey the limits of the human perceptual system. It has not led to the establishment of governmental institutions that force politicians to pay attention to the long-term consequences of their actions. It has not generated TV programs designed to produce a widespread awareness of the diverse limitations and built-in biases imposed upon people by their biological and cultural evolutionary history. It has not provided us with an inventory of tools specifically designed to overcome biases. Cultural evolution has not even allowed most human beings to perceive that their familiar world results from an ongoing evolutionary *process,* even as it has accelerated that process to unprecedented rates of change. It has not, therefore, given us the means of survival.

Section Two

THE MATCHED
AND THE MISMATCHED MIND

4

CARICATURES OF REALITY

How the Mind Is Mismatched

THE WORLD is full of events, be they sudden wind shifts, sunrises, minuscule movements of particles in the air, the swift attacks of hawks. Continents drift slowly along with the Earth's large surface plates, while the Earth itself rotates upon its axis and moves around the sun. Human skin sheds millions of particles daily and hosts whopping populations of bacteria. Large pressure waves (sounds) move through the air. In the modern world radiant electromagnetic energy fills the "air"; if you had the proper sensory equipment, you could receive television programs directly as well as all the telephone calls in your area.

The caricatured "small worlds" of all animals have been biased by evolution to meet the needs of each particular species. To us the small worlds of many of those animals would be strange indeed. Bats live in a world dominated by echoes. As they fly, they orient to their environments by sending out pulses of sound, usually at frequencies too high for our ears to detect. The sound waves are reflected by objects—tree branches, buildings, the flying insects that bats eat. The sensory systems of bats assemble the returning echoes into a "picture" of the world so detailed that in total darkness they can weave rapidly between suspended wires and easily find and catch small moths. Instead of sending out sounds, electric fishes generate an electric field around themselves. Objects, including other fishes upon which they prey, cause distortions in the field that are detected by the electric fish. The world put together by the minds of electric fishes is based in large part on perceptions of distorted electric fields.

While these animals are relatively unusual, familiar creatures also live in worlds quite different from ours. Some up-scale kennels advise the traveling owners of neurotic dogs to send their pets postcards to keep them from getting forlorn. The owners are told to *sit on the postcard for an hour or so before sending it,* since dogs, like many other mammals, are primarily "smell animals." The ability of smell animals to detect chemicals in their environment is much greater than ours. Moles, for example, are virtually blind and live in worlds constructed almost entirely from information received by their chemical and tactile senses. Some male moths are so sensitive to smells that they can detect a female a mile upwind, presumably after running across as little as a single molecule of the chemical signal she emits. Yet the worlds of bats, electric fishes, dogs, moles, and moths are as real to them as our world is to us.

The outside world is silent and dull of itself. There is no color in nature, no sound, no touch, no smell or feel. All these wonders exist inside our nerve circuits. The rich world we perceive is actually within us, even though it is only a shadow of the world that might fill our brains. But suppose your nervous system could generate sensations to correspond with *all* the possible stimuli "out there" in the world? If your nervous system could, your experience would be chaotic, unimaginable, completely overwhelming. "Light" is but a minuscule part of the spectrum of electromagnetic energy. "Sound" is a small splash in the pool of swimming molecules, atoms, and subatomic particles in which we are immersed. Much of what is "out there" is irrelevant to our survival, so minding the world involves both inclusion and exclusion. Senses select what is important and keep the rest of the world out. The entire human mental system is designed to give some events fast access to consciousness and to insulate us from others. And each sense is "designed" to extract a very specific kind of information. You *see* light, you do not taste it.

There is a physical blind spot in the eye, where the optic nerve exits the retina (the light-sensitive tissue at the back of the eye) on the way to the brain. Here there are no photoreceptor cells, so this part of the retina cannot respond to light. When the lens of the eye focuses an image of a small object on the blind spot, the image disappears. We don't notice the loss: our brain simply fills it in, using the context of the rest of the picture. It is not that something that was there is now gone; we don't know that anything is missing.

Vision, our most complex window on the world, is even more limited than this example implies. One reason is that we look out at the world through an almost impenetrable net inside our own eyes. Although the rods and cones are the first retinal cells to receive light, they face *away* from the light and are at the *innermost* layer of the retina. The vessels that supply oxygen to the retina block the light traveling to it. Because our nervous system is structured to respond to changes, we never see these blood vessels, since they are always there.

You can see for yourself that you look at the world through blood vessels. Get a pen flashlight, a blank piece of paper, and a pencil. Turn on the flashlight and hold it near the outer edge of your eye and jiggle it around until the light shines inside your eye. At one point you will see a luminous red "spiderweb," which is a reflection of the blood vessels. By looking at the paper immediately, you can trace a map of these vessels with your pencil.

Have you ever passed a sheepdog whose hair completely covers its eyes? It is hard to imagine how it can ever see anything. If you were from another planet and looked at the human nervous system, you would have the same feeling. The blind spots and the thicket of blood vessels in our eyes ultimately don't interfere with our perception of the outside world. Because they are always present, we never "mind" them.

With all this confusion and blockage of perception, how, then, does the human mind decide which parts of the incoming information are important and which are irrelevant? Consider an analogy: when you make a telephone call, you do not wish to hear all possible voices on the circuit; you want to hear only the voice of the person you called. All animals need to limit the information they receive. Our sensory systems do this by restricting incoming data to very little of what is actually present in the outside world. And our minds therefore must extract from the received cacophony of the entire "big" world a specialized "small world" in which an individual can act and live. For most animals, and for most of humanity, this radical mental filtration, or caricature, has clearly been successful. Organisms adapt to their small world, which in turn lets them succeed in their particular environmental niche.

In this chapter we examine the ways the mind simplifies and caricatures reality so that we might begin to make conscious changes in the way we perceive. The caricatures are created by all parts of the mind; by the design of the senses themselves; by the wiring of the nerve circuits; by processing information in the brain; by interpreting information. And they are involved in making decisions, even life-and-death decisions. The abundant different processes at work within the mind serve one major end: to simplify the outside world so that it can be responded to properly and immediately.

This is not the way we ordinarily think about the nature of our own experience, so it is an important point to consider in some detail. The world seems, to the ordinary observer, to consist of discrete objects: cats and chocolate cakes, shoes and sealing wax, even cabbages and kings. But think about it. How could a cat, or an image of a cat, get inside the brain? The "big" outside world doesn't enter in directly.

It is easy for us to ignore how limited our view of the world is. After all, our eyes reveal a brilliant, colorful world; our ears help us appreciate the complexities of Mozart; our noses allow us to tell a '45 Mouton from cheap red wine. Other people and even other organisms act as if they live in the same world. In spite of its seeming limitlessness, the world of human experience and the world of any animal's experience is in truth Lilliputian. Modern analysis of the nervous system and the mind yields a surprising conclusion: instead of experiencing the world as it is, people experience only about one trillionth of outside events: a small world indeed!

The assembly of the caricatures we create begins with the first receptors that actually sense the world. The primary "method" of selecting information is determined by the nature of the senses themselves. Although there are an amazing variety of ways of extracting information from the world, only the operations of sight, hearing, taste, smell, and touch are available to us. These senses evolved, among other things, to detect threats—sudden darkness, unusual noises, off tastes, new smells, unexpected contacts—and they kept our ancestors out of danger. Each sense captures a tiny bit of the outside world and relays it to the brain. The ability to taste the poison in an unfamiliar fruit combines with the capacity to react fast enough to spit it out before it was swallowed.

Like those of other creatures, human sensory systems are economical; only a limited range of stimuli is received through each sense. We also have senses that keep us informed about temperature and about a very few features of our internal world, in order to help us maintain balance, coordinate and control limb movements, and detect internal difficulties through signals we interpret as pain and nausea. At each step in the pathway from sensory nerve cell to the brain the world becomes more organized and simplified in the mind. The external world, in truth so chaotic and changing, becomes to us a stable simple caricature. Instead of becoming confused by seeing thousands of reflecting bits of glass, thousands of blocks of gray concrete, scores of doors leading to the street, we perceive *one* skyscraper. The parts fit together. So from a relative trickle of sensory information, the brain computes its caricature. The brain then monitors our sensory input, scanning for information that doesn't fit the current small world. Lack of fit, such as noise where it was previously silent, would signal a significant change or threat to which the brain would need to react.

The nervous system then organizes information so that relatively few responses suffice in a wide variety of settings. We want to fight or flee immediately when we perceive threats, although there are other alternatives, such as freezing or panicking. Much of the intricate network of receptors, ganglia, and analytic cells in the cortex (the enfolded outer part of the brain) serves as part of the selection system. Perception of some events may trigger immediate concerns. Observing a car weaving all over the road may give rise to a message such as "Watch that car in the left lane." Some events, such as the arrival of a bank overdraft notice, may reinforce chronic concerns, repeating a message such as "I'm broke." Other events may simply mark changes: a person entering the room may trigger the message "Here's George."

Our caricatures are useful insofar as they correspond *closely enough* with reality that they help us to survive. For most other organisms, and for the majority of people for most of human history, the process of simplification has clearly been successful. Organisms remain, for the most part, well adapted to their ecological niches. But most animals are able to survive only in their native habitats. A parrot abruptly transported to Antarctica would not survive; a penguin could not live in the Amazon basin. But human beings, as we have seen, are extremely adaptable.

That adaptability, unfortunately, is also a source of dangers. We are extremely sensitive to the legendary "boiled frog" syndrome. Frogs placed in a pan of water that is slowly heated will be unable to detect the gradual but deadly trend; they will sit still until they die. Like the frogs, many people seem unable to detect the gradual but lethal trend in which population and economic growth threaten to boil civilization. They keep working to turn up the heat, because they can't detect its rise.

In the complex world of today people are often agitated by the need to adapt to new situations in their lives. Once an invention becomes widespread, as electronic calculators or jet planes have, everyone is under pressure to adapt to the new situations created by the innovations. Adaptation is stressful, as many travelers who fear flying will instantly agree, and with today's rates of environmental change we are always accelerating our efforts to adapt to our own creations.

The human world, of course, is primarily a sight world and secondarily a sound world. The primacy of sight is, you will recall, a legacy of our ancestors' having been arboreal animals for millions of years and then having reared up on their hind legs. Now the sight-sound world is woefully inadequate, because many of the threats to our lives and future are not simple sensory events that can be incorporated into our caricatures of the world. Indeed many of them aren't directly accessible to our senses at all.

When was the last time you went out in the rain and tasted its acidity? In a few places, including some Chinese cities, it is possible to find rain so acid that you can taste it. In most cases, however, a shift in the acidity of rain is not directly detected by the senses. Instead delicate scientific instruments, which must be used very carefully, are required to determine the acidity of a given rainfall, snowfall, or fog.

The sour rain makes little direct difference to us—rain is not acid enough to hurt our skin, it won't interfere with our reproduction or uptake of nutrients. In fact outside of rotting away beautiful old stone carvings in such places as the Acropolis and polluting drinking water, acid rain appears to have little direct impact on people or their artifacts.

The indirect effects of acid rain and related problems make themselves evident slowly and thus are readily tuned out by built-in filters. One episode of acid rain does not turn trout belly-up or cause trees to keel over. Only when large expanses of forest in Europe began to die did the media begin to give extensive coverage to the problem, thus attracting the attention of a substantial portion of the public in the nations affected. Previously acid rain had been largely a concern of ecologists, trout and salmon fishers, and owners of resorts on newly dead, acidified lakes.

Some of the causes of acid rain are even more difficult for us to perceive than the effects. A few gigantic, belching smokestacks create a rather obvious stimulus; there is nothing subtle about them at all. The colorless gases escaping from the exhausts of our cars as we zip along freeways pass virtually undetected at the source. It is only when they accumulate and are converted by sunlight into photochemical smog that they command notice. And even there they are usually tuned out.

The famed smog of Los Angeles provides a classic example of the adaptability of the human nervous system. A visitor to the L.A. basin, arriving on a smoggy day, is often immediately appalled by the quality of air he or she is expected to breathe. But, as with many other constant phenomena, the locals hardly notice. A few years ago one of us arrived at John Wayne Airport in Orange County in the early evening to give a lecture. Every streetlight was surrounded by a halo of smog, and his eyes immediately began watering profusely. As a visitor from the (relatively) smog-free San Francisco area, he felt obliged to kid his host: "Well, at least we have a nice clear night for the lecture." His host's serious response: "Yeah—you should have been here a couple of weeks ago. We had a lot of smog then."

The nervous system of the Orange County resident had adjusted to a high level of noxious air pollution. Until the smog got so bad that coughing and wheezing resulted, he was unaware of its presence. He paid no more attention to minor eye irritation than one does to a persistent cough; he was thoroughly habituated.

Indeed smog in the L.A. basin is not generally viewed as a problem with its roots in human behavior. Its origin in a decision made by auto makers and tire companies in the 1930s is largely unrecognized. People with a stake in the automobile industry decided shortly before World War II to dismantle the Los Angeles area's quite effective mass transit system in order to enhance the market for cars and tires. They did a good job. But to most Angelenos, the affliction of smog is an act of God, not an act of *Homo sapiens.* They think of smog in terms of temperature inversions and Santa Ana winds, rather than decisions by auto moguls and short-sighted politicians. It is even included in the *weather report,* something originally urged by environmentalists to raise public consciousness, but which now has the effect of making it seem all the more natural. The contributions of auto exhausts—in Los Angeles and elsewhere—to the problem of acid rain registers on our old minds not at all.

Even more difficult to perceive, and probably even more serious than the acid-rain problem, is the buildup of carbon dioxide (CO_2) in the atmosphere. With every breath, you exhale the product of your slow metabolic fires. You can't taste, smell, or see that carbon dioxide, but it's there nonetheless. When you stand by a wood fire or sniff the exhaust of a car, you can smell some of the by-products of combustion—but not the CO_2 that is being given off. Your brain *can* detect CO_2—its buildup in your lungs triggers your breathing —but not in any conscious way.

CO_2 is thus an insidious environmental threat, and it is also one of the most potentially deadly. It contributes to the "greenhouse effect," which warms the planet. This, in turn, will alter the climate, changing it in ways that are unpredictable, but that almost certainly will be catastrophic for agriculture. Significant, long-term, and unpredictable changes in climate would almost certainly produce immense famines.

In the long run CO_2-induced warming would melt the polar ice caps, thus flooding many areas, putting New York City, Washington, D.C., and Sacramento, California, under water. Much of eastern England and the low countries would be inundated, and millions of people would be forced by rising waters out of the Tokyo-Yokohama area of Japan. Bangladesh would become submerged, and Rangoon, Calcutta, and Buenos Aires would be gone. Florida would largely disappear, and much of the lower Mississippi River Valley would become an inland sea.

Yet, even for environmental scientists, the CO_2 threat does not produce a strong danger signal. The warning consists of a wobbly line on a graph produced by a sensitive instrument on Mauna Loa volcano in Hawaii. But there is a lot of natural variation in the climate, so that right now it is difficult to sort out climatic changes caused by an enhanced greenhouse effect from natural fluctuations. Nonetheless climatologists are virtually unanimous in thinking that the threat should be taken very seriously. Our old minds, however, don't have the capacity to recognize the threat of CO_2 increase. After all, a squiggly line on a chart is hard to translate into a portent of catastrophe. Until catastrophic effects are evident, old minds will have trouble registering the problem. It took the drought of the summer of 1988 (which may or may not have been related to the greenhouse effect) to start to focus the attention of the public and decision makers on this issue.

A similar account could be produced about the threats to Earth's fragile ozone shield, which is equally obscure to most people. The average person doesn't know what ozone is (it's a rare compound of oxygen in which three oxygen molecules are combined instead of the usual two). You can't see it, although you can smell it—ozone produces that "electric" smell after a lightning bolt or electric arc has occurred. It is also an important component of air pollution.

Obscure as it may be, ozone plays a critical role in our lives. It has the most useful property of absorbing certain wavelengths of (UV) light, a range known as UV-B. UV-B is nasty stuff. If there were not enough ozone very high in the atmosphere screening out the sun's UV-B, the incidence of skin cancer would go way up, plants would have trouble photosynthesizing, and some animals that can see ultraviolet light might be disoriented, among other effects.

Our nervous systems cannot measure the amount of ozone in the atmosphere or detect ultraviolet radiation of any kind. That is why it's called *ultra*violet—it consists of wavelengths of the electromagnetic spectrum slightly shorter than those of the violet light we can perceive. "Light" is merely the name we give to that part of the electromagnetic spectrum we can detect with our eyes. Wavelengths longer than those of visible red light—infrared—cannot be seen by us but can be felt as warmth.

So we're not equipped to detect either ozone or the radiation that it shields us from. In addition, chlorofluorocarbons and some of the other chemicals that will destroy ozone are also not detectable by the senses. In this case scientists are not agreed on the seriousness of the threat, although the consensus is that it shouldn't be taken lightly. Like acid rain and CO_2, however, the problem is that the old mind can't grasp it.

We'll spare you the discussion on pesticides, especially the modern synthetic ones, which can be both extremely poisonous and extremely long-lasting. They can produce obvious short-term benefits and cryptic long-term hazards. The death of pests following spraying is a short-term event, easily perceived and with an obvious cause-and-effect relationship. The consequences that appear later on, often involving the disruption of ecosystems and worsening of pest problems may or may not be dramatic, but accurately identifying the connections cannot be done by the untutored senses.

Other serious threats, such as radiation, can't be detected by the senses at all. Imagine the shock of the Lapps when they discovered that their way of life had been destroyed by an invisible menace originating more than a thousand miles away. Defending reindeer from wolves comes easy to Lapps; defending the lichen-reindeer food chain from Chernobyl proved impossible, not only for them but for the cream of the Soviet scientific community. The human senses also cannot detect a few parts per million (ppm) of the deadly cancer-causing agent dioxin in our drinking water, or a very thin film of residual chlorinated hydrocarbon pesticide on a peach.

Our original caricatures of reality sufficed for quite a while: evolution equipped us with chemical-detection systems sufficiently refined to deal with most of the toxins of the world that made us. That's why unripe apples taste sour and spoiled meat tastes awful. But in that old world, carcinogens (cancer-causing substances) were of little evolutionary significance, since most individuals did not survive long enough to get cancer, and our distant mammalian ancestors may have evolved some resistance to natural carcinogens. Preventing cancer is especially difficult for old minds to deal with, since decades may pass between first exposure to cancer-causing agents and the appearance of the disease, and not all exposures result in cancer. Note how many people still smoke, since taking up the habit is usually separated by decades from the consequences.

Thus we caricature the world in part because we're unable to detect many aspects of it. Another source of our caricature is the nervous system's tendency to focus primarily upon *new* events—the fact of something happening compared with nothing happening. The rising sun is bright compared with the previous night's darkness, a sudden loud noise contrasts with the silence earlier. But during the day we don't notice the sun, and during the silence we are unaware of the absence of sound. The senses notify the brain about the *changes* in the external environment; they announce the beginnings and endings of events and cease responding in between. When an air conditioner is turned on in a room, you notice the hum at first, but soon you don't notice it. You become habituated (accustomed) to, and hence ignore, the noise. When the machine is turned off, you again take note, this time because of the *absence* of the noise.

Airline pilots grow habituated to everything working correctly in their largely computer-automated jets. They have a great deal of difficulty continually checking and rechecking dozens of similar dials and carefully scanning skies in which no other aircraft are usually visible. Habituation keeps them from being alert in an unchanging environment. Their minds tend to "wander" because of the numbing routine: the inertial guidance system worked perfectly on the last five hundred flights, the flaps were "always" extended for takeoff, the pointers on the gauges are in familiar positions. Old minds are poor monitors of the routine. In an airplane, depending on them to do so frequently leads to disaster—"human engineering" has a long way to go in the cockpit.

Habituation is built into our sensory neurons. It provides the basis for the mind's ability to ignore continuing phenomena and to seize instead upon short-term incidents. Most vertebrate nervous systems are geared to "news": loosely speaking, their motto is "Call me when something new happens."

Habituation is only one aspect of the caricaturing process of which we must be aware. To get some understanding of the entire system through which we perceive everything up to and including atomic bombs, let's look at a less complex mental apparatus than the human mind. In 1959 Jerome Lettvin and his colleagues at MIT devised an experiment in which visual stimulation could be offered to one eye of an immobilized frog. The frog was placed so that its eye was at the center of a hemisphere seven inches in radius. Small metal objects were placed in different positions on the inner surface of the hemisphere and moved around from the outside by magnets.

The investigators measured "what the frog's eye tells the frog's brain," by using microelectrodes to detect the electrical impulses sent to the brain by the eye. Infinite distinct visual patterns can be presented to a frog—colors, shapes, movements, and various combinations of all these. When various objects, colors, and patterns were presented to the frog, however, the investigators noticed a remarkable phenomenon. Out of all the stimulation, *only four kinds of "messages" were sent to the brain.*

These four kinds of messages contained information relating directly to the two most important aspects of a frog's survival: obtaining food and escaping danger. One message provided a general outline of the environment. Two of the messages formed a kind of bug-perceiving system: one detected moving edges; the other responded to small dark objects entering the field of vision. Frogs only capture and eat live insects. A frog surrounded by piles of dead flies would starve to death, because it has no means for detecting stationary objects. The fourth message reported sudden decreases in light, as would happen when a large enemy rapidly approached.

The frog's brain is thus "wired" to ignore all but extremely limited types of information. Higher animals, ourselves included, are not as restricted in sensory experience as is the frog. The visual system of a cat selects for edges, angles, and objects moving in different directions. In monkeys some cells seem to respond to specific aspects of the environment. In one study experimenters used a microscopically fine electrode to probe one cell in the cortex of a rhesus monkey. They couldn't find a stimulus that would make it respond by generating an electrical nerve impulse. They placed food in front of the monkey, showed the monkey cards, moving objects, and so on. They tried everything they could think of and found no response from the cell. Finally as a joke they waved their hands "good-bye" to the cell, in front of the monkey's eye. The cell responded wildly.

Then they showed lots of new handlike things to the monkey. The more similar a stimulus was to a monkey's hand, the greater was the response in that cell. At least in the monkey, we can identify a single cell that responds strongly to an extremely specific feature—moving monkeys' hands.

So, as you can see, each element of the visual system of most animals, including the visual cortex, is designed to select information about only some kinds of changes in the environment, to transmit and analyze that information, and ignore the rest. The human nervous system evolved in the old world to work in the same manner.

As does a sculptor who whittles away excess material, the "hardware" of our nervous system contains many mechanisms that reduce the information that reaches us. But even this drastically reduced flow of selected information, to which we respond mostly when there is a sharp change in the information, is still too much for the mind to act upon. So the caricature process goes further; most organisms have "caricatured responses" to specific signals. These reactions are called fixed action patterns by ethologists—students of behavior in natural conditions. When the selected information appears, the animals are set to respond almost automatically.

When a newly hatched duckling or gosling is twelve to eighteen hours old, something quite remarkable can happen. If it follows something moving for ten minutes, the duckling then continues to follow the object anywhere. Psychologists say the duckling becomes "imprinted" on the moving object. In nature, of course, the most likely moving "object" that a duckling of that age sees is its mother, so this "prepared reaction" is an adaptive strategy—it leads to a greater chance of survival.

If, however, someone intervenes, and shows the duckling anything that moves during that period, be it a rectangle or a decoy on wheels, the duckling will imprint on it. In an early dramatic demonstration of imprinting, Konrad Lorenz, one of the most influential ethologists, himself appeared in front of a flock of goslings at the right time. Presto! The tiny goslings followed him as if he were their mother.

Please note that the "neural program" for imprinting is a simple way to deal with the world. In nature the duckling usually automatically follows and bonds to its mother, but there is no strict stipulation in the nervous system that the mother be specified precisely; this would be far too complex. The caricature seems to be: "Follow anything that appears within twelve to eighteen hours after you hatch."

Fixed action patterns such as imprinting are unlearned behaviors that appear or are "released" in the presence of certain stimuli. Niko Tinbergen, another leading ethologist, identified the simple stimulus that caused males of a small freshwater fish, the three-spined stickleback, to attack other males. If you show a male a perfect but colorless model of a stickleback, it will not attack. But show it a model with a red-painted belly and it will attack vigorously. Even very poor models with red bellies are assaulted. The models that spark a stickleback attack do not have to look at all like the fish, but they do have to have the critical sign. Again there is a caricature here. It is probably more economical in the world of the stickleback for the male to attack anything with a red belly than for it to be more discriminating.

Many reactions have a similar innate basis in human beings. Success in child rearing is the final goal of biological evolution and is too important to be left to finicky individual choices. What if a mother didn't like her child? Evolution has built into the perceptual systems of adult human beings interesting ways of bonding them to babies. A key one is a phenomenon we know as "cuteness." Note that babies have much larger foreheads, eyes, and cheeks than do adults. This is called the neotenic face: the more a face approaches the proportions of baby's face, the more we goo and gaa, ooh and ahh.

These same facial-proportion relationships exist in other mammals as well. Our seemingly built-in tendency to like these proportions is taken advantage of in the media. Advertisers select attractive female faces that show similar proportions: large eyes and forehead. Facial characteristics are not only a ticket to success in the fashion industry—Dwight Eisenhower's "neotenic" face won the public's trust, and Mickey Mouse is beloved throughout the world, not only because of his antics but also because of his high brow and large eyes. Teddy bears share the same characteristics.

Evolution has bestowed many other ways of ensuring that mothers love their children. Many innate reactions of a child, among them giving distress calls, bring up the "correct" reaction in the mother. The child cries and thus "trains" the mother to respond appropriately by picking it up, feeding, or cuddling it.

As in the case of the duckling, the world of the infant is simpler and more selected than is the adult world; a baby's small world is assumed to be quite similar to that of most nonhuman vertebrates. Newborns are biologically unprepared to function in the adult world, but they are well designed to function in their own limited world. Their extreme egocentrism is adaptive. An extremely narrow perspective is important for survival; newborns notice objects that are physically very close to them. At birth, human beings can focus their eyes only to about ten inches away, about the distance from the breast to the mother's face. As months pass, their very small world progressively expands, and so do their thought and perspective. They also become less egocentric. Within a few years the range of vision expands to the larger world of the adult.

Human beings, however, while having genetically programmed responses to certain stimuli, also have a second and more flexible portion of the mental system, which quickly comes into play as babies turn into children, and children into adults. What distinguishes even young children from frogs is that their sensory systems present them with a much greater diversity of perceptions. The diversity is so great that it is difficult to accept that adults, too, have built-in tunnel vision, that our nervous systems severely limit our view of the world.

The *flexibility* that human beings enjoy in interpreting experience is also much greater than that of frogs due to the increased complexity of the human brain and sensory nervous systems. Images move in and out of consciousness, like programs in a small computer. Human beings can "retune" their sensory systems to a degree impossible for frogs or any other nonhuman animal.

To experience this, close your eyes at a gathering where several people are talking at the same time. Listen to one person speaking, then "tune" him or her out and listen to another person. It is surprising how easy it is to tune our attention in this way. In fact we have little reason to be surprised at this ability, since we tune ourselves continuously to suit our needs and expectations. The mild surprise comes because we are not usually aware of such self-tuning. The tuning process is programmable, within the fixed sensory limits. It is often driven by need. After we perspire during the summer, we like the taste of foods that are saltier than usual. We don't consciously reason that we need salt and that we should take more salt in with the diet; we simply *like* foods that at other times we would consider grossly oversalted.

To deal with the abundance of information floating around inside it, the mental system organizes sensory stimuli into the simplest *meaningful* pattern. We do not experience a "semirectangular expanse of red with many fine lines along the edge," but a single "red book." When we hear a siren getting louder, we experience an emergency vehicle approaching; when a retreating object becomes smaller and smaller, we don't think it is miraculously shrinking, but that it is going farther away from us. In any situation we tend to experience the simplest organization of the stimuli registered based on previous experience with similar stimuli.

Look at the two drawings of a cube, but from different angles. The one on the left we see in two dimensions, and we would not normally identify it as a cube. It is simpler to see it as a hexagon than as a cube viewed from one of its points. We see the drawing on the right as a cube in three dimensions because that is a simpler object to see than a group of quadrangles and triangles would be.

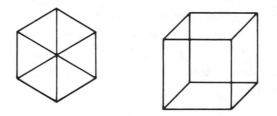

The perceptual system is so specialized for organizing sensory information that it attempts to organize things into a meaningful pattern even when we know there is none. We look up at a cloud and see shapes in it—a whale, a bird. Op art, popular in the 1960s, played with this predisposition to organize. Op art is at once intriguing and unsettling because we continually try to organize certain figures that are designed by the artist to have no organization.

The organization of the world, as shown by such art, changes according to our interpretation of the sensory input. Different cultures, because of the worlds they live in, also develop different caricatures, and it is always instructive to observe them. Pygmies of the Congo dwell primarily in dense forest and thus rarely see across large distances. As a result they do not develop as strong a concept of size constancy as we do. Colin Turnbull, an anthropologist who studied Pygmies, once took his Pygmy guide on a trip out of the forest. As they were crossing a wide plain, they saw a herd of buffalo in the distance.

Kenge looked over the plain and down to a herd of buffalo some miles away. He asked me what kind of insects they were, and I told him buffalo, twice as big as the forest buffalo known to him. He laughed loudly and told me not to tell him such stupid stories. . . . We got into the car and drove down to where the animals were grazing. He watched them getting larger and larger, and though he was as courageous as any pygmy, he moved over and sat close to me and muttered that it was witchcraft. . . . When he realized they were real buffalo he was no longer afraid, but what puzzled him was why they had been so small, and whether they had really been small and suddenly grown larger or whether it had been some kind of trickery.

How do we learn to see in such different ways? Studies with animals reveal the immense adaptability of the system, especially in infancy. Early on we settle on many of the rules that will be used throughout life to form our caricatures. For any animal to interpret visual information, it must be able to register immediately what it is doing and what is changing in the world so as to relate body movements and visual experience. At MIT Richard Held and Harry Hein investigated this relationship using kittens. They raised a group of kittens in total darkness except for an hour each day. During this hour one group was allowed to move freely around a patterned cylinder; another sat passively in a gondola pulled by a cat from the active group. Later both groups were exposed to the same visual stimulation. The kittens with an "active" experience with light learned to see normally, but the vision of the other kittens was permanently impaired. Visual information coming in must in some way be correlated, through early experience, with body movements, or a nonadaptive caricature will result.

Look straight ahead, then move your eyes sharply to the left. Your *view* of the scene has changed dramatically, but the "world" remains stable. If you analyze it closely, you find that the eyes are *always* in motion anyway. We hardly ever gaze at any one point too long. Even if you try to fix vision at one point on an object, very small involuntary movements occur. Portions of the retina are constantly stimulated as a result of both large sweeps and small movements, although at any given moment only some receptor cells are stimulated. The brain keeps a record of current movements in order to account for the visual changes caused by the motion of the eye.

Jiggle your right eye on the right side with your right index finger, so that your eye moves to the left. When it does, the world seems to jump. The difference between this and the previous movement is that we rarely, if ever, move our eye with our hand, so there is no record of movement signals to account for the change in stimulation. We are surprised when a videotape we shot by panning a hand-held camera is jumpy because while shooting, our vision automatically compensated for our eye movement as we panned across the scene. When we view the tape, there is no such compensation.

At the turn of the century George Stratton reasoned that if perception is a process of adaptation to the environment, then it ought to be possible to learn to adapt to an entirely different arrangement of visual information, *as long as it was consistent.* To test this hypothesis, Stratton wore a special prism lens, so that he saw the world turned 180 degrees. The world was topsy-turvy: up/down and left/right were reversed.

Stratton had great difficulty at first doing even simple things such as reaching for or grasping an object. He felt very dizzy when he walked, and he bumped into things. Soon he began to adapt. After only three days of wearing the inverted lens, he wrote, "Walking through the narrow spaces between pieces of furniture required much less art than hitherto. I could watch my hands as they wrote, without hesitating or becoming embarrassed thereby."

By the fifth day he could move around the house easily. On the seventh day he enjoyed his evening walk as usual. On the eighth day he removed the lens and wrote, "The reversal of everything from the order to which I had grown accustomed during the last week gave the scene a surprisingly bewildering air which lasted for several hours." Once Stratton had adapted to the new relationship between information and perception, it took some time to unlearn it.

More than sixty years later Ivo Kohler in Germany conducted further experiments in the effects of optical rearrangement. His observers wore various kinds of distorting lenses for weeks. At first they all had great difficulty seeing the world. But in a few weeks they had adapted. One of Kohler's subjects was able to ski and drive a motorcycle through town while wearing distorting lenses! People can also adapt to color distortions. In another of Kohler's demonstrations his subjects wore glasses in which one lens was green and one red. In a few hours they were aware of no difference in color between the lenses. Instead of bifocals Paul Ehrlich wears a distance-correcting contact lens in the left eye and uses his nearsighted right eye for reading. He becomes aware of the lens only when the left eye is blocked when viewing a distant object or the right is blocked when viewing a near one. Our caricatures can be adapted quite quickly when the stimulus to do so is sufficient.

But is it just our perceptions that are subject to the simplifying processes of the mind? No, our thought processes themselves work in the same way, as the mind further simplifies and pigeonholes perceptions into "categories of thought." Certain aspects of the world seem to "go together," and our categories reflect this: dogs are considered more similar to cats than to airplanes.

Systems of classification (or taxonomies) ordinarily organize things according to similarities and differences. As a result relationships become explicit. By yielding a quick table of relationships and associations among many disparate objects and events, the categories enable people to operate in a time-limited, close-proximity world. Because they work and seem natural, we don't think about the process—but considering an unnatural classification quickly emphasizes the utility of the natural. Here is a classification of the animal kingdom attributed to an ancient Chinese encyclopedia, the *Celestial Emporium of Benevolent Knowledge:*

ANIMALS ARE DIVIDED INTO

a. Those that belong to the emperor
b. Embalmed ones
c. Those that are trained
d. Suckling pigs
e. Mermaids
f. Fabulous ones
g. Stray dogs
h. Those that are included in this classification
i. Those that tremble as if they were mad
j. Innumerable ones
k. Those drawn with a very fine camel's-hair brush
l. Others
m. Those that have broken a flower vase
n. Those that resemble flies from a distance

Needless to say, this system has little or no functional value. The *Celestial Emporium* was the creation of the contemporary Argentine author Jorge Luis Borges. It shows us that there might be innumerable categories in the world, but most would not be helpful in organizing our small world and haven't survived as cultural entities.

Categories not only reflect the structure of the physical world, but many categories are peculiar to individual cultures and can be observed in the structure of different languages. For instance, Argentine gauchos have some two hundred words to describe the colors of horses, but divide the world of plants into only four categories: *"pasta"* (fodder), *"paja"* (bedding), *"cardo"* (woody materials), and *"yuyos"* (all other plants). Eskimos have no generic term for water, but dozens of words to describe various kinds of liquid and frozen water.

We use the categories of our own culture as standards for judgments. An American traveling in Japan would probably have to convert the 125,000 yen bar charge into dollars to get a feel for how much a weekend's entertainment would cost. If we find that the empty lot we want to buy is half a hectare in area, we may have to convert to acres or square feet to know whether it is large enough to hold the house we had planned to build.

The way thoughts are categorized is similar to the way our senses limit perception. Our caricatures are partly composed of stereotypes (standardized mental pictures that credit the same characteristics to all members of a group), and we use these stereotypes in making quick judgments. We may think of a strong, well-coordinated man as a "typical athlete," or love of fine wine as "typically French." The match of categories to experience works especially well in stable societies marked by little innovation. The match is often quite poor in the new world. For example, love of fine wine is now more typically Californian than French, the change having taken place in the last two decades.

However, it is not just the structure of the mind that influences sensory inputs. Our previous experiences and present attitudes strongly affect what we perceive. In one study students in a class were asked to draw a picture of the teacher and themselves. The majority of the honor students drew the teacher slightly smaller than the students in the picture. But the pictures by less-than-average students depicted the teacher as much taller than the students. In another study a group of students attended a lecture; in the questionnaire that followed, they were asked about the speaker. Some were told that he was a student, some that he was a graduate, some that he was a young professor. The "professor" was rated as taller than the graduate, and the graduate was seen as taller than the student. The professor was seen as "a big man"!

When you "boot up," or start, a computer, it begins with a set of what are clumsily called default positions, procedures it will follow unless someone deliberately replaces them with different instructions. So it seems to be with the human mind. While it is flexible in the extreme compared with those of most other animals, the human mind's "defaults" have been highly influenced by our biological evolution, and they take over if other routines are not consciously "called up." In the new world, in this complex world we made, there are now too many hazardous situations for us to go on safely with business as usual. Humanity is suffering from a serious case of dangerous defaults.

Among the default positions of the human mind are a tendency to analyze everything as an immediate, personal phenomenon: what does this mean to me? A personal insult dominates attention, yet "in time" the insult is forgotten. Whatever gets close to us, in space or time, is immediately overemphasized. Viewers of violent movies believe there is more violence in the world than do people who do not see such films. The fans of violent films may therefore also be readier to respond violently to perceived threats, which may or may not be real.

Because of the time factor current information is automatically given high weight in making decisions, whether they are a response to an insult, a change in weather, or a matter of statecraft. During the Geneva summit between Reagan and Gorbachev in 1985, Secretary of Defense Caspar Weinberger wrote a letter warning the President to oppose summit accords. The letter was front-page news in the international media, and many commentators felt that it threatened the talks.

Yet the letter contained no real change in policy or novel information or "news" of any kind—it simply restated already known positions. It was *perceived* as potentially damaging because it was leaked in close proximity to the talks. Thus the letter was incorrectly perceived as "current" information. Had it been made public two weeks earlier, it would have had no effect. Short-term information influences elections, and politicians seem to get elected or reelected on the basis of the activities of the previous few months, not the long term.

It happens in life-and-death matters, too. When the wife of President Ford was reported to have breast cancer, all over the United States women went to their physicians to get examined. They should, of course, have been getting routine breast examinations; Betty Ford's misfortune had nothing to do with other women's probability of contracting cancer. Similarly the sudden announcement that the artificial sweetener aspartame may be bad for health is "news" and gets full scrutiny while the enormous, well-known dangers of smoking cigarettes get less emphasis than they deserve. These reactions (among thousands of other examples that could be given) are based on our caricatures of the world.

People in contemporary society have inherited and learned unconsciously an enormous number of ancient modes of thought, some of which can be traced back for many millions of years. These derive from our predecessors throughout human biological and cultural evolution. We think it is about time these modes of thought were uncovered, assessed, and evaluated for their relevance to today. Even if they are deeply ingrained, some of the ancient styles of thinking and actions *can* be modified, as the variety of behavior and attitudes seen in different cultures today clearly demonstrates.

To sum up, the most important "defaults" of the human mind are to look for discrepancies in the world, to ignore what is going on constantly, and to respond quickly to sudden shifts, to emergencies, to scarcity, to the immediate and personal, to "news." For millions of years these "defaults" of the mind have worked well. They do not work well in a world where 2 billion people could be killed by a simple misjudgment, and our defaults do not even work so well in the day-to-day world of modern life, as we shall see.

5

WHERE DEFAULTS HARM

Daily Life Decisions

A T LAST you get the report from the planning committee; it says that a large capital expense is essential to correct a number of hazards on the town highway. Repaving is needed and a guardrail should be put up at Goose Curve. But the report from the financial consultants cautions that the $100,000 assessment would mean raising property taxes a little or floating new bonds at a disadvantageous rate. We can't do it; it is irresponsible to spend so much at a time of tight bucks, you think; and so you vote to postpone the renovation and the new safety commitments.

You drive home from the budget meeting, thinking it's too bad the funds aren't there for the highway safety measures. They're important. Maybe next year. Then you decide to go two miles out of your way and look at Goose Curve yourself. It's dark and raining, quiet outside. The boring budget battles still pack your mind.

Then you see it.

Skid marks swerving all over the road. You follow slowly and hope. It is probably old Johnson, drunk again, most likely driving too fast under the influence. You hope that he didn't go over the edge of the cliff.

But he did. Wild slashing tire tracks lead to a spot where the lip of the gully was recently broken off. The accident probably happened not too long ago. It's pouring and late, but you slam on the brakes and leap out of the car, your mind filled with fear. You begin to climb down the hill and you see Johnson, lying in a pool of blood, thrown out of his car, his arm and head bleeding.

You struggle back up the hill carrying Johnson over your shoulder, blood splattering over your suit and shoes, but you don't notice. Your heart is pounding, strength comes from you know not where, but you trudge up, step by slippery step.

You breathe a sigh of relief as you reach your car at the top, open the door, gently lay Johnson on the backseat, and race to the hospital as fast as you can. The admitting physician at the emergency room says, "Where's his health insurance?" Johnson, you find, has none. You say that you will pay any amount if it is critical, as you watch him unconscious. You don't mind, you just hope he will live, that's all you can think about.

He is saved, and it winds up costing you $5,000. You are pleased, even a little proud, to have saved his life, and don't dwell on the cost of the medical bill.

The trains of thought in both the budget meeting and the emergency exemplify the old mind in action. In both circumstances the thought processes seem logical and lead to obvious conclusions.

From the perspective of the large budget and one's fiscal responsibilities, the need for the guardrail seems a trivial and minor concern in comparison with the major financial problems of the moment. It is not prudent to increase expenses even a little while there are deficits in the budget. Our old minds can all agree with that.

The mind is not stable, however, and an individual's point of view about events shifts from encounter to encounter. The need for a guardrail appears to be a minor issue when you are sitting at a meeting looking at pages of numbers. When there is an emergency (which could have been prevented by the rail), the single event is magnified to fill your perspective, and it becomes virtually impossible to ignore someone in desperate need of aid.

During an emergency nothing seems to matter except saving lives. Almost any normal person will give his or her all. After saving Johnson you feel much better than you would have about winning a political battle for a guardrail that would have forestalled the imminent tragedy and probably prevented others like it. Nonetheless you now fight for a new guardrail. You no longer care anymore about the budget committee compromise. But your share of the tax increase would have been about only $10, and Johnson's lawsuit might well cost the county more than $100,000.

But it is only when the two situations are connected that the mismatches and misapplications of the quick mental judgments are evident. The cost of the guardrail, compared with other expenses, doesn't merit much attention or concern. It is just one more item in a complex budget. It is judged by short-term blinders, which compare only the budget expenses with income, taking into account the consequences for immediate financial planning while ignoring the reality of possible long-term costs.

One cost, involving the possible death of a single person, literally changes your mind on the spot. The positions and criteria for judgments shift so suddenly that you don't even notice that your assumptions have a different basis, and a new, even shorter-term "mind" is in place. The emergency triggers another of the caricatures of the mind, shoving everything else off the stage, and you rush to rescue Johnson.

Comparable shifts in thought and judgment happen all the time with respect to social issues, in the way we respond to the media, and in the way we understand others. This case history only highlights the inconsistency. The old mind is mismatched and sometimes utterly inadequate in the modern world. Some of the errors of misperception and misjudgment are silly, but many have serious consequences. The problem is that human beings, having the same kind of nervous system as tarsiers, frogs, chimps, and cats, are ready to respond to Johnson's accident but not to commit themselves to the long-term preventative measure of the guardrail. And, like those of other animals, human "small worlds" are not the same as the real world. Sudden unexpected events go to the forefront.

A single accident, the tragic and preventable loss of seven lives in the space shuttle, captured the attention of the world; ignored are the thousands who die equally tragic, preventable, but dull deaths daily. Consider the following annual American statistics:

43,500 killed in automobile accidents in the United States (1985)
1,384 murdered in New York City (1985)
36 murdered in Honolulu (1985)
150 died in accidents in their own bathtubs (1984)
1,063 killed in boating accidents (1984)
3,100 died choking on food (1984)

A single murder, that of hostage Leon Klinghoffer in 1985, commanded the front pages of almost every newspaper in the Western world. Extreme political demands have been met because of the importance that individuals, the media, and governments give to such actions. The threat of terrorism made millions of Americans change their travel plans in the summer of 1986. During the time it takes you to read this book, more people will die in automobile accidents in the United States than have *ever* (up until this writing) been killed by terrorists.

Late in 1985 national attention was suddenly focused on medicines bought over the counter. A few cyanide-tainted Tylenol capsules were discovered in drugstores. The threat is still remembered. But *hundreds of daily murders* in the United States, before, during, and after the tamperings remain almost unnoticed.

The way the mind caricatures reality to focus on the new and unusual is what makes terrorism good value. We believe that terrorism will be a recurring strategy of the otherwise powerless until people realize that its effect depends upon the emphasis automatically given to it by the default positions of the "old minds," and, by extension, in the media. Terrorism taps into the nervous-system program that originated to register short-term changes in a steady state. The steady flow of murders is "tuned out," just as the sound of an air conditioner is tuned out shortly after it starts. But terrorism, or the discovery of a serial killer, is like an occasional squeak in the air conditioner's motor; each time it sounds, it rivets our attention on the machine.

There isn't that much we can do to alter human evolutionary history. We can't rewire the nervous system. But most people are ignorant of the automatic caricatures of mind and its constant short-term emphasis. This ignorance leads otherwise rational people to misjudge life-and-death situations.

Wouldn't Americans, if they were in their "right minds," understand that hundreds of murders each and every day in the United States are a more serious threat to their lives than the murder of one hostage by terrorists? Put that way, read in a book in cold type, it seems quite obvious. But most of us don't "see" it this way. Another well-publicized hijacking or bombing immediately changes our viewpoint.

A group of Americans was "held hostage" at the U.S. embassy in Iran from late 1979 to early 1981. The President of the United States said that he would make this act "the center of the consciousness of the American people." After fourteen months of yellow ribbons and unceasing media attention, all the hostages were released, and the country went into a joyous celebration—even though hundreds of millions of dollars had been spent on an abortive rescue mission and several Marines had died in the Iranian desert.

During the period of that hostage crisis, many other events in the United States did not attract much public notice:

About 15,000 civilians died by the gun.

About 25,000 people were slaughtered senselessly in highway accidents, most of which could have been prevented.

About 100,000 people died from preventable heart attacks.

The Iran hostage crisis was followed day by day on television; there was a *new* angle every day. So much interest was generated that an entirely new TV show, which became *Nightline,* was created. Contrast another event involving Iran, the Iran-Iraq war. It has already resulted in *one million* dead, but was relatively ignored until the U.S. involvement in the Persian Gulf increased.

That war, involving alien peoples, and in which we seemed to have little stake, was not brought continually to our attention by the media. Events that change significantly only in years or decades, such as the size of the world population and the assault of acid rain, are notably difficult to come to grips with unless they are somehow made into "news" and frequently made to "squeak" like the air-conditioner motor. The involvement of American naval forces in the Persian Gulf was that squeak for the Iran-Iraq war.

The human mental system has cleverly evolved a few major strategies to steer people through the kinds of day-to-day conditions that challenged our forebears. But these strategies, as well as our self-deception that we are largely rational thinkers, often underlie personal, social, and political problems. Consider how the mind's caricatures lead to many daily decisions that are mismatched with reality.

The default positions of our minds that give priority to the short term make us easy pickings for exploitation. It happens in sales every day, because advertisers recognize and manipulate the vulnerable points of the mind.

One of these is a partiality toward immediately valuing and searching out scarce items, exemplifying short-term thinking at its purest. Social psychologist Robert Cialdini noticed this reaction in himself:

The city of Mesa, Arizona, is a suburb in the Phoenix area where I live. Perhaps the most notable features of Mesa are its sizable Mormon population—next to Salt Lake City, the largest in the world—and a huge Mormon temple located on exquisitely kept grounds in the center of the city. Although I had appreciated the landscaping and architecture from a distance, I had never been interested enough in the temple to go inside, until the day I read a newspaper article that told of a special inner sector of Mormon temples to which no one has access but faithful members of the church. Even potential converts must not see it. There is one exception to the rule, however. For a few days immediately after a temple is newly constructed, nonmembers are allowed to tour the entire structure, including the otherwise restricted section.

The newspaper story reported that the Mesa temple had been recently refurbished and that the renovations had been extensive enough to classify it as "new" by church standards. Thus, for the next several days only, non-Mormon visitors could see the temple area traditionally banned to them. I remember quite well the effect this article had on me: I immediately resolved to take a tour. But when I phoned a friend to ask if he wanted to come along, I came to understand something that changed my decision just as quickly.

After declining the invitation, my friend wondered why I seemed so intent on a visit. I was forced to admit that, no, I had never been inclined toward the idea of a temple tour before, that I had no questions about the Mormon religion I wanted answered, that I had no general interest in church architecture, and that I expected to find nothing more spectacular or stirring than what I might see at a number of other churches or cathedrals in the area. It became clear as I spoke that the special lure of the temple had a sole cause: If I did not experience the restricted sector soon, I would never again have the chance. Something that, on its own merits, held little appeal for me had become decidedly more attractive merely because it was rapidly becoming less available.

Sensitivity to an immediate scarcity of resources—especially a sudden change leading to scarcity—is a default program in all animals. It is part of how the world made us. Before the Agricultural Revolution, an eye blink in evolutionary history, food supplies were not under human control. The unexpected sudden departure of a herd of game animals or a drought that resulted in the failure of

fruit crops would require immediate action. Because such short-
term changes are recorded quickly by the nervous system, many of
our human ancestors probably avoided starvation by responding to
shortage immediately, gobbling up the last of a declining resource
and then changing their diet or shifting their foraging area.

Waiters seem to have learned to take advantage of this old-mind
tendency. Columnist Jon Carrol of the San Francisco *Chronicle* took
over as head waiter for one day in an East Bay restaurant. He
learned about responses to scarcity quickly. The title of his article
(November 13, 1986) was "Only a Few Clams Left." He says,

> About halfway through my one-night tenure as the substitute maitre d'
> (or host) at the Bay Wolf, an Oakland restaurant of sole and heart, I
> checked in with the kitchen.
> "The clams aren't moving," said Stephen, chef in charge of first
> courses. "Tell them about the clams."
> Why not? The clams were swell; they just weren't selling. East Bay
> diners had developed an unaccountable craving for spinach salad. So the
> next five times I did my small tap dance at the beginning of the meal—
> "Let me direct your attention to a few special items on the menu"—I
> described the clams in loving detail. Still nothing.
> With the next party, I tried a different approach. "The clams are very
> popular tonight," I said. "So if you want to start with them, I suggest you
> tell me now,"
> Marketing heaven. The clams began walking out the door like little
> soldiers. Rebecca, one of the waitresses told me: "Gold star on your chart.
> My whole table ordered clams."
> I walked into the kitchen again. "I've got a great way to sell anything,"
> I told Lee, the head chef, "Just say it's going fast."
> Lee considered carefully. Finally, she said:
> "Gee, do you think I could sell myself that way?"

(She probably could, because people who are perceived as hard to
get are usually thought of as being quite attractive.)

This built-in default of the mind, automatically amplifying short-
term changes, makes us liable to manipulation by claims of scarcity.
The best evidence comes from advertising. About twenty years ago
Robert Ornstein decided to get his car painted. He noticed an at-

tractive price in an ad for Earl Scheib Auto Painting. The ad listed a "special low price" for paint jobs and said that it was the "last three days" for this price. Ornstein went right out and had the job done.

Recently he was looking for a new paint job on another car and happened to notice the current ad for Earl Scheib Auto Painting. The price was still low (in the context of twenty years of inflation). What had also not changed was the pitch: it still announced it was the "last three days" for the low price. This must be the longest three days in history! The pitch works because of people's propensity to rush to take advantage of sudden scarcity (in this case scarcity is signaled by shortage of *time*). Of course people are not continuously in the market for paint jobs on their car and don't really notice that in Earl Scheib Land it is always the last three days.

But even when advertised items are bought more often, the "special, limited-time offer" attracts us as a result of the defaults of our mismatched mind. One school-portrait company urges parents to buy as many poses as possible because "stocking limitations force us to burn the unsold pictures of your children within twenty-four hours." Of course stocking limitations do not really exist, but this ploy has evolved to suit the old mind of the purchaser. When something is available for a limited period only, people are more likely to value it. A limited performance of a stage play can often attract a larger total audience than an extended run. The same thing happens in the new shop-by-TV programs. Virtually every item is available for only a "limited time," in some cases as little as four minutes!

Psychologist Stephen Worchel demonstrated the importance of perceived scarcity in a simple test. Individuals in a "consumer preference" study were given a chocolate chip cookie, taken from a jar. They were then asked to rate its quality, its probable price, and how tasty they thought it would be. In the first study half the people got cookies drawn from a jar that contained ten cookies, half from a jar that contained two cookies. The cookies from the jar that contained two (in short supply) were thought more tempting to eat and were expected to be more costly than were the abundant cookies. When something we need or want is growing scarce, our mind's default positions immediately consider it more desirable.

So scarce cookies, identical to those in greater supply, are immediately more highly valued. But the mind is even more vulnerable to its defaults than this indicates. What about a sudden scarcity of a previously abundant cookie? Worchel ran the experiment again. One group of people first were given their cookies from the jar of two and the second group were given a cookie from the jar containing ten. But the jar containing ten was immediately removed and replaced with the jar of two.

So we now have, in our terms, a comparison between (relatively) consistently scarce cookies and newly scarce cookies. Both groups had considered their cookies in front of a jar containing two. Which is valued more? Again people valued the *newly scarce* cookies more than the "old" scarce cookies, estimating, for instance, that the newly scarce cookies would be 20 percent more expensive than the old scarce cookies if sold.

This "cookie" experiment is not just another laboratory demonstration of something trivial. It ties in with the fundamental caricatures of the old mind: respond to emergencies—food is becoming scarce—look to the short term and maximize gain. And the same default positions influence all sorts of decisions, in business as well as in cookie evaluation.

In 1973 ABC decided to pay the unheard-of sum of $3.3 million for a network television broadcast of a movie, *The Poseidon Adventure*. It was an amount that ABC and other networks admitted, at the time, could not be justified. ABC stood to lose $1 million on the deal. Why did they do it?

The selling of this movie was different from previous leases of films to television. It was the subject of an open-bid auction, the first of its kind. In an auction the commodity, in this case a single broadcast of a film, automatically becomes scarce. Like the cookies, scarce movies automatically get higher value in the mind. One competing bidder, CBS president Robert Wood, said, "Logic goes right out the window."

Wood described the feeling:

We were very rational at the start. We priced the movie out, in terms of what it could bring in for us, then allowed a certain value on top of that for exploitation.

But then the bidding started. ABC opened with $2 million. I came back with $2.4. ABC went to $2.8. And the fever of the thing caught us. Like a guy who had lost his mind, I kept bidding . . . there came a moment when I said to myself, "Good grief, if I get it, what the heck am I going to do with it?"

The "winner's" reaction was straightforward, and their later statement said, "ABC has decided regarding its policy for the future that it would never again enter into an auction situation."

The manipulation of this short-term spotlight on something rare is a way of life, from the crush of shoppers at opening-hour specials ("prices good for the first hour" of the store's business day) to the continued popularity of auction houses. It costs us daily, this vestige of the past. And it also determines how we judge other people.

The immediate highlight on the short term makes anyone who is difficult to meet seem more desirable to meet. In one study in a singles bar, researchers in Virginia randomly selected customers and asked them to rate the attractiveness of the opposite-sex individuals present, at three hours, then two hours, and then one-half hour before closing. The results were surprising. Those remaining a half hour before closing, when the chances of meeting and striking up a conversation were becoming scarcer, were judged the best-looking.

The automatic defaults of the mind seem to operate everywhere, especially in how people respond to others. First impressions of other people are difficult to change. Our minds are made up in the first social encounter because our attention is focused on beginnings of events (as it is on the air conditioner starting up). After the first impression, acquaintances seem to fade into the background, like the continuing hum of the air conditioner.

One of the quickest ways of judging the people we meet is by their appearance. In our visually dominated small world, clothes, skin color, and physical attractiveness often dominate our first impressions. This means that many long-held stereotypes may be influenced by the overwhelming amount of exterior—appearance—information we receive about people.

It is easy, then, for us to misconstrue the applicability of the immediate impressions we receive from the surface physical features of others. One survey of University of Pittsburgh graduates showed that men six feet two inches and over had a starting salary $125 per week higher than those below six feet. Tall people are judged more trustworthy and generous as well. But does this bias affect only matters such as job security? Not at all. The same processes are at work in judging job worth and political capabilities.

In all presidential elections from 1900 through 1968, the taller candidate won. So impressed were Jimmy Carter's campaign managers about this that when Carter had to meet the taller Gerald Ford in debate, he insisted on their lecterns being placed far enough apart so that they would never be on screen together at the same time. Even the ritual handshake was carefully choreographed. Carter stood far away and extended his hand as far as possible, then walked away, immediately minimizing the exposure. We may "read" height as being so significant because, in the small world of a small tribe, it may well have signified one well suited to lead others in battle. Biological and cultural evolution have made tall people those we "look up to."

Surface attractiveness is part of our caricature because it is important to us in selecting a mate and starting a family. In truth, beauty is often more than skin-deep; it may indicate good health and thus good reproductive potential. A clear skin may signify freedom from disease. Weight also is important. In cultures where food is sometimes scarce, males prefer females who are quite heavy, even obese by Western standards, presumably as a sign of their capacity to carry children through to term and nurse them. In Western societies as the general level of affluence increases, thinner and thinner women are preferred, as a sign that they "don't have to carry their own bags." Higher-income groups tend to prefer thinness: as they say, You can never be too thin or too rich.

The unconscious high value given to immediate surface information causes many mismatches. Most people claim that appearance should not be important in the courtroom. But there is clear evidence that most people are unable to put their default positions aside and act on this belief. Criminologists have collected evidence showing that if criminals are good-looking people, they are less likely to get caught in illicit activities; if caught, they are less likely to be reported to the police; even if the case does come to court, judges and jurors are more likely to be lenient with them. We might call this the Oliver North principle.

In an unusual study psychologists persuaded 440 young men and women to go in and shoplift merchandise from ten supermarkets in a large city. The results were clear. Clerks were less likely to accuse shoplifters who were well groomed and neatly dressed than those who were unkempt.

Clerks are not the only ones who observe shoplifters. Another experiment showed that customers, too, are more likely to report shabby shoplifters. In grocery stores of two different chains and in a discount department store, two sorts of people blatantly shoplifted in the presence of customers. One variety looked like typical professionals out on a shopping break. The others were "hippie" shoplifters (this study took place in the mid-1970s). One male hippie was described in the following way: "He wore soiled, patched blue jeans, blue workman's shirt, and blue denim jacket; well-worn, scuffed shoes with no socks. He had long and unruly hair with a ribbon tied around his forehead. He was unshaven and had a small beard."

Hippie shoplifters were not only more likely to be reported, they were reported with more enthusiasm. "That son-of-a-bitch hippie over there stuffed a banana down his coat." Good looks pay off: salespeople and customers (and the rest of us, presumably) are less suspicious of an attractive person's every move.

What effect does a person's attractiveness have on others' judgment of them? In another study people were asked to watch a well-dressed woman and one who was slovenly shoplifting. The "detectives" were asked how upset the woman would probably be if she were caught, tried, and convicted of shoplifting. Observers felt that the well-dressed woman would suffer more, that she would be more emotionally upset and concerned about what her family and friends would think of her than the scruffy woman would be.

Whenever juries decide, they are presumed to use all the information they acquire to come to the right decision. Because of the tendency of the mind to ignore the familiar, the unusual may get special attention. Psychologists Solomon and Schopler hypothesized that unusually attractive defendants might be judged most leniently on the assumption that "what is beautiful is good." Homely defendants may also be judged compassionately out of pity. An average-looking defendant, however, does not get the benefit of the doubt for either reason; thus he or she may get the harshest sentence.

In a study designed to test this possibility male students at the University of North Carolina evaluated a case of a young woman accused of hustling ten thousand dollars. The woman was described to the "jury" as attractive, average-looking, or unattractive. The attractive woman got the most magnanimous sentence, of 12 months. The unattractive woman had an average prison sentence of 18½ months. The average-looking woman, however, received the most restrictive sentence of all. The men wanted to lock her up for 19½ months!

The sentencing of a rapist may depend not only on his crime but additionally on his looks. Test subjects heard the following description:

It was ten o'clock at night, and Judy W. was getting out of an evening class at a large midwestern university. She walked across the campus toward her car, which was parked two blocks off campus. A man was walking across the campus in the same direction as Judy W. and began to follow her.

Less than a block from Judy W.'s car, the man accosted her. In the ensuing struggle, he stripped her and raped her. A passerby heard her screams and called the police. They arrived at the scene within minutes.

Judy W. told the police that she had never seen her attacker before that night. Based on her description, the police arrested Charles E., a student whom they found in the vicinity of the attack. Judy W. positively identified Charles E. as the man who raped her. Charles E. swears that he is innocent. He testified that he was just taking a break from studying by going out for a walk and that it was just a series of coincidences that he was in the vicinity and that he matched Judy W.'s description of her attacker.

Again, as in all such psychology experiments, different people were given different information about the attractiveness of Charles E. If Charles E. was described as a handsome man, both men and women judges were likely to think he was just out for a walk and that his resemblance to the rapist was coincidental. Not so if Charles E. was ugly. Then he was likely to be seen as guilty. It's assumed that a handsome man can attract women and doesn't need to attack them—a misperception of rapists' motives.

Judges were also asked how long a prison sentence they would recommend for Charles E. if he were actually guilty. If these "judges" had really judged, the good-looking Charles E. would have had to spend about ten years in prison, while the homely version would be locked up for almost fourteen years. Ugliness may be dangerous to your freedom.

The victim's beauty was also important. Judges were more likely to assume Charles E. was guilty when told that Judy W. was attractive. They were also less sympathetic to a rapist of an attractive woman than to a rapist of an unattractive woman. Attractive women and men have great advantages, because skin-deep differences, easy to see, easy to classify quickly, have a great effect on the mind.

The old mind tells us that intelligence is a single, fixed quantity —someone is either "smart" in almost all things or not. But this viewpoint is just another caricature of the mind. Another person's intelligence is largely a creation of the *perceiver*. Someone is often judged intelligent who acts with excellence and originality—in what is considered, by those judging, the best way.

Different societies also have quite different concepts of intelligence. In most societies the individuals who are most useful are considered the most intelligent. Western society values high verbal skills and rational thinking, but when we use these values in a formal assessment of other minds, our mental caricatures lead us astray.

IQ is the most abused of all the caricatures of mental abilities. IQ is an abbreviation for "intelligence quotient" and is thought by many to be a genuine and almost physical component of a person, the way height is. In certain school systems and in the military, people are sorted and sent into different streams of education and eventually different lives on the basis of a paper-and-pencil test lasting a few hours at most.

We use IQ measurements extensively because of World War I. In the United States, the Army needed a quick measure of the capability of its unknown, untrained, and untried soldiers. Psychologists such as Alfred Binet in France had developed tests to determine the capacities of different children for schooling. Binet's tests gave a "mental age" usable for school programs. The test could also be administered simultaneously to large groups and could be easily scored.

But once established, Binet's simple expedient took on a life of its own. Later the scores became more important than they had been in Binet's original tests; designed to predict the academic performance of children, they now became the primary factor in determining the assignments of soldiers. Group administration of tests (a wartime necessity) and the strong reliance on the test score as the measure of "intelligence" *remained the norm even after the war ended.*

Lewis Terman of Stanford University revised Binet's test into the Stanford-Binet, noted that "high grade moronity" was "very common among Spanish, Indian, and Mexican families . . . and among Negroes." But he said this in 1919, before much was understood about tests, minds, or cultural differences.

Then, in a celebrated article in 1969, Arthur Jensen, a psychologist at the University of California at Berkeley, argued that compensatory education programs that attempted to improve the intelligence of black children failed because the children were genetically programmed to have low IQs. Although many scientists, including ourselves, regard this as scientific nonsense, these views are still widely maintained. (Japan's former Prime Minister Yasuhiro

Nakasone recently succumbed to this kind of thinking when he attributed Japan's success to its racial unity and superiority of intelligence.)

Racial and ethnic stereotypes easily arise in people because "in-group, out-group" hostility served the needs of the original small human groups and because of the mind's built-in tendency to establish categories of thought. Ethnic stereotypes are established: sexy French, materialistic Americans, dumb blondes, wise elders, drunken Irishmen. They are very difficult to erase. Every ethnic group that has migrated to the United States—the Italians, the Poles, the Irish, the Mexicans, the Vietnamese—have been subject to prejudices based on ethnic stereotypes. Prejudice against those with different skin colors is amplified by another of the defaults of the old mind: if it *looks* different in the caricature, then it *is* different.

Intergroup differences in average IQ score primarily reflect the prejudices of the white, upper-middle-class people who constructed the tests. The idea that complex human intelligence can be accounted for by a single, simple quotient has long since been given up by most thoughtful researchers. It has been replaced by investigations of the multiple components of the mind. But the defaults of the mind tend to keep information simple and stable, so myths about IQ persist.

The recognition of races is another good example of the tendency to categorize, to produce stereotypes, for which there is little or no basis. The races of human beings were first formally classified by Carolus Linnaeus (1707–78), founder of the science of taxonomy (which deals with the classification of organisms). He believed that human races differed not only in color but also in personality characteristics. However, Linneaus's "racial" classification, like those that have followed, was artificial.

He arbitrarily based it on surface appearance—especially skin color—which is just one of many geographically variable human characteristics. Any number of characteristics that vary from place to place could have been used for the primary division, including height, hair color, eye color, head shape, nose size, blood type, and so on. Each of these tends to vary in its own pattern, delineating different sets of "races."

The major differences classically used to differentiate races are truly only skin-deep. In addition to skin color, they consist of superficial features such as hair type and presence or absence of folds in the upper eyelid. There is, however, no evidence of people with different skin characteristics having brains of different sizes, shapes, organization, structure, or basic intellectual ability. A person's skin color, contrary to myth, tells you nothing about intelligence, nor do hair color or the prominence of the nose. But surface appearances overwhelm our poor old minds.

Unfortunately there is a profound confusion between the knowledge that genes can influence certain important characteristics and the automatic inference that therefore "races" have different inherited mental capacities. Predispositions toward certain mental characteristics can be inherited by individuals. That does not mean that differences between groups of people with regard to the same characteristics are necessarily due to genetic differences. This is a difficult point to understand when discussing mental attributes, but a parallel example using skin color will clarify it. An individual's skin color is partly inherited, but the average difference in skin color between groups of people, one riding in a New York subway and another sunning on Miami Beach, could have been produced entirely by those different environments.

People get their genes from their parents, not from a group. There is no way to extrapolate from inherited differences between individuals to inherited differences between groups. Ordinarily there are much greater inherited differences between individuals within a "racial group" than there are between group averages.

The word "prejudice" literally means "to prejudge." In the mind, prejudice derives from the instant caricatures we use to get on in the world, to judge many different objects and people quickly and act on these judgments. We sort the infinite variety of things we encounter into categories in our small world and assume that all members of a category are similar. It works well most of the time. This old-mind tendency caused little trouble within tribal groups;

however, it can cause serious trouble in the new world. The problem comes when we overextend our caricatures and develop rigid stereotypes.

Using simplifying processes to judge others leads to constant misinterpretations. "Extrovert" is a common stereotype—outgoing, boisterous, gregarious, loud. In one study people read a description of a person that used several descriptors, such as "extroverted," "calm," "intelligent," and the like. Later on, people not only recalled more of the traits that had been mentioned and fit the stereotype (such as "loud" in an extrovert) *but they also remembered traits that had not been presented,* traits that also fit the stereotype. So we are likely to experience people as caricatures. We are more likely to believe that someone is "excitable" if we are told he is an extrovert than if we're told he's an introvert. We fill in the gaps in experiencing other people, just as we do in experiencing objects.

If a stereotype is widely accepted, it can have lasting effects on the group so stereotyped. One study, done in the days before people became sensitive to racial issues, showed that black children, even as young as three years old, felt that whiteness was superior. They rejected black dolls in favor of white ones and classified the white dolls as better than the black.

In our society women have been stereotyped as intellectually inferior to men. In one study, male college students were asked to judge the accomplishments of highly successful physicians, male and female. Even though the accomplishments presented were identical, the males rated the females as less competent than the males. Women also seemed to believe the female stereotype. A number of female students were asked to read several scholarly articles and to evaluate them. The articles were signed by either John T. McKay or Joan T. McKay. The articles were rated more highly when written by John than by Joan.

The old mind hurts us in ways other than translating our caricatures into stereotypes. Its tendency to emphasize the immediate often leads us astray in the new world. Something that we see or hear firsthand is given much more weight than evidence reported by others. The nearly catastrophic accident at the Three Mile Island nuclear reactor in 1979, brought into people's living rooms by television, stimulated many people to protest against the use of power from nuclear fission. The accident was judged to be representative of nuclear power plants, and it entirely overwhelmed the nuclear power industry's claim that these plants were perfectly safe. It changed opinions much more than years of warnings by many scientists about the potential for catastrophe in poorly designed nuclear power plants. The Three Mile Island event was seen as strong support for their claims, and Chernobyl as proving them right. Those frightening accidents may well have removed all fission power from the future energy options available to Americans, even though well-designed plants might eventually prove acceptably safe.

One or two dramatic events can have a striking influence; statistics can be easily ignored. It is a phenomenon that psychologists Daniel Kahneman and Amos Tversky call representativeness. Social scientist Charles Murray gives a good example of representativeness in his controversial book *Losing Ground,* which deals with the results of social welfare programs. He writes that the programs "lent themselves to upbeat anecdotes about individual success stories: John Jones, an ex-con who had never had a job in his life, became employed because of program X and is saving money to send his child to college. Such anecdotes, filmed for the evening news, were much more interesting than economic analyses. . . . Tacit or explicit, a generalization went with the anecdote: John Jones' story is typical of what this project is accomplishing or will accomplish for a large number of people. That such success stories were extremely rare, and that depressingly often John Jones would be out of his job and back in jail in a few months after his moment in the spotlight—these facts were not commonly publicized. The anecdotes made good copy."

For our ancestors, the focus on current and short-term, close-proximity changes was certainly adaptive. Those of our forebears who reacted strongly to sudden threats had a better chance of survival than others who pondered the evidence more calmly. Someone who responded to any sign of an approaching leopard or other large predator would be more likely to survive than someone who was nonchalant. The "payoff" of the two kinds of blunders is quite different: there would be less penalty for running from a "false alarm" than for a lack of concern when the threat was genuine.

Threats in our world have changed, but not our responses to them. Individuals and society as a whole are especially susceptible to anyone who can exploit the parochial focus of the old mind. In the modern world that focus leads to the vulnerability to terrorism, to brutality spreading as a result of watching violence in movies and on television, and to the election of incompetent politicians who look good and sound good and thus make us feel good. But its focus also leads to the slighting of the hazards of acid rain, CO_2 buildup, desertification, and other unprecedented perils approaching too gradually to trigger our "fight-or-flight" responses.

Besides leading us to ignore certain dangerous trends and make maladaptive day-to-day decisions, our old minds threaten our bodies directly. Remember the branch cracking underfoot? Imagine that you are a nurse who works in the evening. To get home, you must walk a couple of blocks to your car through a dangerous area. It's dark, and there are few people around. You begin to hear footsteps behind you, but when you turn around, there doesn't seem to be anyone there.

You start walking faster, but the footsteps keep pace. You remember that a nurse was mugged last week not too far from where you are and you begin to feel afraid—your heart starts to pound, your mouth gets dry, your stomach may churn, and your hands get clammy. The footsteps get closer, and you can't decide if you should run for it or turn and face the mugger.

Suddenly you whirl around and the person in the shadows seems to be huge and menacing. A man steps into the light, and you see it's just the security guard, who offers to escort you to your car. Although you feel relieved, you worry about the next night and wonder if you shouldn't try again to transfer to the day shift.

Your immediate reaction includes *physiological* changes in heart rate and respiration, in skin conductance, as well as more subtle, hormonal changes and *psychological* reactions, such as fear, anger, guilt, and anxiety. In this case the reaction was adaptive in the modern world—even though the danger was not real. But a similar reaction to a divorce or a murder seen on television is maladaptive, since there is no need to activate mind and body to deal with those events, no reason to see them as destabilizing.

The formation of caricatures by the old mind is enhanced by the thoroughly skewed "small world" that is created by the media. The average television watcher sees thousands of murders every year and forms a caricature much more violent than the environment actually is. TV caricatures society, and our minds caricature the input from TV. In the complex world of today, people are often overwhelmed by such short-term assaults on their senses and lose their ability to create a stable small world. Too many "life changes," such as the death of a spouse, a new job, or a move to a new city, can tax a person's ability to adapt and can result in illness or even death. The common word for the deleterious effects caused by an overload of perceived changes, a collapse of the stabilizing process, is "stress."

These physical reactions, evolved to facilitate immediate responses to sudden changes, are called up too often within complex modern life, and one's heart can actually be "broken" by them. Worse yet, much entertainment is *designed* to elicit arousal, which can lead to too much stress and an acceptance of extreme actions. Many young criminals in urban slums see nothing wrong with murder. They see it as a common, normal occurrence in television and receive no counteracting training at home. Committing acts of violence does not signal an important change in their small worlds.

The focus on short-term changes can even determine the selection of a wife or husband. Under "pressure" or the stress of war, many people suddenly find individuals whom they meet quite attractive. In films or novels it is the daring hero, the one who takes chances, who always gets the girl. Seducers know this. They typically pick exciting locales for evenings out. On dates people often go to horror movies, drive like maniacs, and ride on roller coasters.

One experiment was done to determine the degree to which short-term signals of danger, even subtle ones, influence a man's attraction to a woman. A woman interviewed two groups of men, each on a different footbridge near Vancouver: one bridge is safe, the other very precarious. One is a solid wood structure 10 feet above a stream. The other is the Capilano Suspension Bridge; it is 450 feet long, 5 feet wide, and sways and wobbles 230 feet above rapids and rocks.

Men crossing the bridges were met by an attractive woman interviewer. To each man on both bridges she said she was researching "the effects of scenic attraction on creative expression." She then asked the man to write a brief story based on a picture she showed him of a young woman covering her face with one hand while reaching out with the other.

When he finished writing, she gave the man her name and number and invited him to call her if he wanted more information about the experiment. The stories were also scored for sexual imagery.

Of the men who crossed the secure bridge, 12.5 percent called the woman for more information. Of the men who crossed the wobbly bridge, 50 percent called. Those who met the woman on the wobbly bridge wrote stories with far more sexual imagery than those on the secure bridge. Fear is related to sexual arousal. Here the excitement, technically termed arousal, was a signal to the old mind to note that what was going on was important; but in this situation, which is more common than we might like to think, the excitement is "transferred" to the other person, in this case an attractive one. The reverse can also happen, when excitement is mismatched as hate.

Excitement thus not only penetrates the small world, it prepares it for change. Chronic problems, in contrast, do not. Consider a tragedy of the sort that happens twenty times per day in the United States, yet has little effect on decisions. Three-year-old Sarah Wilson hit her head on the windshield of her parents' Chevrolet when it careened into a dump truck. Her mother and father are dead, killed in the collision. Sarah is forever brain damaged. The tires on the family car had not been able to grip the road properly and stop when the truck abruptly pulled into the road ahead and George Wilson slammed on the brakes.

Every month, hundreds of Americans are severely injured or killed because of underinflated tires and other results of poor maintenance on their cars. This is far more important for us to recognize than is a single terrorist murder. It does not register much in the caricatured mind, since tire inflation is scarcely as exciting as the exploits of the Symbionese Liberation Army, the hijacking of the *Achille Lauro,* the explosion of the *Challenger* space shuttle, or even crossing a swaying suspension bridge over a deep chasm.

But this kind of inconsistent thinking is not isolated. The Food and Drug Administration (FDA) has rigid requirements for the toxicity of novel food additives. In its testing procedures such sweeteners as aspartame are given in massive doses to laboratory animals and the incidence of toxic reactions or cancer is recorded. If a new additive increases the risk of cancer, say, by one in a million, it is not allowed on the market. But a whole series of long-used additives are placed on the GRAS (Generally Recognized As Safe) list and not tested at all. This is partially a consequence of the mind's tendency to ignore the familiar, even though that may be extremely hazardous, and to focus on the new! (It was also partly a political decision to avoid expense and uproar that would result from testing substances that have been marketed for a long time.)

And, of course, despite government warnings, the hundreds of billions of cigarettes smoked annually cause much more cancer (and heart disease) than could any possible increase in the use of artificial sweeteners. Cigarette production is heavily *subsidized* through governmental support of tobacco prices. Without those supports, less tobacco would be grown, and the price of killing yourself with lung or bladder cancer, emphysema, or heart disease would rise.

And these problems are hardly the limit of the cost of our mismatched mind. We dispatch jet fighters to apprehend terrorists who have killed a single man, but we will not lift a finger to save thousands of families like the Wilsons, or improve the lives of many like Sarah, who are injured permanently and lost to society. It seems senseless, absurd, and bizarre, but people ignore the constant, familiar dangers of daily life, even dangers that threaten death.

The old mind not only has difficulty perceiving gradual changes, it seems actively to suppress them. The capability to destroy humanity and most of life on earth, only a few decades old, seems "natural," just part of the everyday environmental reality, like the smog in Los Angeles. These threats slip by our old mind. Instead of reacting with horror and with rapid remedial action, as we would to the appearance of a bear at our cave's entrance, we easily incorporate the specter of possible human annihilation into daily life as if it were slightly more threatening than a temporary power blackout. Or we subconsciously reject that specter as too horrifying—an approach that is no more likely to protect us from nuclear war than it would from a cave bear. Paradoxically, the old mind is, in a way, *too adaptable.* Think how quickly ricocheting through the air at five hundred miles per hour in jet planes became "normal" for a species that for most of its existence rarely traveled faster than five miles per hour. And think how quickly airport security checks became routine.

Unnecessary deaths and living close to the brink of annihilation are just two of the prices we pay for not having adapted to the world we have made. We will go on, needing disasters like the space shuttle crash or the Detroit airline disaster to get us to demand action to increase the safety of the space program or of air travel. There may have to be another nuclear bomb dropped in anger before we will work seriously to prevent a large-scale nuclear war. The probability of global disaster goes up each year, but our consciousness of it does not. We seem to need shocks and tragedies to goad us into action. The old mind quickly tires of being cautioned, especially about dangers that cannot be averted by immediate *personal* action.

But if blindness to threatening gradual change continues, eventually a weather report might sound like this: "Clear skies on Thursday, followed by scattered nuclear explosions in the Northwest—with possible unseasonable freezes for a few months."

6

OUTGROWING THE TRUTH FAIRY

Medico-, Psycho-, and Mystico-Therapies

THE MIND'S instantaneous emphasis on short-term events leads to all kinds of hilarious misreadings of the prices we pay for some decisions, the allure of others; it even leads to a misunderstanding of our own thought processes. But these daily difficulties are not, in truth, critical to our society, and there is no crucial need for "a new mind" to avoid these daily minor bungles. We would just muddle through, chasing scarce cookies and cuties; misjudging people on the basis of their veneer, gender, and race; falling in love when we're frightened; and having stress-related diseases. Humanity has presumably made it through the ages this way, responding with its immediate consciousness.

More serious and more general problems, however, follow from the mismatches of the mind. One set is the major social misjudgments that have developed about matters of life and death: our physical, mental, and spiritual health. Many people suffer and die because they, or their society, caricature and thus misrepresent reality. Events that fit easily into the caricatured world, such as dramatic therapeutic techniques, fantastic "cures," and dramatic "states of mind," are, like vivid emergencies, overemphasized. This leads us to distort our perceptions of some of the most important institutions in our lives, such as medicine, psychotherapy, and religion.

Today in the United States billions of dollars are spent annually on psychotherapy, hundreds of billions on health care, and many more billions on various forms of religion. Have people somehow blinded themselves into accepting the continuous growth of big medicine, big subconscious therapy, and big religion while letting the bombs pile up? We are afraid so. Our society has radically miscalculated the kind of therapy we need and misunderstands the kinds of spirituality we do have and the kinds we might have.

It seems obvious to most people that the improved medical care of sick people has been responsible for the modern improvement in health. Western society is by far the most medicalized in history, and the prevalent belief is that medical care has made it healthy. Many of the common diseases that have plagued humanity, such as tuberculosis and cholera, have almost disappeared from the developed world, and death rates have dropped. But suppose we ask, *How much* of the decline in death rates in the past century is due to medical care? Some people we questioned about this assumed that all the improvement was due to medicine, and most have said, "Much more than half."

A few striking successes, such as the use of salvarsan and, later, penicillin against syphilis, streptomycin against tuberculosis, and the

polio vaccine, have led an entire medical establishment to believe
that chemical "magic bullets" or immunization techniques can be
found to cure cancer and heart diseases. Maybe they can, but the
idea has taken hold that if we just spend money to fight our disease
"enemies," we will conquer them. A "war" on cancer was declared
by President Richard Nixon under this illusion. Hundreds of millions of dollars were spent long before there was any real hope of
finding cures, since a basic understanding of this family of diseases
had not been reached. It was like trying to go to the moon before
Isaac Newton formulated his laws of motion. The head of the Food
and Drug Administration wrote in 1978 of this campaign, "The
War on Cancer is a medical Vietnam." That war got started because
of the way the idea of cancer fit into the mind, not because that was
the most promising way to deal with it.

Cancers are dramatic: an invading set of cells multiplies out of
control. After AIDS they are the most feared diseases of our time.
But are cancers so important? If all cancers *could* be cured by a
magic bullet overnight, then the average life expectancy would increase by a mere two years, according to estimates by Beverly
Winikoff, a physician at Rockefeller University. If good nutrition,
exercise, and good health habits (especially not smoking) were followed, average life expectancy would increase by seven years. But
cancer catches attention; diverticulosis does not. A surgeon staying
up all night to save a life is visible and commands respect, attention,
and funding, whereas a nutritionist has a slow and subtle, but possibly more significant impact on health.

A visitor from outer space would probably wonder about the
endless series of arguments over supplying ever-increasing amounts
of a nonexistent substance called health care. The United States
spends more than $400 billion annually, some 13 percent of the
gross national product, on the medical enterprise. But how much of
it is just the old mind's reaction to the constant promotion of medical marvels, especially "news events," such as liver transplants for
cute toddlers and plastic artificial hearts for middle-aged men?

To approve of this massive effort, one would first have to believe
that organized "health care" is quite important to people's health. It

is not. To justify such a massive social investment, one would also have to believe that the entire medical enterprise, including all the accumulated research evidence and training of the past century, has produced a meaningful extension of life. It has not.

Medical care has *not,* on the average, notably lengthened the life of those who survive early childhood. Between the middle of the nineteenth and twentieth centuries, in societies for which good health statistics exist, such as England, Wales, and the United States, the average age at death rose from fifty to seventy-four. But about one hundred years ago a forty-five-year-old white English male could expect to live for about another twenty-five years. In other words, a similar male living a century later can expect to live only four or five years longer than his ancestor who lived before all these highly visible and dramatic developments had taken place.

Death rates first dropped mainly because of something quite boring: advances in sanitation. Interventions such as water purification, better sewage disposal systems, and generally improved hygiene greatly decreased mortality from infectious disease. Later, death rates continued to fall because people began to have fewer children and could care for them better; they also fell as the infectious diseases of youth were conquered. It was only in the twentieth century that much of the success in reducing diseases resulted from advances in what we think of today as "medical care."

The death rate from tuberculosis declined drastically well before the existence of modern medicine as we know it, dropping *97 percent* between 1850 and 1945. The effect of streptomycin in 1947, the first effective medical treatment, caused a sensation, but it only effected a further 3 percent drop in death rates. In spite of the small real decline due to the drug, the vivid emptying of the hospitals, so fresh in recent memory, makes most people credit the conquest of tuberculosis to the "wonder drug." However, malaria had largely disappeared from Europe, and yellow fever had vanished from the United States before the causative agents were even discovered.

If death rates did not decline much because of medical care of sick people (of course, increasing scientifically based environmental and public health measures greatly helped), then perhaps a better question is, How much is medicine responsible for the good health and vigor that people enjoy while they are alive? This question is appropriate, as it would get us away from being "mind-blinded" by the success of the wonder drugs, the miracles of many surgical techniques, and the intricate diagnostic and life-support devices that are used in modern hospitals. However, when we switch from the simple caricature view—spending money will produce health, and "tremendous advances have been made"—to a calm, cold analysis of the absolute contribution of medicine, we begin to see a different picture.

Such an analysis was done by epidemiologists John and Sonia McKinlay. They used sophisticated statistics to assess the role of medicine in maintaining health. In their analysis, medical intervention in infectious diseases such as tuberculosis, diphtheria, whooping cough, influenza, and the like is responsible for only *3.5 percent* of the total decline in mortality since 1900. The major elements in enhancing resistance to disease were improved nutrition and environmental changes that made food purer and safer, especially for infants.

Epidemiologists Lee and Alexandra Benham considered the impact on health of the recent great expansion of the availability of medical services. *They found no effect of expanded medical care on health.* Other studies have found some effect, but the effects are relatively small, in the 5 to 10 percent range, results of much less consequence than such day-to-day factors as marital status, employment, happiness in relationships, and the availability of care givers. Of the factors that determine the state of our health, more than 80 percent, probably much more, derive from our environment: our relationships with friends and enemies, our status in society, the quality of our education, our thoughts about ourselves. Our moods —boom or gloom—have much more to do with health than do the interventions of physicians when we get sick.

Minor social changes cause enormous changes in the functioning of a person's body. The heart responds quite quickly to changed circumstances. Thomas Scotch found that Zulus living in an urban environment were likely to have much higher blood pressure levels

than their relatives in rural settings, even when diet and other factors stayed the same. Biologist Harold Morowitz analyzed data from
the original United States surgeon general's report on smoking and
found that a divorce was as likely to cause heart disease as years of
smoking two packs of cigarettes per day!

Our caricatures make us attribute the improvement of health care
to medical technology. We even title that technology and those who
employ it a health care delivery system, as if health care were a
specific item that could be packaged and delivered like pepperoni
pizza. In fact many hospitals are now called health centers, instead
of medical centers, just as the War Department of the United States
Government became the Department of Defense.

But "health care" is not an object and, as such, is hardly even
taught in medical schools. The defaults of the old mind cause people to confuse the spectacular short-term new developments in medical technology with "health care"; even though the fancy new
techniques affect only a minuscule portion of the population. Most
people, even in very highly medicalized societies, do *not* use medicine (not to be confused with taking medicines, such as aspirin) for
most of their ills.

The mechanizing of medicine has led to rather horrifying mismatches, such as that embodied in the statement "The patient died
in perfect electrolyte balance." It has led, too, to a mechanical "biomedicine" that all too often ignores the very real problems of its
living patients, such as the social and emotional components of
disease. It might surprise many people to learn that it was only
about fifty years ago that medicine began to become a science in the
modern sense and that only thirty years ago could it be considered,
on balance, to do more good for the average patient than harm.

The old mind focuses on the immediate behaviors and actions
that save the lives of individuals, not on long-term improvements to
health or the gradual growth of an unbalanced, incredibly expensive
health care system. Health care may be "delivered," but it is largely
delivered by sufficient nutritious food, soaps, toilets, water-treatment
systems, window screens, milkmen (especially for children), and,
increasingly, condoms. It has been delivered gradually, undetectable

by the unaided nervous system. The struggle to preserve the individual for his or her biological life span has been largely won in Western societies. One of today's most pressing medical problems is how to accommodate death when it is unavoidable and proper—how to let people die right the first time. It is not a problem earlier societies, lacking the technology to suspend the desperately ill on the brink of death, had to face.

AIDS, of course, is a long-term medical problem that has forcefully brought itself to the attention of society, but the true magnitude of the threat has not yet registered on the old mind. One little boy gets AIDS from a blood transfusion, and of course we immediately want to help him. But in allowing him to go to school, there is a tiny chance that we may endanger other people. His case thus becomes "news," and civil libertarians fight to get him admitted. They fail to recognize that they may hasten the boy's own death by exposing *him* to many infectious diseases.

To protect the anonymity of AIDS victims, laws have been promulgated that forbid surgeons from finding out whether their patients are infected with the AIDS virus. This exposes surgical teams and their families, as well as society as a whole, to greater risks. During operations, physicians and nurses are often splashed with large amounts of blood, and the surgeons frequently are cut. Wearing two sets of gloves provides a surgeon with added protection, but reduces the sense of feel that is critical in delicate procedures. But the old mind is most sympathetic with the immediate victim. It does not ordinarily register the secondary costs—more people getting the disease and thus adding to the chances that AIDS will propagate in the heterosexual population, surgeons refusing to operate on "suspicious" patients, hematologists and other physicians forced to break the law to protect their colleagues, and so on. The old mind wants to keep AIDS in the familiar arena of civil rights rather than in unfamiliar domains such as epidemiology and medical ethics. But AIDS must become a matter primarily of *public health,* albeit one in which civil rights are guarded as zealously as possible within the constraints set by the need to protect society from a catastrophic breakdown.

AIDS is killing tens of thousands of people and threatens to kill tens of millions. It may well have the greatest potential, outside of nuclear war, for killing people over the next few decades. AIDS will probably do so unless there is a radical change in human behavior (and considerable good luck). We need a stimulus to change behavior, since the dry statistics, even of mounting deaths, don't seem to help in the heat of the moment of transmission of the virus. Pictures of people wasting away, shown daily on television, are exactly the kind of signal needed to register on old minds. But, like many other possible campaigns, it needs to shock us continually so that we don't forget it, as we seem to have forgotten genital herpes in the wake of the much more horrific AIDS problem.

Every slim hope of a cure for AIDS receives immediate and wide coverage, as it should; but the truly catastrophic potential of the disease is rarely discussed, and some behavioral changes we need to make to reduce the spread of the virus have collided with opposing barriers of the old mind.

In his classic book *The Plague,* Albert Camus noted the incapacity of old minds to project the consequences of trends:

> Everybody knows that pestilences have a way of recurring in the world; yet somehow we find it hard to believe in ones that crash down on our heads from a blue sky. . . . A pestilence isn't a thing made to man's measure; therefore we tell ourselves that pestilence is a mere bogy of the mind, a bad dream that will pass away. But it doesn't always pass away and, from one bad dream to another, it is men who pass away, and the humanists first of all, because they haven't taken their precautions.

People just don't believe it can happen to them—unless "it" appears suddenly next door. Few events in modern times have illuminated the human capacity for tuning out the significance of trends more than the growing incidence of AIDS. The example is especially stark, for in spite of widespread media coverage, including frequent pictures of dying victims, many people are still denying that they could become involved. A true grasp of the potential magnitude of the disaster is restricted to the few with appropriate training. Many biologists and epidemiologists can see what a few million infections and a few thousand deaths this year may portend for the human condition around the turn of the century.

For decades now humanity has been setting itself up as a progressively ideal target for a worldwide epidemic. The combination of rapidly increasing numbers of malnourished people, who live in conditions of poor sanitation and with impure water, with ever-more-rapid transportation systems has been making the human epidemiological environment ever more precarious. We have created a giant, crowded, "monoculture" of human beings, millions of whom are especially vulnerable to disease and among whom carriers can move with unprecedented speed.

Humanity has already had some close calls, but they have generally not entered old-mind consciousness.

AIDS is actually the third in a serious of serious viral diseases that seem to have recently transferred into the human population.* There is, unfortunately, much uncertainty about this disease. What is known is that it is caused by a special kind of virus, known as a

---

* In Africa as human populations have expanded, pathogens have shifted from animal reservoirs to the human population and begun to cause serious diseases. The first of these new diseases to be recognized was Marburg disease, caused by a virus that infected vervet monkeys. In 1967 a consignment of these monkeys infected with the virus passed through Heathrow Airport, in London, on their way to a laboratory in Marburg, Germany. In the laboratory twenty-five people in contact with the monkeys or their tissues were infected by the virus, and seven died almost immediately. They managed to pass it on to a few additional people, all of whom survived their bouts with the disease.

Humanity had two strokes of luck in this case. First, the incubation period for the disease was short—usually only four to seven days. Victims had little chance to contact others and pass on the disease before they became sick and died. This allowed epidemiologists to trace the course of the disease and quickly limit it by isolating the sick. If, on the other hand, the virus had infected workers at the London airport, it might have been disseminated around the globe before anything could be done to stop it.

Humanity's second near-miss was Lassa fever, caused by another African virus that originated in nonhuman mammals (in this case, a rat). It first appeared in the Nigerian village of Lassa in 1969 in the form of a highly lethal, contagious hemorrhagic disease. A small but nasty epidemic ensued (twelve of twenty-three patients died in the Nigerian town of Jos), and the disease was even transferred to the United States when sick medical missionary workers were evacuated. But luck held again. The originally lethal virus became less virulent as it passed from person to person, and a serum containing antibodies produced by survivors has helped cure subsequent victims.

retrovirus, which invades a particular kind of white blood cell that plays a crucial role in providing immunity to disease.

Some consensus about AIDS, however, now seems to be emerging from the scientific community. First of all, it is an extremely deadly disease. The recovery rate of people who show symptoms of the full-blown disease is essentially zero. More problematic is estimating the percentage of people now only carriers who will eventually display the symptoms and die. Early estimates of a conversion rate of 10 percent are now uniformly viewed as much too optimistic. Informed opinion appears to be moving toward expecting that if you are infected with the virus and some other cause of death does not intervene, AIDS will eventually kill you (unless a cure is found). And developing a satisfactory vaccine or cure is expected to be at best a long and difficult task.

It is also clear that certain groups within the populations of Western countries, specifically homosexuals, intravenous-drug users, people who receive blood transfusions, and those (primarily those with hemophilia) dependent on blood products, remain at higher risk than the general population. The disease has, however, by no means been limited to these groups. At the very least it can be transmitted by heterosexual intercourse, and other forms of blood-to-blood or fluid-to-fluid transmission are possible. The virus can also be passed on from mother to offspring before or during birth or in mothers' milk, so there is a substantial probability that a child born to an AIDS victim will contract the disease.

While most of the AIDS cases in the United States and Europe are in the "high risk" groups, in Africa (where the virus has been in the human population the longest) it appears to infect men and women about equally. Reliable statistics from that continent are hard to come by, but in some areas of central Africa as much as one quarter of the population has been claimed to be carrying the virus. Even the conservative estimate of the Center for Disease Control in Atlanta is a still-horrifying 7 percent. It seems certain that the death rate in Africa from AIDS will move very rapidly upward.

The reason for the different distribution of the virus in the African population is at the moment unclear. It is possible that a high incidence of other sexually transmitted diseases (STDs) produces a frequency of genital lesions that eases the transfer of the virus. Widespread use of shared, unsterilized needles and transfusion with untested blood are clearly important factors. Heterosexual anal intercourse is also reported to be much more commonly practiced in Africa, in part as a means of birth control, than elsewhere. Bleeding as an aftereffect of female circumcision may also have some small influence. Most frightening of all, the commonest strains of the virus in Africa may simply be more easily transmitted heterosexually than those now found in the rest of the world.

In spite of the old-mind tendency to ignore slow-motion catastrophes, no one should doubt that AIDS already represents, at the very least, a public health disaster unsurpassed since the great flu epidemic of 1918–19, which killed more than 500,000 Americans. An estimated 1 to 2 million people are already infected in the United States, which in itself implies a horrendous economic cost to be borne in the future. Suppose just 1 million are infected with the virus and half of them contract the disease; and suppose the average loss of productivity and cost of care per person were $100,000. This would amount to an economic cost to the nation of $50 billion, even if not one more person were infected. That very conservative estimate, of course, does not even consider the loss of the economic productivity of the victim, or the incredible human costs that are not economic in nature, such as the suffering of half a million individuals and their families and friends.

In fact there is every reason to believe that even these enormous costs are just the tip of the iceberg. AIDS clearly has the *potential* for decimating the human population. In addition to its extreme virulence, the AIDS virus can be carried for many years without producing symptoms. For part or all of that period the carrier is infectious, and that makes the situation much worse. People carrying the virus can infect person after person, and no one need be the wiser. A prostitute infected with AIDS could stay in business for five years or more, killing thousands of people (her clients and their other contacts) without being aware she was doing it. Under present public health policies in many nations there is no way of ending the sequence.

More frightening is the extreme mutability (the ability to change form) of the virus. Many different strains exist already, which, along with other properties of AIDS, may make the development of cheap, permanent immunization procedures quite difficult. Furthermore few drugs so far exist to combat viruses, and there is little reason to believe that a biochemical cure for AIDS will be found readily, even though substantial progress has been made in understanding how to design antiviral drugs. Among other things, the virus may be able to evolve resistance to drugs that are initially effective. Last, as more and more people are infected, strains of the virus may evolve that are more readily transmittible than those already circulating in the population. That is a very real possibility that terrifies biologists who understand the evolutionary potential of viruses.

It is even therefore conceivable that humanity will sooner or later have to deal with strains of AIDS that can be transmitted by the bites of arthropods (perhaps by the bites of mosquitos that were interrupted while feeding on someone carrying the virus). Worse yet, a variety of AIDS virus might evolve that can be transmitted by relatively casual, nonsexual physical contact or even by inhaling droplets sneezed into the air. The odds of it happening seem very small, but the consequences if it did occur would be, to say the least, daunting. With millions virtually certain to die in Africa, the possibility that the virus, if uncontrolled, could result in extremely high death rates in the developed countries should not be overlooked.

Nonetheless, overlooking such possibilities is precisely what our nervous systems are designed to do. Even with all the publicity, most people haven't grasped the fact that a few people dying today may portend their own premature demise in the future. As a result society has been much too slow in responding to the building catastrophe. Scientists and governments have not made it clear to the general public that AIDS is a potentially lethal threat to *everyone*— not just members of a limited number of high-risk groups. Instead a "head-in-the-sand" approach has to be countered. A statement in early 1987 by a British government official that "Christians don't get AIDS" is typical of widespread old-mind attitudes.

By 1985 governments should have already instigated large-scale crash programs to find ways of protecting people against acquiring the virus, of building up the resistance of those who are already infected, and of treating those who already are showing symptoms. Developing a means of immunization should have been made a top research priority. Major programs should have been launched aimed at understanding patterns of transmission of AIDS and its overall epidemiology. Compulsory testing of everyone between the ages of twelve and thirty has been suggested. By making testing universal, some of the problems of discriminating against certain groups could be avoided, while the seriousness of the problem could be brought home to the public. Carriers could be identified quickly and counseled, and epidemiologists would have sound data on which to base recommendations. A system could be devised that would make both testing and counseling anonymous, but any such mass testing program would best wait until more reliable tests are available.

Meanwhile massive programs of public education are needed worldwide on the threat of AIDS and on behavioral changes that can reduce that threat. Mismatches in social reactions have made such programs pathetically slow in coming. As soon as it was clear that the virus was primarily transmitted sexually, people should have been urged to eliminate promiscuous behavior and (since many were unlikely to take that advice) made aware of ways to make sex safer. The use of condoms, combined with spermicidal jellies, could reduce (but not eliminate) the chances of acquiring or passing on the virus. Most important, condom use could slow down the spread of the virus and thus buy time to find ways of stopping the virus from infecting people. It could even lead to the disease eventually disappearing from populations in which most sexually active males employ condoms. A relatively small drop in the chances of passing on an infectious disease can be the difference between the disease propagating in a population or dying out.

Education in the use of condoms did not reach the proper scale in Europe until 1986. Great Britain then finally mounted a massive campaign to promote condoms, including demonstrations on television using model erections to show a generation largely unfamiliar with them how rubbers should be applied and rock songs about always going to bed with "your Johnny [condom] on." On Swedish television, ads show the rolling of uninflated balloons onto bananas.

The United States has lagged far behind many European nations. American television networks, for whom sex is the staff of life, strongly resisted broadcasting condom ads, and the ones first shown by local stations were so "tasteful" that a naive viewer might think them either promotions for vacations in scenic surroundings or ads for life insurance. The networks claimed that condom ads would offend viewers, who are regularly treated to dinner-time ads about hemorrhoids, diarrhea, armpit stench, bad breath, incontinence, unsightly and odorous dentures, and the problems, embarrassment, and conundrums of those "difficult days" of the menstrual cycle.

The media have invaded Ronald Reagan's privacy by having details of his colon spread throughout the newspapers, and animated diagrams illuminated and itemized by a journalist about the details of his intimate urinary discomfort have been featured on the TV news. But a forthright announcement that slipping a rubber sheath over the penis before sexual intercourse might save your life is unacceptable. However, there are hopeful signs that new-mindedness may be found even within the Reagan administration. In 1986 the very conservative surgeon general of the United States, C. Everett Koop, recommended education about condoms in the schools. He found himself ostracized by many previous supporters (who agreed with his opposition to abortion) for proposing such a realistic and straightforward approach. In contrast, the Catholic Church, some of whose priests are dying of AIDS, remained steadfastly opposed to the use of condoms, even during heterosexual intercourse.

In summary, because of ingrained, outdated attitudes, society is making tragic mistakes in its handling of the AIDS epidemic, even though it has many characteristics that easily penetrate the old mind. Too often the focus in AIDS has been on the rescue of the miserable individual victims, be they waiters or schoolchildren, and on the victim's civil rights, rather than on the infected person's potential role in disseminating the disease. Part of this is due to the standard journalistic device of using individuals in distress to make more general points. But the new mind needs to develop dual empathy: an immediate empathy for individual victims and a sustained empathy for those who will *become* victims if proper steps are not taken to contain the disease.

The AIDS epidemic, like the nuclear arms race, is one place that the price of old-mindedness can be easily seen. Because of the slowness of our old minds to project the possible long-term consequences of the disease, it may now be too late to contain the epidemic. Even if humanity is fortunate and succeeds in developing adequate immunizations or treatments and somehow delivers them to the poor as well as the rich, so that deaths are limited to a "few" million worldwide, we must be aware that victory will not necessarily be permanent. A new-minded approach to public health would also recognize the increasing vulnerability of an expanding human population to other plagues and would moreover recognize that medical science is unlikely ever to conquer totally the various microorganisms that can cause disease. If this were part of our consciousness, we could vastly improve our ability to react to the threat of epidemics. Viruses, bacteria, the plasmodia that cause malaria,* and other pathogens do not register on our senses and so are not easily recognized enemies, but they are deadly ones.

---

* Unhappily, AIDS is hardly the only infectious disease that is misunderstood. Malaria is another. The old-mind approach to its control is to focus on protecting individuals from being infected and to provide relief of individual suffering. We try to eliminate the immediately visible and obviously annoying threat of mosquitos by "broadcast" spraying of pesticides, giving toxic drugs to travelers as prophylaxis, and applying even higher doses of these drugs to the unfortunate individuals who become victims of the disease.

But malaria, once thought to be nearly "conquered," will be with us for the foreseeable future. It is now making a comeback throughout much of the Tropics, thanks in large part to the evolution of drug resistance in the malarial organisms themselves and pesticide resistance in the mosquitoes that transmit the disease. A new-minded approach to its control would be to focus on the system of which the disease is a part. It would involve a program of careful ecological management designed to suppress the disease. That program would include many steps to prevent or discourage mosquito breeding, keeping people indoors when malarial mosquitos are abroad, and using window screens and bed nets to prevent mosquitos from reaching people. Other measures would include enhancing immu-

Our perceptions often distort the significance not just of diseases but of various drugs as well. Vivid public relations makes us believe that some drugs are more dangerous, while social acceptance makes us assume that other drugs are less dangerous, than they actually are. Robert Ornstein has attended many government councils on drug abuse, conferences in which concerned professionals discussed the dangers of marijuana, heroin, and amphetamine while at the same time they smoked cigarettes and drank coffee and alcohol, three drugs that not only change consciousness but also have very harmful physical effects. Sometimes those everyday drugs are more injurious than the substances that are subjects of the convention!

Smoking tobacco, as everyone knows, leads to severe health consequences, such as lung cancer and heart attacks, and withdrawal from tobacco can be as painful and difficult as withdrawal from heroin. Excessive alcohol consumption causes brain and liver damage and other organ degeneration. The physiological effect of coffee is quite similar to that of amphetamine. Coffee was not always familiar and thus seen as safe. Here is an extract from an early Arabic writer on the abuse of a new drug:

The sale of coffee has been forbidden. The vessels used for this beverage . . . have been broken to pieces. The dealers in coffee have received the bastinado, and have undergone other ill-treatment without even a plausible excuse. . . . The husks of the plant . . . have been more than once devoted to the flames and in several instances persons making use of it . . . have been severely handled.

---

nological resistance to malaria in people and regulating the use of antimalarial drugs and insecticides to avoid the buildup of chemical resistance in the disease-causing malarial parasites and the mosquitos. Some of those steps are now, fortunately, being taken. The tragedies caused by the improper use of pesticides against malarial mosquitos and too much dependence on antimalarial drugs may well, in the long run, eventually outweigh their benefits. A side effect of that dependence has been less attention to ecological management that, while not so dramatic (and thus appealing to old minds), could provide better control of the disease in the long run. Related difficulties have developed thanks to the prescribing of antibiotics inappropriately without sufficient consideration of the medium-term evolutionary consequences. Drug resistance is now a major problem in the treatment of many diseases.

If coffee were scarce, unknown, and offered under conditions of great expectation, its impact on society and the person ingesting it would be very different than it is when the same substance is offered everywhere in anonymous plastic cups in vending machines. We constantly underestimate the danger of the familiar and overestimate the danger of the unfamiliar.

Consider our attitude toward heroin. Opium is an unrefined extract of the poppy seed pod; morphine is a refined extract of opium and is stronger in its effects. Heroin is derived from morphine and is even more potent in its pure form. ("Street" heroin, however, is usually diluted to below the strength of opium.) Opiate drugs kill pain by fitting into receptors that stop pain from reaching the brain's cortex. The user not only feels no pain but also no signals of normal physiological needs, such as hunger telling him it's time to eat. So while physical pain is relieved, there is also a decrease in anxiety and often a reduced interest in food, sex, and work.

But heroin, taken orally at least, is more dangerous psychologically and socially than physiologically. Of course the body did not evolve to receive injections of substances, so *anything* shot up is likely to be dangerous. One important physical danger of heroin is that people who use it often neglect their health by not eating, drinking, or attending to pain. It is not, however, *in itself* an extremely toxic substance. People can be reasonably well "maintained" on it for years without much damage. The damage comes from the social situation, from having to steal to get a drug that is addictive and illegal, from dropping out of society to support this kind of habit, and from self-neglect. However, other drugs well tolerated by society, such as caffeine, nicotine, and alcohol, are inherently more poisonous substances. Because the carriers of these poisons have long been accepted by society and their use promoted by powerful economic interests, they are viewed as nonthreatening parts of our small worlds.

Old-mind attitudes control not just how we deal with the health of our bodies but how we treat disorders of the mind. Mental therapies grow because of the mismatches in the mind—striking cases capture attention the way a sudden noise does. Dramatic cures of phobias and the remissions of schizophrenics make for great cinema, as in the famous film *The Three Faces of Eve.*

Psychotherapy illustrates this growth of mental therapies; it has become a major preoccupation of our culture. About 35 million people, one out of every seven in the United States, will consult a professional for a psychological problem during his or her lifetime. Americans see psychotherapists more often than do people in any other society. It is costing society billions of dollars per year and has much less effectiveness than most assume.

What is the real outcome of all the storm and stress of psychotherapy? Does psychotherapy work? Does one type of therapy perform better than another? If they improve people, do we know why?

The effectiveness of psychotherapy has been the subject of great controversy within the scientific community. Some universities, such as Stanford, have given up entirely the training of clinical psychologists on the grounds that the benefits of psychotherapy have not been demonstrated. But 35 million people spend a lot of money and time seeking it out.

Everybody has a favorite brand of treatment: emotional, dynamic, nondirective, cognitive, cognitive-behavioral, drug-behavioral, behavioral-cognitive, emotional-dynamic-behavioral, and the like. It is difficult to imagine that so many different kinds of treatment could spring up if the phenomena being treated were well understood.

Empirical evidence about therapy is surprisingly scarce given the enormous number of people in treatment. Trying to appraise therapies is mind-boggling; there is little agreement among therapists on basic issues, such as what is wrong with a specific patient.

One difficulty lies in how the training of the therapist affects his or her perception of the problem. This was illustrated when Perry Turner of the magazine *Science 86* asked four therapists, representing a tiny sample of the four hundred kinds of therapy practiced today, to consider treating a fictional "George." This setting allows us almost perfect examples of the way the therapists with mismatched minds, especially trained mismatched minds, see a small part of the whole, make a caricature out of a patient's problems, and then go on to prescribe very different treatments based only on the caricature.

The case, "The Shrinking of George" was presented to different therapists as follows:

George is 31 years old and has been married for five years. . . . His wife, who is 30, is four months pregnant with their first child. George came in complaining of insomnia, "testiness," and anxiety caused by fantasies about another woman and by fears that he would prove inadequate as a father, husband, and musician. George reports no history of significant acute or chronic physical illness. He takes no prescribed or over-the-counter medications. His last physical was seven months ago; all findings were normal.

His childhood was "as happy as anyone's," he says, and his parents were loving and fair. . . . About seven months ago, a new typist named Laura started working in George's office. Laura, a poor typist and a very pretty young woman, behaved quite seductively around George. . . . The night he planned to tell her they had a fight. . . . He ended up not telling Ann about Laura, and he remembers feeling a moment of satisfaction in keeping this part of his life to himself. He and Ann made up shortly, but he "never got around to telling her" about Laura, who made it progressively clearer to George that she wanted to sleep with him.

About two months after she had started working in his office, George played a concert in a nearby park with several coworkers. Laura and Ann showed up, though separately. When he saw them, he felt suddenly humiliated by his "artistic pretensions." . . . One night, having awakened at 4:00 A.M., he resolved to get his life in order: the next day he began suggesting to Ann that they start a family, and he asked a coworker to complain about Laura's performance to the office manager and see about getting her transferred. Within three weeks, Laura had been reassigned to an office on another floor and Ann had conceived.

George . . . began to grow frustrated. He started waking up regularly in the middle of the night and could not fall asleep. He feared Laura would discover he had engineered her transfer. . . . One night while making love to Ann he fantasized he was with Laura, and subsequently he has been unable to stop doing this whenever he and Ann make love.

In this fictional case, George sought help three weeks after the fantasies began. He wanted more self-discipline and did not want to resent his child as an intrusion in his life, but feared that he might. And he wanted to sleep through the night. How did four different therapists respond?

Behavior therapist Marcia Chambers would try to get George to define his complaints as specifically as possible. What do "self-discipline" and "testiness" mean to him? Then George would isolate the behaviors he would like to change.

"I would spend maybe four sessions teaching George relaxation. . . . Once he'd learned that, we could really use it for many different things . . . once he's very relaxed, have him think about being in bed and having sex with Ann. And then see if he could do it again at home." . . .

With practice, George would come to relax when he made love to Ann, and the deeper his relaxation, the higher his resistance to distress—to thoughts of Laura, specifically. As Chambers points out, "It's physiologically impossible to feel relaxed and anxious at the same time." . . . And she would encourage him to devise his own incentives, especially ones that he could work into his day-to-day routines, such as taking Ann to dinner after a week of faithfully practicing his bassoon. "My goal," she explains, "is to put myself out of business." Not all share this goal.

In a different kind of treatment, cognitive therapist Dean Schuyler would jot down the critical events in George's life and the accompanying thoughts and feelings. He would ask George to record his reactions in a journal between sessions, to reveal how George's thoughts set off distress. Cognitive therapy challenges these thoughts. Here is how it might go:

S: What is so bad about thinking of someone else while making love to your wife?

G: Your marriage is a hoax—this person isn't who you wanted.

S: So what if your marriage is a hoax?

G: Well—then you're destroying someone's chances for happiness because—you bound her into this arrangement under false pretenses.

S: So what if you did that?

G: It's hard enough for each person in the world to be happy— why drag someone else down with your lies?

S: Okay, so all of this miserable stuff that you're doing has resulted from your having thought about someone else while making love to your wife?

G: No, no, but—

S: (smiling a little): Certainly seems what you've been saying.

Schuyler says that six months of once-a-week therapy would be required.

Family therapist Joseph Lorio would talk to George about the symptoms and record the relationship between George and Ann. He would involve Ann in therapy. He would try to get George to analyze what's going on between him and his wife so that he can understand how he can change.

The key thing is to change from being an emotional reactor to a better observer. The better you can observe and learn about the interplay between self and relationships, the less you react emotionally to it and the faster you make progress. Oftentimes people with just six sessions feel less anxious, calmer, better in control of their lives. But he could be in therapy a year or two, or even longer, if I could get him to bridge his current situations to his extended family.

Psychoanalyst Robert Winer was struck that George's job is managing other people's development. He recalled the cliché "Those who can, do; those who can't, teach." The "restiness" indicates that he is simply reporting someone else's accusation about himself. Winer sees George as having an oversensitivity to others' opinions derived from his early family life about keeping up with the Joneses.

. . . the whole business of getting Laura transferred represents an overriding concern with his own security and a lack of a reasonable effort to be concerned with someone else's. Laura is nothing to get nervous about. She's being flirtatious, that's all. She's entitled to that in life. He can always say . . . "Look I'm a married man, we're not going to have anything happen." . . .

"And now he becomes obsessed with Laura. Usually obsessions are a way of controlling aggression. You wonder how much anger toward his wife about the pregnancy is tied up in that. And men can experience intercourse with a pregnant wife as an attack on the baby, if they're already feeling aggression toward it, so maybe the obsessive thoughts about Laura are some way of blocking out that aggression. . . .

"It may be that just seeing him through the end of the pregnancy will be enough to help him make some kind of adjustment around the baby. But if his goal is to realize himself more fully as a man, given that he's been ducking that all his life," concludes Winer, "you're talking about analysis: four or five sessions a week, probably for several years."

Turner's excellent article, which we extracted at length because it shows caricatures in action, gives a good idea of outright lack of agreement in the field. What should be the aim of the treatment? How should we go about it? What do we want to come out of it? And remember, the therapies described for "George" are only 4 of the 400 "brands" of treatment available in America today.

The various forms of psychotherapy have existed since the beginning of the century, but the first study to show that psychotherapy has even a slight positive result was not published until 1980. Basing our judgment simply on the evidence presented in scientific research journals so far, we do not believe that the practice of psychotherapy would pass the conventional requirements the Food and Drug Administration imposes for a new medical therapy. All that should be concluded now is that further study of its effects is certainly justified. It may prove worthwhile, but it has, like the medical industry, grown up without regulation and remained unanalyzed because of the prominence assumed by some individual "cures," such as the famous hypnosis demonstrations of Freud and his teachers and the "fusing" of the multiple personalities of "the three faces of Eve."

What about the basis of therapies? The most influential psychotherapist and inventor of psychoanalysis, Sigmund Freud, set out a hydraulic model of personality, explaining it in the context of the operations of simple nineteenth-century machinery and of early developments in physiology. This model postulated a mental "energy" that shifts from a consciousness exclusively verbal and rational to an uncharted, feared "unconscious" that contains everything from "repressed" hatred, ancient memories, unsocial lusts, to irrational religious experiences.

Freud's synthesis was brilliant, given the lack of scientific knowledge about human nature in the late nineteenth century. Freud linked the anxieties of his patients to the growing understanding of human beings as evolutionary creatures, with lusts and urges suited to a different time. If this view of Freud as a "biologist of the mind" seems controversial, we suggest a reading of *Civilization and Its Discontents,* which contains a long discussion about the upright, bipedal structure of humanity and the problems our evolutionary baggage causes in modern life. Freud's discussions could have been written by Charles Darwin (they were certainly influenced by him), or they could have concerned the life of *Lucy.* Freud understood quite well that the human mind is profoundly mismatched in modern civilization. But Freud conceived the mismatch too dramatically, as one of a clash between fundamental instinctual urges and the restraints of modern life. Good writing, good theater, not such good science.

And it was a fine start at understanding of the mind. But after his early work, Freud did not develop his ideas in line with advancing knowledge, and psychoanalytic theory did not change as did the other sciences of the time. Contemporary scientists don't nowadays write about "phlogiston" or "ether wind," but psychoanalysis, instead of maturing and changing along with new developments, has simply aged into an outmoded practice. Notwithstanding, it has been embraced by the culture.

There were virtually no objective data on the effectiveness of psychotherapy until the mid-1940s. There have been several studies since. In 1952 Hans Eysenck of the Maudsley Hospital in London initiated research on the question of the effectiveness of psychoanalysis. Eysenck divided those seeking psychotherapy into two groups. The members of one group were put on a waiting list; the others received therapy. The study showed that "roughly two-thirds of a group of neurotic patients will recover or improve to a marked extent within about two years of the onset of their illness. This improvement or recovery was the case whether the person had received therapy or not."

But this was not the only surprising result. Ernest Poser, of McGill University in Montreal, found in treating schizophrenic pa-

tients that randomly selected undergraduates with almost no training used as therapists produced more positive change than did
psychiatrists and psychiatric social workers. We would be surprised
if those untrained in neurosurgery performed more successful brain
operations than those who had gone through medical school, resi-
dency, and a decade of practice. Dr. Poser's and others' studies
indicate that the "training" of psychotherapists is not very relevant
to their efficacy.

It appears, in fact, that the different "brands" of psychotherapeutic treatments all work in much the same way, their different doc-
trines notwithstanding. And, as Jerome Frank's analysis in *Persuasion and Healing* makes clear, the similarity also applies to
treatments available in cultures very different from ours: psychiatrists, priests, rabbis, faith healers, witch doctors, shamans and medicine men all help heal in the same way. Patients enter their therapy
—psycho-, shamanic, or mystical—very demoralized and are given
hope by the process. It is as if all medicines used to treat physical ills
were placebos. Their use is of help only so long as doctors can
convince patients of their potency.

Carl Rogers, an influential psychotherapist, initiated careful studies and found that the specific qualities that make for successful
therapy involve the *personality* of the therapist, not the efficacy of
the therapy's theory or dogma. These personal characteristics include empathy, spontaneity, and the therapist's "unconditional positive regard" for the client. Rogers concludes that "Intellectual training [for psychotherapists] and the acquiring of information has, I
believe, many valuable results—but becoming a therapist is not one
of those results." Psychotherapeutic training may weed out just
those who might be best!

When treatments work, we do not know why. Some of the successes may be due simply to attention, some to the specific technique, some due to drugs. The main point in the end is that psychotherapy, on the average, could possibly help some if the right
treatments could somehow be applied at the right time by the right
therapist to the right people. But we don't know now what the
important factors are, certainly not well enough to charge someone

$150 per hour three and four times per week (unless this expense enhances the placebo effect).

There is often no agreed-upon standard diagnosis, no matching of problem to treatment. The chance to compare alternatives, as in the case of George, is rare. Often, troubled people seek help and may well find sincere, competent therapists who want to help. Yet the treatment may not work as well as it could because of the lack of a match between the problem and the kind of therapy. In some cases the mismatch is so great that it is as if you broke your arm and went to a heart surgeon for treatment. With the current recognition of the dominant role played by the therapist's personality, psychotherapy researchers may be able to develop a more balanced spectrum of treatments for different difficulties and different people. But clearly there is much research still to be done in evaluating treatments and determining how best to prescribe one of the many therapies for any given problem. Nonetheless, this is necessary before psychotherapy can move from a cult with hit-or-miss results to one that provides assured assistance in most cases. And it is also not certain that the problems can be overcome until the caricatures instilled by narrow training can be fleshed out.

Think about what has happened. Think about all the effort, time, and money spent. Psychotherapy, as a practice and as a body of knowledge, is in an infant stage of development, a stage in which responsible investigators are attempting quite reasonably to discover and to develop a proper discipline of treatment. To a great degree, the wrong people, we feel, are getting treatment. The amount of time spent by clients in psychotherapy and by professionals in careers chasing a dramatized, romantic ideal of a "cure" for relatively well-off people could much more profitably be directed to assisting the homeless, the refugee population, and the victims of torture throughout the world. These are all people who have quite serious difficulties that could be helped by financial support and simple counseling.

Another way countless people try to come to grips with the nature of their minds is in disciplines designated as spiritual. Unfortunately, we can just as easily be misled when searching for transcendental experience as we can seeking psychotherapeutic experiences. If the sciences of medicine and psychotherapy are not yet enough, then spiritual disciplines as we know them today are too much. Too much because, like psychotherapy, they have extended themselves into an area left largely empty by our culture: training in knowledge of the mind.

Organized religions, in the main, are products of an ancient time, when the spiritual component of human life was of necessity mixed in with social and political components. Religious and spiritual leaders controlled many aspects of people's lives, in part because sensible guidance on matters of food, marriage, and family life were otherwise unavailable. Dietary rules and modes of dress, as well as in-groups and out-groups, developed along with the spirituality and the experience of transcendence that today are considered the appropriate realm of religion. But in the modern world, obsolete rules and prejudices hang on, while what is left of the spirituality is usually so degraded as to be unrecognizable.

Antievolutionism is a good example of degraded spirituality—a result of the old mind's search for stability. That human beings evolved from other animals does not provide a foundation for making moral judgments, although it eventually did provide us with a need to make such judgments. The oxymoronic "scientific creationism" is about as "scientific" as the notion that the sun circles the earth. In the Soviet Union the acceptance of a creationist viewpoint is partly responsible for the disastrous state of their agriculture—an excellent example of how the old mind plagues the U.S.S.R. as well as the United States.

Many of the classic "mystical" techniques work by opposing bodily desires and needs. Why? The answer lies in the nature of the old mind, designed to serve its owner by "minding" all the functions of the body. This is probably what was meant, in more archaic terminology, by saying that the human mind is encased in a "coil of flesh." Thus many attempts to "break the bonds" of human consciousness do so by trying to break the controlling links to the body.

For centuries people have tried to "mortify the flesh": to free the mind from bodily restraints on its operation. It has been done by dozens of methods—by flagellation, torture, marathon races, starvation, uncomfortable lotus positions, sitting on nails, clapping one hand, or by depriving oneself of everything agreeable, taking away sexuality, power, sensuality, food, and all other sources of fun!

Countless regimes have been designed, in a simplified, idealistic, and well-meaning way, to accomplish this. Over the millennia one of the most popular methods has been the establishment of monasteries that feature a release from all "worldly" desires, often including regimes of restricted diets and reduced stimulation, all for the purpose of "freeing the conscious mind" to go elsewhere. The problem is that most people's minds do not know where to go.

Moreover, what is the use of a select group transcending the normal bounds of knowledge if their insights are not disseminated into society? It is indeed unfortunate that so many have had to suffer for so long, and often for so little. It is also unfortunate that many of the important "ways of knowledge" that might have vital importance for our society have been separated into the side stream of religions.

To us most religions and spiritual groups have, at their core, a vital message: that all human beings are connected to one another, affecting one another's fate and that of the world, and that people must find within themselves a moral compass for orienting both people and their environments. It is a message that is often obscured in the trappings of religion; the short-term thinking that leads to fund-raising on television (as Jackie Gleason said, if all these preachers want you to ask God for healing or for a new car, why can't they ask God for money?); to costumes, hierarchies, and rituals; to archaic dietary and sexual proscriptions.

There is something important to be reclaimed from religion for our culture, since science has so far proven a rather poor source of moral guidance. The problem in finding out about spiritual thought is that the practitioners are usually as confused as the rest of us. Both organized mainline religions and the smaller centers of mysticism share the same old-mind blinders: they focus on the immediately available, or what worked millennia ago for their founder, and then stick to it, just as the psychoanalysts stick to Freud's brilliant but now outdated notions.

The same process holds in religious groups as in medical and psychotherapeutic ones. One cult may find that a certain technique, such as chanting or meditation, works well in a given situation, be it a technique to achieve relaxation or concentration. Its members may sometimes apply the technique in situations that are inappropriate or with people for whom it is ineffective. Because the technique works for them personally, they come to believe that it *ought* to work for everyone at all times. Thus the technique becomes the end, even an obsession, both in small cults, such as meditation societies, and in big cults, such as the established churches. One man's sacred is another's cult.

Instead of concentrating on really understanding the human soul, mind, and body, religionizers often become mere adherents of an organization. Thus the virtue of generosity is often taken as the end point in the esoteric traditions and may even become a moral imperative. This personal attitude should not be an end in itself, but it is a *technique* for attaining a state of enhanced understanding or well-being. Indeed, recent research indicates that even a person *watching* another person perform a selfless act may derive profound improvements in immune system functioning. Such altruism has been shown to be beneficial not only for society but for the individuals themselves.

Similarly, specific diets developed for a certain community at one time may be promulgated across cultures and epochs; the style may remain but the original context is lost, and the diet persists as an empty tradition. The same thing happens with specific exercises designed for one community. Many people travel miles today to see "dervish dances" by the troupe of Konia, and the troupe now makes its own world tours. It is impressive entertainment, but these exercises were originally prescribed because their originator, Jalaluddin Rumi, considered the people of Persia of the fourteenth century to be so dull that they needed to dance around a bit. But there are enough moderns wishing to give mysticism a whirl, and the dance still turns them on!

Members of the rational-scientific traditions often disdain reli-
gious-spiritual psychologies and vice versa. Many who subscribe to
rational thought see religious or spiritual people as following a path
of self-indulgence, performing useless and ridiculous rituals and
withdrawing from life while others around them suffer. From adherents of the spiritual often come hysterical attacks on rational
"materialism" and on the "world" as an "illusion." So spiritual
concerns have moved further and further from the center of contemporary life.

The spiritually inclined hang on at the fringe of society as church
attendance becomes social and perfunctory, and the humane and
transcendent knowledge of the spiritual traditions—about loving
one's brother as oneself, about turning the other cheek, about generosity to others—is almost ignored. Instead we find crooked TV
preachers who time their fund-raising appeals to the arrival of Social Security checks and then use the money extracted from gener-
ous souls on the pretext of serving the needs of crippled children to
support a regal life-style for themselves. Instead we find old men
dictating the details of the sexual behavior of young women. Instead
we find descriptions of the "efficacy" of various spiritual techniques
displayed on bumper stickers, in brochures, and on posters in laun-
dromats and pizza parlors. "Improve awareness! Get in tune with
nature! Get relaxation, restful alertness, brain wave synchrony,
faster reaction time! Increase your perceptual ability, learning ability, academic performance, productivity, job satisfaction, job performance, self-actualization, inner control, mental health, psychology,"
and so on.

Indeed lay cults seem to be replacing the frankly religious. The
innumerable brochures and posters that promote the so-called TM
(Transcendental Meditation) movement often contain claims that
go beyond any reasonable evidence. "Increased synchrony" of the
brain waves recorded on an electroencephalograph (EEG) is often
claimed as a result of TM. This kind of propaganda is supposed to
connote to those versed neither in meditation nor in brain research a
measure of the mind's "increased harmony"—that both hemispheres are working together. In truth such "synchrony" (a finding

largely unrepeated) derives from the brain's producing more alpha rhythm in times of quiescence. Alpha rhythm is a kind of "idling wave" of the brain. So when the two halves of the brain are on "idle," the correlation of the two hemispheres of the brain is increased. But this is no more significant than your television being in perfect sync with your car because both are currently turned off.

These and other attempts to "validate" spirituality exploit science to sell a product; they use promotions similar to the pharmaceutical-company television commercials that show one product entering the bloodstream faster than others, even though speed of entry is not significant. However, the real question for research should be, What are the real effects of meditation? Popular forms of meditation are, most likely, a quite reduced and sanitized form of a more advanced exercise, no more useful than repeating the word "money" over and over again for relaxation.

Self-proclaimed experts, often former car salesmen, now send brochures offering weekend self-improvement courses promoting a particular amalgam of techniques chosen by the expert himself. They commonly involve a little meditation, a little indoctrination, a little scientology, and a little "validation," with the audience softened up (as in brainwashing) by fatigue, fasting, full bladders, and fatuous insults. Such courses bear the same relationship to a real spiritual experience as a sex manual has to real love.

The franchised weekends take advantage of the gaps in our education about who we are, what our minds can do, and how we might improve ourselves to fit into our world. We don't train people to understand and control their bodies, minds, and selves—topics that should be part of basic education. These gaps permit enthusiasts to take an archaic exercise, such as meditation, which was meant for a particular community in another era, and offer it via mass indoctrination to everyone. Not everyone needs to meditate, not everyone needs to calm down, not everyone needs to turn off his or her rational thought processes every day.

The weekend cults are artificial and have to be kept going with much effort and activity. Social gratification begins to substitute for the development of the mental system, with parties, mixers, investment clubs, phone solicitation, uniform dress, and jargon designed to create an exclusive in-group. Continual reminders are given to stragglers by mass mailings, phone calls, and various opportunities to "serve" the huckster who is posing as the "guru" at the head of the organization.

So we have abdicated responsible training in the area of religion and left it to be filled with the irrelevant, the loonies, or to "science" (which makes a poor cult, even though some of its practitioners treat it as such). Some of our most distinguished contemporary institutions have their foundations in the shortcomings of mismatched minds. The mismatches cost us billions in medical care, billions in delayed emotional relief and continued dysfunction, billions in contributions to TV hucksters, evangelists distinguished mainly by their weird sex lives, and more in lost lives in this world and probably the next world, if there is one.

7

MANAGING A WORLD LONG GONE

The Old Mind in Politics,
the Environment, and War

O NE AMERICAN PRESIDENT was not reelected primarily because he "allowed" 54 hostages to be held in
Iran for 14 months, even though all were eventually freed relatively
unharmed. The next president was responsible for the deaths of 241
marines in Lebanon. One of his generals explained it: "We can't be
prepared to fight someone who will give up his life for a cause."

That president was reelected by an enormous majority, on the basis of his charming personality.

Politicians are the ultimate creatures of the moment. Their post confronts them with a constant stream of problems that must be solved *now,* without regard for next year. At most their time horizons reach until the next election, which in most Western democracies means a maximum of six years in the future and which for the majority of politicians in the United States is only two or four years down the line.

As a result politicians have little incentive to tackle or even to identify and analyze long-term trends. Even if elected officials could perceive those trends, they are unlikely to be able to influence such "slow events" before the next election. And since their constituencies see only short-term caricatures, politicos garner little credit if they try to do something for posterity. Better to wage a quick, clean "war" on something that has already registered on our old minds, such as poverty or drug abuse, make bellicose speeches about the death penalty, or simply serve the day-to-day needs of the most powerful voters. That requires much less perspicacity than trying to solve long-term social problems and is much more likely to lead to reelection. And reelection is what it's all about; after all, being an attorney or a successful real estate developer offers nowhere near the perks and prestige of being a congressman, governor, or even a state legislator.

The perceptual horizon of politicians tends to be confined in space as well as in time. The nearby wins out, and so to the degree that other peoples and nations enter the thinking of most national leaders, they enter as stereotypes. Foreigners are enemies or allies, customers or competitors. Officials still weigh the effects of their actions on *national* security in a world in which *global* security is at risk. Even when events highlight that global risk, politicians lead the public in taking a provincial and short-term view of the situation.

The focus on the immediate leaves the long-term perils untended. As the human population has increased, so has the vulnerability of peoples living in marginal areas to starvation, flood, and other natural disasters. In the last two decades, for example, the media carried stories about massive flood disasters in Bangladesh. Some 106 million people are crammed into Bangladesh's 56,000 square miles, giving a population density of 1,900 people per square mile. That density is more than twenty-eight times that of the United States, and there are some ten times as many Bangladeshis per acre of land in cultivation as there are Americans. Because of the severe shortage of agricultural land, Bangladeshis have moved in large numbers onto *chars,* silt bars in the Brahmaputra-Ganges delta. The fertile *chars* have risen from the waters of the delta, formed from soil eroded from the deforested slopes of the Himalayas.

Existence on the *chars* is precarious; cyclone-driven flood waters periodically wash over them. Hundreds of thousands of people in Bangladesh were killed in 1970, and tens of thousands more in the same areas in 1984. But there is little recognition by politicians in Bangladesh, let alone in rich nations, of overpopulation as the root source of the problem. Although the world annually adds a record number of people to its population, the demographic situation evolves too slowly for the old minds to register the changes. Progressive politicians, especially in poor nations, have come to recognize population growth as a serious problem and have periodically spoken out on it. But even those relatively new-minded leaders do not regularly proclaim overpopulation to be a threat to civilization.

The tendency to focus on immediate, local events made rich nations partially responsible for, and lax in responding to, the ongoing famine in Africa's Sahel, the region just south of the Sahara. In the Sahel tragedy, the growing overpopulation of both people and their domestic animals combined with the disappearance of monsoon rains (which was not an unprecedented occurrence) to produce severe overgrazing. Loss of plant cover worsened the drought, and people and animals starved in large numbers. The ways of life of some nomadic groups, such as the Tuaregs, the famous "blue men" of the desert, probably were destroyed forever. With desertification heightening the climatic effects, the drought spread to much of the rest of Africa in the early 1980s.

Shortsighted development policies had helped to create the disaster. In the Sahel, funds from developed countries had been used to drill wells. The water they supplied permitted herds to be increased to beyond the long-term "carrying capacity" (ability to support animals) of the range and assured that overgrazing would follow. Furthermore, in giving aid to countries in sub-Saharan Africa (as in many poor nations), donors had failed to give proper attention to agricultural development. Farmers were already in bad shape because food prices in cities had been kept artificially low. Coups tend to start in cities, and politicians don't like having their heads cut off. Keeping city-dwellers satisfied, therefore, tends to be high on the agenda of politicians in the Third World. Development-program administrators did little to change this situation, and the resultant weakening of the farm sector of the economy resulted in grave food shortages when drought arrived, since farmers in less-stricken areas were in a poor position to aid starving nomads.

Development policies in the Sahel destroyed a fragile ecosystem that for centuries had supported nomadic grazing and lowered the long-term carrying capacity of an entire region. The short-term interests of politicians in Sahelian nations were well served, however. The surviving Tuaregs and other wandering tribes were forced to settle down near agricultural villages, where some food was available. The nomads, previously difficult to control and tax, thus finally came under the thumb of central governments.

The immediate reaction to the African famines of most governments, private agencies, and concerned individuals in rich countries was to send food. The old mind reacted to a "sudden" crisis (which it had created) and responded with the "obvious" solution—massive shipments of food for the starving victims. In the new world, however, the obvious solution can be a recipe for disaster. By itself the humanitarian response was likely only to increase suffering in the medium and long term. The arrival of free food would only further undermine the already weak agricultural sectors of national economies. In poor countries there is too little demand for food—

that is, too little money to buy food. The arrival of free food only serves to dampen demand, driving food prices even lower and further reducing the incentive for farmers to produce.

However, there was some new-mind thinking, and some people were able to see that other steps were required if short-term aid was not to lead to further disaster. A number of economists pointed out that food aid alone was unlikely to provide a permanent solution to the problem. One often heard the saying that if you gave a man a fish, you would feed him for a day, but if you taught him to fish, you would feed him for the rest of his life.

But as often occurs, the attempts in the mid-1970s to stimulate sound agricultural development in sub-Saharan Africa were too little, too late, and showed a characteristically old-mind lack of foresight. Trucks were sent to nations with utterly inadequate farm-to-market roads. No provisions were made for mechanics to maintain the trucks or for building roads. Public and political attention in the developed world only focused on the problem intermittently, when the mass media found themselves short of programming material. Television networks periodically rediscovered hunger in Africa as "news," even though the famines have been more or less continuous.

Most revealing of all, not one powerful leader seemed to associate the dramatic and immediate plight of Africa with the slowly increasing population of that continent (and the rest of the earth). Neither Ronald Reagan nor Margaret Thatcher nor Chou En-Lai nor Pope Paul decried the growing dependence of humanity on spending its inheritance of "capital." No political leader proclaimed that humanity was living far beyond its income. Indeed, the African famine highlights the tendency of our species—and especially its political leaders—to focus on spur-of-the-moment action alone. As usual, there were pathetically few careful analyses or follow-up measures to alter long-range trends. The caricatures that afflict political *Homo sapiens* were exemplified by the Pope's traveling to famine-stricken Africa, where population growth rates were at record-high rates, urging people to have large families!

But at least the West had humanitarian instincts. There were

"Band-Aid" (appropriately named) rock concerts to raise millions of dollars for relief funds, and governmental donations of food and transport. Some politics were played, as when the United States focused on the plight of Ethiopians, who were subject to a bungling and cruel Marxist government, while ignoring similar suffering that occurred in nations with bungling and cruel capitalist governments.

The Soviets, however, showed an astounding indifference to the plight of African peoples. They supplied arms to the Ethiopian government, which was engaged in a bloody attempt to suppress Eritrean rebels, and extracted payment from that starvation-racked nation in the form of shipments of wheat. Both East and West sought (and still seek) short-term (old-mind) stability and advantage in sub-Saharan Africa, rather than sustainable societies that would increase everyone's long-term security.

Our region, the San Francisco Bay Area, is not threatened with starvation like the Sahel, but it *is* paying the costs of overpopulation. If you are a San Franciscan, the impact of population growth is most dramatically felt through brute increases in local numbers. The rush hour, which once was just a short time around 5:00 P.M., now begins at 3:20 P.M. and ends at 6:45 P.M.

Environmental problems related to overpopulation also plague the Bay Area. Mountains are obscured by smog whenever there is an atmospheric inversion. People notice how clean the air is just after a rainstorm, but it was clean every day before the rise of air pollution. Orchards and fields of wildflowers have been replaced with crowded suburbs and freeways. Sewage spills make swimming or fishing in the bay and local rivers dangerous. The papers are full of stories of new groundwater pollution originating in the computer-related industries of Silicon Valley.

As in Bangladesh, more and more people are, often unwittingly, forced to live in hazardous situations. Homes proliferate on unstable landfills in San Francisco Bay. Others are built on sawtooth projections of coastline cliffs, with steep gullies on either side where other chunks of cliff have previously dropped into the Pacific. When the inevitable next large earthquake occurs, many of the people living in these marginal situations are likely to perish.

Growing numbers of residents and visitors in San Francisco and its suburbs are destroying the very values that attracted people to the Bay Area. The same thing is happening in other regions that are considered desirable places to live or vacation. Cheek-by-jowl living (and sometimes the stench of untreated sewage) is overtaking not just the central California coast, but also the once-lovely, palm-lined shores of Florida and the Caribbean islands, the increasingly smoggy ski resorts of Colorado, the sewage-soaked Costa del Sol in Spain, and even the reef-fringed beaches of Bora-Bora. The last remnants of the great game herds of East Africa are threatened not just by the land hunger of rapidly expanding local populations, but also by mobs of tourists roaring around in open-topped vans.

In all these cases, the default positions of the old mind make recognition of the basic problem difficult, especially since the slide downhill is slow and undergoes temporary reversals. Resolute enforcement of emission rules temporarily reduces the load of atmospheric pollutants, a new sewage treatment plant reduces the stench, or a new freeway briefly improves traffic conditions, but then standards are relaxed or further population growth overwhelms the capacity of the corrective systems.

Since it is *people* who run the system of pollution controls and standards, and the caricatures of their old minds depend heavily on comparisons, it is hard to maintain environmental standards. We all tend to compare today with yesterday much more readily than with twenty years ago. Few residents of the Bay Area know what it was like before World War II. Tourists, lacking any basis for comparison, are largely unaware of environmental decay in resort areas.

New visitors faced with the ranks of boxlike condominiums, high rises, and proliferating hotels that now warehouse tourists along Kaanapali Beach on Hawaii's island of Maui cannot compare today's scene with that of 1970, when the beautiful beach was relatively uncrowded and not lined with ugly concrete buildings. Even residents of Maui are only marginally aware that one of the beauty spots of the planet has been destroyed—converted into Miami Beach West—because the destruction took two decades. And probably tourists in the year 2000 will still enjoy themselves in spite of even more crowding and sewage pollution. Even then, an overdeveloped Maui in the winter would still be a fine place to which to flee from Chicago, London, or Tokyo.

Of course, global population growth influences San Francisco, Maui, and Kenya in ways other than by lowering their environmental quality and by creating an ever-larger pool of people who can arrive as visitors or new residents. Overpopulation contributes to the deterioration of the international economic system. It is partly responsible for increases in the prices of food, automobiles, Rembrandt sketches, and building materials. It helps to increase the risk of both regional and world wars. But it does all of these things in ways that can only be traced by careful analysis, in ways that the mind must be trained to see.

Overpopulation causes no cracking branches, no thunderclaps, no darkening of the cave door. It leads to small annual changes in columns of numbers, hidden in reports. Curiously, the lethal threats of overpopulation are not even signaled by demographic statistics. Those statistics—birth rates, death rates, growth rates, population-age compositions, life expectancies, and the like—were all very well known to demographers a generation ago. The numbers were there, but to the old mind they signified little. Sure, the population was growing, and fast, but so what?

Even environmental scientists had to learn how to combine population statistics with other information on resource depletion and environmental deterioration. They had to find answers to such questions as, How much further down do we have to drill on average to strike oil today than in 1950? How fast is the Ogallala aquifer being drained? What proportion of Europe's forests are dying from acid precipitation or climate change? How much fertilizer is needed to double crop yields now, as opposed to three decades ago? And how soon will additions of carbon dioxide to the atmosphere raise the global temperature by 2 degrees Celsius? Looking at data on many such issues at once, a few environmental scientists, starting in the 1950s, began to see in the numbers the equivalent of a bear lumbering into the cave. It is a learning process that has barely begun for most scholars with the training required to understand the state of the planet.

The American political system is, as we have indicated, beautifully designed to focus the attention and activities of politicians on the short term. Legislation promoting population control in the United States is very badly needed, but it is highly unlikely that such a controversial topic will even be seriously discussed by the Congress or advocated by the President. If a move were made toward limiting and then lowering the population size of the United States, at least several decades and perhaps a century or more would pass before the program's effects could be felt. By then, the wise politicians who initiated population control would not only be retired from office, they would most likely be dead. Why take a stand on a highly controversial issue when the voters most likely to benefit from your position are not yet even born?

The shrunken time horizons of politicians are evident today in how they handle a wide range of issues. In the 1980s a small, temporary reversal in the rise of fuel prices (partly a result of earlier success in establishing conservation and alternative energy programs) permitted the Reagan administration to relax fuel-economy standards on American automobiles—just at a time when they should have been tightened. Indeed, Chrysler had demonstrated the feasibility of producing fuel-efficient vehicles that met the standards, but Ford and General Motors claimed they were too stringent. Such a popular president as Ronald Reagan might have persuaded insecure American males that their machismo, love lives, and economic image would be enhanced by driving *small* cars as efficient as their computers rather than clunky Detroit gas guzzlers. But the immediate bottom line for powerful business interests took precedence over the long-term interests of the nation—hardly surprising in a "now" society.

Similarly the extremely serious long-term threats of continued acid precipitation, the accumulation of CO_2 and other greenhouse gases in the atmosphere, and the accelerating destruction of the ozone layer by chlorofluorocarbons (CFCs) cannot be easily dealt with by a political system designed, like the old mind, to blot out long-term trends. These trends threaten not only the United States but much or all of the planet with immense disruption. Nonetheless, the call from most politicians, who now at least realize that there might be a problem, is for "more research," not action. We must wait for "proof," they say—which is roughly like saying you won't worry about danger in the game of Russian roulette you're playing until you hear a "bang" in your ear.

The situation in other developed countries is similarly grim. Great Britain is busily spending her North Sea oil revenues to support a growing population of untrained, unemployed young people who have little hope for a productive future. Gradually Britain is slipping into a situation where her main exports are antiques and soccer rioters.

Instead of trying to rebuild its decaying nation into a viable entity and make it a center of intelligent moral leadership, the Thatcher government is squandering its limited resources on two new nuclear submarines to carry Trident II D5 missiles. These contraptions, which have a "counterforce" capability, will simply push the Soviet Union into a more hair-trigger military posture and *reduce* the security of Great Britain and the rest of the world. The rest of Western Europe is much the same, as growth-manic economic systems lose momentum and environmental problems escalate. Astounding as it may seem, politicians elsewhere are often worse than those in the United States at dealing with gradually changing environments.

Japan can serve as an early warning system for other overdeveloped countries. That nation is so short of indigenous resources and so far advanced in its abuse of the environment that it may be the first rich country to go down the drain. Japan is utterly dependent on the world trade system remaining functional and on maintaining her competitiveness within that system. And the nation has already suffered many deaths and much illness from environmental disasters, such as Minimata disease and Itai-Itai (mercury and cadmium poisoning, respectively). Japan's vulnerability is greatly increased because her government and industry are so tightly intertwined that there is essentially no chance of detecting the long-term trends that are leading that nation to disaster. Ironically, that same intertwining has contributed greatly to Japan's temporary economic success.

In most capitalist nations "planning" is selective and caricatured. It consists of projecting future economic activities based on past performance while failing to perceive the gradual deterioration of the resource-environment "capital" that makes those activities possible. Politicians generally share with economists the view that the world will always operate by the rules that applied when they were young, although the politicians generally have a more realistic view of political interactions than economists have of the factors controlling the economic system. Unhappily, though, the politicians usually accept the judgment of the economists—a point noted long ago by John Maynard Keynes, who said, "Practical men, who believe themselves to be quite exempt from any intellectual influences, are usually slaves of some defunct economist."

In the Soviet Union things have been much worse. There politicians are wedded to an inefficient economic system whose main purported advantage is an ability to generate relative economic equity. But instead in the hands of Soviet politicians it has created a society dominated by a single class. Politicians in the Soviet Union, even more than their counterparts in the United States, are utterly committed to their own perpetuation in office. They can be removed at any moment by the machinations of their colleagues; they cannot enjoy even the two-four-six-year horizons of their counterparts in the United States. Whatever ability Soviet politicians have had to perceive gradual change has tended to be concentrated on forecasting changes in the political climate. Furthermore, the U.S.S.R., thanks largely to Stalinist purges, is largely devoid of ecologists and evolutionists, the scientists most likely to detect and call to public attention the environmental transformations that threaten all of humanity. So those who are successful within the Soviet political system are very unlikely candidates for either developing new minds or being willing to retrain their perceptual systems. It is therefore all the more cheering to see that such a system can produce a seemingly new-minded leader such as Mikhail Gorbachev. It remains to be seen, however, whether he can persuade a significant fraction of his countrymen to become new-minded too.

Perhaps the best place to see the old mind at work in politics is in the arena of foreign affairs—in the attempts of national leaders to create a stable, secure international situation. Seeking short-term international stability is a tradition that probably traces to the earliest city-states. Security has classically been sought by what Prussian general and military historian Karl von Clausewitz called "nothing more than the continuation of politics by other means." Resorting to war, conquering the enemies of the moment, or being ready to fight was probably the only sensible approach to keeping the state safe in days of yore. Military power and proper alliances were what stood between you and being raped and pillaged. For centuries cities, nations, and entire peoples appeared and disappeared with no apparent effect on the system as a whole. Even at the time of the Congress of Vienna, which in 1815 restructured Europe after Napoleon's final defeat, security could legitimately be seen as residing primarily in a balance of power. It would continue to work that way for more than a century, but the old world of international politics was already on its way out.

Napoleon's invention of the citizen army was one of the harbingers of that change. War, which in the past had often affected entire populations of nations (sometimes killing millions of civilians through plague, famine, or slaughter), now started to become the *business* of entire populations. Instead of small professional armies pitted against one another in a conflict governed by carefully prescribed rules, the world moved toward no-holds-barred, population-against-population, total war. The accelerating Industrial Revolution made this possible.

The supplies, transport, and communications necessary to maintain and maneuver large forces in the field became increasingly available after 1800. In the American Civil War, rifles, railroads, and telegraph lines helped create a conflict in which a quarter of all those who entered the armed forces lost their lives. While a smoothbore musket ball could kill regularly at two hundred yards, the conical minié ball spun by the spiral grooves of a Confederate or

Union muzzle loading rifle reached out accurately over four times as far.

Confederate and Union generals, however, still used massed infantry charges as a standard tactic, and as a result more Americans died in the Civil War than in both World Wars, Korea, and Vietnam combined, even though the population during those later conflicts was several times as large. The minié was the great killer, accounting for about three quarters of the deaths in the Civil War. Inventive humanity had remade the world of war with an idea as simple as spiral grooves designed to spin a conical projectile; old minds could not see the significance of the change or what it portended.

The change signaled that technology, industrial power, and manpower were becoming dominant factors in national security. The North triumphed in the Civil War primarily because of its much greater industrial capacity and larger population, even though it was out-generaled by Robert E. Lee and his lieutenants with astonishing regularity. The handwriting was on the wall in other ways—with the ironclad ships *Monitor* and *Merrimack*, the Gatling gun, repeating rifles, primitive submarines, air reconnaissance by balloon, and, near the end, with infantry digging in as they would in the future in the trenches of Verdun and the foxholes of the Kasserine Pass, Stalingrad, and Okinawa.

The horrendous slaughter of boys from both North and South in the American Civil War is just one example of the old mind at work in the military, unable to design new tactics to respond to new weapons. This inability to analyze trends that decade by decade would transform warfare would be obvious time and again for the next century. The French general staff decided after their defeat in the Franco-Prussian War in the 1870s that they had not been aggressive enough on the offense. They developed a policy of "attaque à l'outrance" (attack to the extreme) that served them ill in World War I, a conflict dominated by the defensive capabilities of the machine gun (which by then had been perfected) and modern artillery.

A generation of young Frenchmen was destroyed on the Western Front, which is still affecting France today. In that war French soldiers, pushed beyond endurance, finally mutinied when repeatedly ordered to launch hopeless attacks. Artillery and machine guns also wrote finis to horse cavalry, since, as one analyst put it, horses could not be trained to crawl from bush to bush. Nonetheless the old-minded generals of most nations retained cavalry units in their armies through the beginning of World War II. Then enormously brave Polish cavalry units were destroyed by strafing Messerschmitts of the German Luftwaffe and the artillery and automatic weapons of the Wehrmacht. And an American cavalry troop retreated on horseback before invading Japanese tanks on Luzon in the Philippines.

World War I made clear to all but the marginally mindless that the human capacity to destroy life and property had increased so much that the people had created a new world. Machine gun and cannon technology had caught up with and surpassed the death-dealing capabilities of rifles, and even generals finally realized it was no longer necessary or useful to put men literally shoulder to shoulder to defend a battle line.

One soldier every few yards could do the job, and with large populations and conscription millions of soldiers were available. The generals did not, however, predict the seemingly obvious consequence of this, and the "surprise" result in World War I was the development of continuous fronts of opposing trenches that snaked across major chunks of continents.

The human and material wealth of the warring nations was drained away in cascades of men and cannon shells that rarely changed the configuration of the front by more than a few hundred yards. The British bombardment at the third battle of Ypres in 1917 consisted of over 4 million shells, whose total weight was more than 100,000 tons. Nineteen days of cannon fire used up a year's production by 55,000 workers. In the battle of the Somme, England lost more than 400,000 soldiers. The costs of war were becoming so high that even the victors would soon be unable to afford them.

The lesson that French generals then drew from World War I was that defense would reign supreme. Although they built many of the newfangled tanks that would replace horses as the mounts for cavalrymen, unlike German panzer leaders, the French appeared to have no notion of how armored vehicles would change the shape of warfare. Instead, old-minded to the bitter end, they behaved as if the world of 1940 would be the same as that of 1914 and created a massive system of static defenses known as the Maginot Line. The Belgians took similar steps, building the "impregnable" Fort Eban Emael. The Germans made short work of both. They sent panzer columns crashing through the "impassible" Argonne Forest, out-flanking the Maginot Line and destroying much of the French army and with it the French government's will to fight, in the first blitz-krieg (lightning war). Similarly, the Germans used specially trained assault troops landed by gliders to surprise and capture the Belgian fort in a matter of hours. Indeed it was only a miscalculation on the part of Adolf Hitler and the German high command that permitted the British to retrieve a substantial portion of their expeditionary force from Dunkirk.

It is disturbing for those who loathe everything that Nazism stood for to recognize that the minority of military men who *did* have the capability of breaking out of the old mind-set were best represented in the German military of that time. The allies had some too; they just were ignored. One of the most new-minded American officers, Billy Mitchell, was effectively run out of the U.S. Army Air Corps. Mitchell's career was ended by people who could not comprehend that the role played by air power in World War I was but a shadow of the role it would play in World War II. In the 1920s Mitchell had sufficient knowledge about the strategic position in the Pacific that he even predicted that the Japanese would make war on the United States, starting with a surprise attack by carrier-based aircraft on the Pacific fleet at Pearl Harbor—and on a Sunday morning!

When the Japanese fulfilled Mitchell's predictions, they had bad luck. They slaughtered the battleships lying at anchor beside Ford Island, but the U.S. aircraft carriers were not home on that fateful December 7th morning. They also made a colossal tactical blunder by not bombing the fleet's vulnerable fuel stores. Had they done that, the war in the Pacific might have lasted considerably longer. But the end would have been the same.

The Japanese naval genius Isoroku Yamamoto was new-minded. He understood gradual trends in the world; he knew the role that industrial might would play in the coming war. During World War II, American propagandists reported that Yamamoto had bragged that he would "march to Washington and dictate the terms of peace in the White House." Actually he had told the Japanese warlords that his fleet could run riot in the Pacific for about six months, after which the industrial power of the United States would turn the tide of battle. Based on knowledge of American attitudes and capabilities, Yamamoto knew that Japan was unlikely to win the war. He was making that point when he said sarcastically that *in order to win* he would have to invade the United States, march across the continent, and dictate the terms of peace in the White House.

The military men of the superpowers act as if the same ancient patterns of conflict can still be used to achieve foreign-policy goals, even though now-opposing sides have tens of thousands of enormously destructive nuclear weapons. Too many people still seem unable to recognize that what seemed practical reasons to go to war for several thousand years no longer are. Attacking another nuclear-armed nation cannot be justified now, since, regardless of the "success" of the attack, both aggressor and recipient are certain to receive unacceptable damage. Fortunately, though, enough have recognized this fact to avoid a war between the superpowers for half a century thus far.

But understanding and reacting appropriately to these basic facts of the nuclear age have proven difficult, especially for many key decision makers. Cultural evolution has, in various ways and to a varying degree, prepared us to face humanity's unique and frightening burden: knowledge of the inevitability of our own deaths. People have invented various kinds of afterlives or taken solace in the legacies they leave behind in the genes or memories of those who come after them. But neither biological nor cultural evolution has prepared us to deal with an *end to births*—to the likelihood of the death of society itself. It is a notion we all have difficulty accepting.

Ironically, the threat of the end of births comes from one of humanity's greatest technological triumphs, the epitome of the world we made. The most unprecedented threat of all comes not from your neighborhood mugger, drunk driver, or drug dealer. Instead, it nestles in silos on the steppes of the U.S.S.R., in lush farmlands of the central United States, in the quiet French countryside, and under the deforested surface of China. It berths within the bomb bays of American, British, French, Soviet, and Israeli aircraft. It hides inside the launch tubes of missile submarines of five different nations and in the ammunition lockers of both NATO and Warsaw Pact forces.

Thermonuclear weapons and their delivery systems epitomize the enormous ingenuity and creativity of our species. They also create its worst predicament.

An Intercontinental Ballistic Missile (ICBM) may be as tall as a small office building and weigh at launch almost 100 tons. In a minute or so, it can leave its armored tubular burrow on one continent and depart the atmosphere of the planet, shedding used-up parts as it goes. An ICBM is guided by tiny precision gyroscopes that detect its every move and compare its course with one programmed into its computer memory. It can travel eight thousand miles in half an hour.

A thermonuclear warhead such as the American W56 is itself another marvel. It rides in its Mk-21 advanced ballistic reentry vehicle with up to nine other reentry vehicles in the bus of the MX missile. It contains uranium-235 or (in our example) plutonium-239, a heavy metal by-product of nuclear reactors, carefully configured chemical high explosives and a neutron actuator to start the fast chain reaction required for the fission bomb to go off.

When the chemicals blow up, the explosion compresses the plutonium-239, creating a "critical mass." That leads to conversion, through the splitting (fission) of the nuclei of plutonium atoms, of a microscopic quantity of matter into an enormous amount of energy. That energy, channelled in the right direction, leads to the fusion of the nuclei of the light elements into heavier nuclei, triggering an even greater yield of energy. And finally, fast neutrons from the fusion penetrate the U-238 and cause it to fission, releasing more energy.

To assure that all of these steps occur properly requires an extraordinary understanding of the properties of matter and energy and an extraordinary engineering skill. And the result is extraordinary, too: a heat burst as hot as the core of the sun. A modern "citybuster" can explode with the power of more than a million tons of TNT. Enough blast, heat, and radiation is produced instantly to shred, decapitate, fry, disembowel, vaporize, crush, or otherwise dispose of ten times more men, women, and children than you'll meet in your lifetime.

World War II, basically the second act of World War I, culminated, as the world knows, with the explosions of these first atomic bombs. That should have driven the lesson home. With Fat Man and Little Boy (the Hiroshima and Nagasaki bombs respectively), the nature of national security was irreversibly changed. But the pace of change of our war equipment has been too swift for our neural equipment. Secretary of State John Foster Dulles, wanted to supply atomic bombs to the French to help them out of their self-inflicted disaster at Dienbienphu in Vietnam. The United States has, to this day, never said it would not use nuclear weapons first in the event of a conventional conflict in Europe between NATO and the Warsaw Pact nations.

The old mind seems bogged down in the now-fatal caricature that security still lies in more and better weapons, either offensive or defensive. This is beautifully expressed by the United States government's recent promotion of the Strategic Defense Initiative (SDI), better known as the Star Wars program, of antiballistic missiles.

To understand the mismatch between President Reagan's dream of SDI and the reality, the dream must be put in the context of recent nuclear events. The United States deployed Pershing II medium-range ballistic missiles (MRBMs) in Europe in the early 1980s to counter in kind an old-mind move by Soviet strategists—increasing their "security" by increasing the size of their MRBM force in Europe. The Pershing II missiles can reach the vicinity of Moscow so fast that the Russians would have only about ten minutes' warning, and their warheads can be delivered with extreme accuracy. To the Russians, the Pershing IIs looked like weapons designed to play an important part in building American "first-strike" strategy. They are weapons accurate enough to destroy the bunkers in the vicinity of Moscow from which Soviet missile forces are controlled, perhaps before a Soviet retaliatory strike could even be orchestrated. Fortunately, if the INF treaty provisions are followed, all the Pershing II's will be gone by 1991.

Like Americans, the Soviets live with the fear of a surprise attack by their opponents and make worst-case plans against that possibility. Knowledgeable scientists in the United States as well as in the U.S.S.R. are aware that SDI will not be able to stop a determined first strike by Soviet ICBMs. After an American first strike, however, an antiballistic missile system defending the United States might well shoot down a significant portion of the warheads in the small, ragged return volley that battered Russian missile forces could launch. Accordingly Soviet planners, following their own caricatures, view SDI as one more piece in a pattern that indicates America is planning to attack first.

To counter this perceived first-strike threat, Russian analysts have privately expressed the fear that the Soviet Union was being pushed into a so-called launch-on-warning or launch-under-attack posture. This means the Soviets would, in essence, wire their radars directly to their computers and their computers directly to their launch buttons. Human beings would be removed from the system; if the radars and computers thought an attack had been launched, a robot system would return fire immediately before the opponent's warheads arrived. There would be no time for a person to confirm an order to shoot. This means that if the Russians go to launch-on-warning, their computers would have the power to destroy us.

This is not a cheering prospect. The Soviets lag behind the West in many areas of technology, but they are especially laggard in computer technology. Even state-of-the-art American computers have repeatedly issued false alarms, saying in essence that "the Russians are coming" when in fact they were not. That you are reading this book is only due to the intervention of human beings who could tell the blips of a flock of seagulls on a radar screen from those of incoming Soviet warheads or who could detect that the wrong tape had been mounted on a computer or that a capacitor had blown somewhere. The survival of the United States and the lives of everyone in the Northern Hemisphere may soon depend upon the performance of shoddy Russian computers. Reducing this possibility somewhat is a potential great benefit of the INF Treaty.

If the Soviets were not hooked on the same ways of old-mind thinking as the Americans, they would see that there is no need for them either to fear the SDI or to try to emulate it. They should simply declare that they will take whatever measures are necessary to counteract any SDI deployment. The Soviets have many options, all vastly simpler and cheaper than creating their own Star Wars system. But Russian generals like intricate hardware, too, and doubtless have a nagging fear that perhaps the Americans might make some kind of unimagined breakthrough. So instead of improving the lives of their people, Soviet leaders almost certainly will pour a substantial part of the wealth of their nation down an SDI rathole, if the United States continues toward deployment.

The Star Wars program represents the continuation of a mind-blindness to trends that have long made military thinking one of the clearest examples of the functioning of the old mind. The rigid, unimaginative training of those who choose military careers apparently reinforces the brain's natural tendency to focus on the immediate and the near term and, especially, to count on the environment to remain unchanged. So obvious is this effect that the comment that "generals are always preparing to fight the previous war" has become a textbook commonplace. That the military *does,* in spite of this, include a substantial number of new-minded individuals gives us great hope that minds can be changed throughout society.

Today it appears that the changes made in military technology over the past generation require completely unprecedented and difficult responses. A new-minded military leader needs *not* to find ways to fight wars with new devices and tactics but to find ways not to fight at all.

While some military leaders recognize that nuclear weapons, and the prospect of a nuclear winter, make large-scale warfare obsolete as an instrument of policy, most seem to be unable to avoid the build-more-and-better-weapons syndrome. The notion persists that some hi-tech breakthrough will give us (or them) a permanent, unbeatable edge—even though "edges" are now meaningless.

There is *no* prospect that either the United States or the Soviet Union could win a large-scale thermonuclear war in any meaningful sense or even defend itself against a determined attack by its opponent. In recent years, happily, Mikhail Gorbachev of the Soviet Union has led the way in emphasizing this, and has apparently convinced Ronald Reagan as well. Reagan's administration had previously taken the extraordinarily dangerous old-mind position that nuclear wars could be won.

A key new-minded question is, How much destructive power really matters? If we have ten thousand warheads, does it matter how many more we obtain? The answer is a clear no. The problem here is that the rising stockpile of nuclear weapons has become part of the background, like the noise of an air conditioner, and we are habituated to it. Both sides misperceive each other because of this and misunderstand the actual danger. In fact, as one case history nicely illustrates, much less force is necessary for deterrence than we might think. This case allows us to look at deterrence from a different viewpoint, with the blinders removed.

Consider, then, one expert who had firsthand experience in the meaning of deterrence. Robert S. McNamara was Secretary of Defense during the Kennedy administration, which came to power claiming a "missile gap" existed between the United States and the Russians. McNamara soon found the gap did indeed exist, but that it was to our advantage. False stories of American military inferiority, such as the "missile gap" on which John F. Kennedy rode to office and Ronald Reagan's phony "window of vulnerability," are extremely dangerous. They help fuel an increasingly unstable arms race. Every one of the Joint Chiefs of Staff has denied in congressional testimony the story told by officials of the Reagan administration that somehow the Russians are ahead of us militarily.

But suppose that we were (or are) "behind." Would that destroy deterrence? How large a nuclear force do we actually need to deter an attack? Robert McNamara was the Secretary of Defense during the Cuban missile crisis, and we can learn a great deal from his account of an actual case where deterrence worked. On a recent visit to the Soviet Union he was asked about the number of missiles necessary to achieve parity:

> I replied that parity exists when each side is deterred from initiating a strategic strike by the recognition that such an attack would be followed by a retaliatory strike that would inflict unacceptable damage on the attacker. I went on to say: "I will surprise you by stating that I believe parity existed in October 1962, at the time of the Cuban missile crisis. *The United States then had approximately five thousand strategic warheads, compared to the Soviet's three hundred.* [emphasis ours] Despite an advantage of seventeen to one in our favor, President Kennedy and I were deterred from even considering a nuclear attack on the USSR by the knowledge that, although such a strike would destroy the Soviet Union, tens of their weapons would survive to be launched against the United States. These would kill millions of Americans. No responsible political leader would expose his nation to such a catastrophe."
>
> One conclusion I draw from this story is that the "width" of the "band of parity" is very, very great. In 1962 it would have made no difference in our behavior whether the ratio had been seventeen to one, five to one, two to one in our favor—or even two to one against us. In none of these cases would either we or the Soviets have felt we could use, or threaten to use, nuclear power to achieve a political end. (From *Blundering into Disaster* by Robert S. McNamara, Pantheon, 1986)

Now the Soviet Union has some eleven thousand strategic warheads, some thirty-five times as many as actually deterred the United States in 1962. The U.S. has about twelve thousand. From this perspective, what would be the risks of cutting our numbers of warheads by fifty percent? The risks would be much less than our blinkered minds think. Indeed, if the most destabilizing weapons were disposed of, the risks of cutting both side's strategic forces by ninety percent would be negligible, and the gains in national security enormous.

McNamara, an erstwhile proponent of achieving defense by the numbers, has clearly made the transition to a new way of thinking:

> It is in the best interests of the United States to make its adversary feel more secure. Many argue precisely the opposite: it is important to keep the Soviet Union on the defensive and wary of American strength. But in the age of nuclear weapons, where one country holds the fate of another in its hands, old rules no longer apply.

While some people have learned to make the transition, the majority of political leaders, like their military counterparts, are still planning to fight the last war.

In recent years the old mind has never been so much in evidence in American politics as in the second half of the Reagan administration. In the winter of 1987, President Reagan finally got rid of Donald Regan, who managed the White House with shortsighted incomprehension. Regan did not prevent the public relations disaster at Bitburg, where the President paid homage to dead Nazi SS troops. He sent his boss, famous for his lack of grasp of details, shoddily prepared to the Reykjavík summit. There the President did not remember that the meeting was to be a discussion of general issues, not a bargaining session. The last straw for Regan, as the President's right-hand man, was his management of the Iran-Contra affair.

What was important was not that Regan was ultimately canned but that U.S. credibility in foreign affairs was virtually destroyed. What was also important was the way decision making in the White House, and the media discussions of the White House disasters, were molded by simplified memories of largely irrelevant situations long past. It is frequently proclaimed that Donald Regan's management was inferior to that of his predecessors. James Baker, Edwin Meese, and Michael Deaver were remembered in many newspaper articles in early 1987 as a group who protected and managed the President well. In their regimes, it seemed, there were no PR mistakes, issues were aired with real concern for their validity, and the President was presented with different points of view, all for the benefit of the society. So it was said.

No one seemed to remember, only two years later, that this "troika" of presidential advisers were the individuals responsible for the works of the early Reagan regime, the same crowd who spent hundreds of millions of dollars resurrecting useless antique battle-ships, wasted fortunes on the military, and sent the marines into Lebanon unprotected to be slaughtered. They also established the policies that gave the United States a $200 billion annual deficit. Reagan, the staunch advocate of responsible fiscal government, nev-ertheless managed to borrow more in his first few years than had been borrowed in the entire history of the republic.

There are two points in this situation that illuminate the nature of the mismatched mind. First, our memory is hardly accurate, and there is a bias in memory, above all, to simplify what we do remem-ber. Second, extremely critical matters easily retreat into the back-ground of our memories, to be replaced by mere, minor, transient concerns. To illuminate this, let's look at some basic research on memory.

In 1932 the Cambridge psychologist F. C. Bartlett published an important book, *Remembering,* in which he demonstrated the im-portant simplifying effects of a person's existing knowledge struc-ture on memory. The method he used in his experiments was simi-lar to the child's game "Telephone." A subject was shown an "original stimulus," either a drawing or a story, and asked to repro-duce it from memory. That person then passed on his or her repro-duction to the next person, who reproduced it, and so on. Bartlett called this method serial reproduction. The stimuli Bartlett chose were deliberately exotic, unfamiliar to local residents of England, where he did his research.

One example of such serial reproduction was a series of drawings that begin with an African drawing, *Portrait d'Homme* (portrait of a man). In these drawings, the subjects transformed figures to corre-spond with what was already in memory. According to Bartlett, unfamiliar features *"invariably suffer transformation in the direc-*

tion of the familiar." That is, people have a tendency to change "odd" or unfamiliar figures into conventional or familiar ones. In the final reproductions of the African drawing, all the original unconventional characteristics are gone. The final figure is an ordinary, even schematic representation of a face. The one clue to the exotic qualities of the original was the transformation, as it was copied by person after person of the name *Portrait d'Homme* (portrait of a man) to *L'Homme Egyptien* (Egyptian man).

Bartlett also presented an unusual story to his students, an American Indian tale called "The War of the Ghosts." Again, each subject was asked to reproduce what he or she remembered from the previous subject's version of the story. The original story is recounted below:

> One night two young men from Egulac went down to the river to hunt seals, and while they were there it became foggy and calm. Then they heard war-cries, and they thought: "Maybe this is a war-party." They escaped to the shore, and hid behind a log. Now canoes came up, and they heard the noise of the paddle, and saw one canoe coming up to them. There were five men in the canoe, and they said:
>
> "What do you think? We wish to take you along. We are going up the river to make war on the people."
>
> One of the young men said: "I have no arrows."
>
> "Arrows are in the canoe," they said.
>
> "I will not go along. I might be killed. My relatives do not know where I have gone. But you," he said, turning to the other, "may go with them."
>
> So one of the young men went, but the other returned home.
>
> And the warriors went on up the river to a town on the other side of Kalama. The people came down to the water, and they began to fight, and many were killed. But presently the young man heard one of the warriors say: "Quick, let us go home: that Indian has been hit." Now he thought: "Oh, they are ghosts." He did not feel sick, but they said he had been shot.
>
> So the canoes went back to Egulac, and the young man went ashore to his house, and made a fire. And he told everybody and said: "Behold I accompanied the ghosts, and we went to fight. Many of our fellows were killed, and many of those who attacked us were killed. They said I was hit, and I did not feel sick."

He told it all, and then he became quiet. When the sun rose he fell down. Something black came out of his mouth. His face became contorted. The people jumped up and cried.

He was dead.

Here is one of the final reproductions of the story:

Two Indians from Momapan were fishing for seals when a boat come along containing five warriors. "Come with us," they said to the Indians, "and help us to fight the warriors further on." The first Indian replied: "I have a mother at home, and she would grieve greatly if I were not to return." The other Indian said, "I have no weapons." "We have some in the boat," said the warriors. The Indian stepped into the boat.

In the course of the fight further on, the Indian was mortally wounded, and his spirit fled. "Take me to my home," he said, "at Momapan, for I am going to die." "No, you will not die," said a warrior. In spite of this, however, he died, and before he could be carried back to the boat, his spirit had left this world.

Again the effects of the English student's organization are clear: the story has been transformed into a more conventional one. The original distinctive names are gone, though Momapan is added. Bartlett says, "The story has become more coherent, as well as much shorter. No trace of any odd or supernatural element is left: we have a perfectly straightforward story of a fight and a death." Things that do not match the common schemata of an Englishman are omitted or transformed into the familiar: canoes are changed into boats, references to ghosts are omitted.

Memories are transformed to suit our attitudes, and they are transformed in a way that helps the blinkered mind get on and succeed in life. We tend not to remember how difficult our past life has been and often hold a simplified and healthy optimism about our family or work history and our past in general. These healthy illusions (85 percent of people, for instance, judge themselves as "better than average" in intelligence and life satisfaction) probably evolved to ease the pain of childhood experiences and reduce the inhibiting effects of the past on our lives. But these same caricatures when applied to current political depictions often lead to dangerous comparisons. "The good old days," whether applied to a marriage, a childhood, or James Baker and the indicted Michael Deaver, is just another artifact of how our minds work.

To return to our second point, the ease with which critical matters retreat into the background can be adaptive. Otherwise we might be preoccupied with the inexorable approach of our deaths. But this tendency can be maladaptive too. The budget deficit for 1986 alone was $180 billion, about 15 percent of the total national debt accrued since 1776. This gigantic debt merited almost no media attention, pushed off the newspapers' pages by the Iran-Contra affair and other transient concerns. In fact, there was widespread satisfaction that the deficit was "under control" and was "coming down." Again we and our politicians judge events, even matters of the greatest importance to the future of the United States, through the blinkers of the old mind. The deficit is not easily translated into the kind of dramatic "news" that is so attractive to the old mind. The mounting national debt, even without increases in the annual deficit, represents a substantial danger to the future quality of life in the United States.

The significance of the national debt is a complex technical subject that requires careful analysis, not quick-reflex responses. Its significance is somewhat in dispute, but a few statements can be made with assurance. First, in spite of the rhetoric of politicians, the analogy between private debt and the national debt is invalid. Most of the American national debt is owed to ourselves—to Americans holding government bonds (of course, the remainder of the debt is owed to foreigners, its servicing will reduce the goods and services available to Americans). Such a debt cannot be passed on to our children in the way that a son must assume the mortgage on the house he inherited from his father. There is no way of borrowing from the future; we can only decide to pass less wealth on to posterity.

Deficit financing, even year after year, can be healthy in a modern economy. But too large a national debt, even if owed entirely to United States citizens, can be very harmful. That is especially so when that debt is accumulated to pay for nonproductive (indeed, useless or dangerous) items such as ICBMs and aircraft carriers. Accumulating too much internal debt amounts to using up society's capital today and limiting investment in the future. Many economists tend to be relatively relaxed about the size of the deficit because they expect future growth of the economy to reduce the significance of the national debt (since it will become an ever-shrinking fraction of the GNP). But the rate of growth of the debt during the 1980s has been unprecedented, and the prospects, and desirability, of much more growth in the American economy are questionable. The recent increase in the national debt represents a waste of scarce resources and has the potential for fueling runaway inflation and creating serious problems in the distribution of wealth within the nation.

Because the growth *rate* of the deficit is down, however, and because it represents a relatively constant "problem" compared with juicy tales of the sex life of presidential candidates and hypocritical TV preachers and reports of incompetence and astrologers in the Reagan White House, we don't notice it so much. No one is certain what penalties society will eventually pay for largely ignoring this issue, but new-minded politicians would be paying much closer attention to the mounting debt.

Perhaps the most serious political problem faced by society is the attraction of the old mind of the public to old-minded leaders. It is a problem that plagues all nations, and both the Democratic and Republican leaders in the United States. We'll draw many of our examples from the Reagan administration. That administration, even more than most, was based on caricatures of the world, literally on one-liners on Reagan's famous index cards. But an examination of the Administration's Democratic opposition would turn up precious little in the way of new-mindedness. The greatest errors of the early Reagan administration helped to make it popular. The Administration encouraged the public's chauvinism when a new-minded administration would have worked to reduce it. The Administration concentrated on finding short-term "solutions" to economic problems, with little or no thought about their long-term consequences. The Reaganites encouraged overexploitation of resources for short-term profit—a policy prominently advocated by James Watt as Secretary of the Interior and continued under Watt's successor, the quieter and more effective Donald Hodel.

On the environmental front the Administration's policy focused entirely on the near term. That it did not take effective action on obvious threats, such as toxic wastes and acid precipitation, was symptomatic. The Administration's extreme caricature of the world and global long-term environmental problems and callous attitude toward the poor people of the world was highlighted by Hodel's statement that we should permit ozone depletion to continue and counter the resultant influx of dangerous ultraviolet radiation with suntan lotion and sunglasses! The Administration made a determined and largely successful effort to destroy the laboriously erected federal apparatus designed to provide some protection to the environment, and to discontinue U.S. aid to family-planning programs overseas.

Reagan's caricatured view of the world, even on issues of national defense, has been highlighted by such things as his statement that submarine-launched ballistic missiles could be "recalled" once launched and his childlike faith that the American people could be protected from nuclear destruction with a Star Wars antimissile defense.

Most frightening of all was the President's repeated confusion of events in war movies with events in real life. When you or I get our adrenaline up while watching movies or TV, it stresses us physiologically. Reagan's habit of mistaking John Wayne epics for the real world stressed the entire world. The old mind is easily fooled by the immediacy of movies. It never quite acquires the ability to distinguish tomato juice on celluloid from real blood. The old-minded public saw a caricature; a John Wayne-like Reagan "standing tall," and most did not register the dangers inherent in leaders who are inclined to confuse myth with reality.

The lack of careful analysis and failure to consider long-term consequences of the Reagan administration was finally brought home to much of the general public by the Iran-Contra disaster. It was too blatant a blunder and too-clearly-immediate "news" to be overlooked. It registered even on old minds. The public finally saw the Chief Executive of the United States living in a world of Hollywood fantasies, describing out-of-control Colonel Oliver North as a "national hero" for trading arms to Iran for hostages himself at a time when Reagan had been lecturing America's allies about never giving in to terrorists. It was indicative of the old mind at work that most of the early investigation of the Iran arms deal was focused on the relatively minor issue of the illicit diversion of funds to the Contras. That was a problem of short-term thinking, whereas the damage to the credibility of the United States of trading arms for hostages while lying to the world was virtually certain to make it difficult for the nation to run its foreign policy over the long term. How was it possible to send foreign-service professionals all around the world demanding that our allies not sell arms to Iran while at the same time we were doing so? Did anyone who knew about the sales realize that short-term solutions—in this case, the emphasis given to hostages in danger from terrorists—could wreck a long-term consistent policy? Did anyone realize that the whole mess was certain to become public sooner or later? If anyone did, he or she lacked the sense or courage to blow the whistle.

A similar result came from the domestic policies; the long-term security of Americans was undermined by a waste of resources and environmental degradation, while the people who financed Reagan reaped immediate, rich benefits. In foreign as in domestic policy, the bottom line was the bottom line—short-term gain for a few was substituted for the long-term good of the American people, most of whom got only their share of a record deficit, accumulating toxic wastes, and at least until the INF Treaty, an enhanced probability of being vaporized.

And until the Iran arms disaster, the American people loved it! While many or most disagreed with Reagan's policies, almost everyone admired Ronald Reagan himself. He blended in with the rest of the TV programs, so our old minds painted him harmless because he was a familiar presence in our living rooms, just like Mr. Rogers or the friendly man next door. Reagan did not disturb the brain's ancient small-group focus; he became part of the family, just as do familiar characters on soap operas. His appearances were often models of presence, timing, and humor. Even his quip after the Hinckley assassination attempt was a model of good public relations. He told his wife, "Honey, I forgot to duck." John Wayne couldn't have done it better. Ronald Reagan never left the cinema, never left a milieu that further simplified the world already caricatured by our nervous systems.

Electoral results are getting to be more and more like the television ratings; in every election, our judgments of political figures seem to be moving closer to the most simplistic old-mind caricatures. Quips, sincerity, affability—all good qualities in a neighbor—dominate the impressions made via television. The noted analyst and friend of Reagan, George Burns, recently said about making a good impression, "What counts is sincerity and honesty. If you can fake these, you've got it made." Looks count, too. The bald or the fat need not apply, whatever the value of their ideas. No more Churchills.

While the need for structural reforms in the government was never clearer than during the Reagan administration, the signs of a mismatch between old-mind politicians and the needs of the nation have been building since the presidency of Dwight Eisenhower. John Kennedy attempted to govern by style rather than substance and blundered with his amateur advisers first into the Bay of Pigs and then into the morass of Vietnam. Memories of him have been somewhat distorted by his tragic death and the rhetoric written for him by Ted Sorenson. Like most politicians today, Kennedy saw the nuclear world through old-mind glasses. Lyndon Johnson, compassionate as he was about the poor, completed the plunge into the Vietnam swamp and pursued bankrupt policies into bankruptcy.

Richard Nixon was better informed than most, did us an enormous favor by opening China, but was morally deeply flawed and seemed to have visions of becoming emperor. Gerald Ford was honest but with little vision, and at least did not turn back the clock dramatically in the position that was thrust upon him by the Nixon disaster. Jimmy Carter had brains, ideas, and a sincere moral outlook, but was unfamiliar with how the federal government functioned, with who worked where and what they did, and with who could influence what. And he didn't know how to use television to manipulate old minds. Because he was so much more capable and still failed, Carter, even more than Ronald Reagan, highlighted the need for structural changes that would preserve *experience* in the executive branch so that vital long-term issues could be dealt with coherently.

How might we close what seems to be an ever-expanding gap between the competence needed by the Chief Executive of the United States and the competence of the people who can actually reach that exalted position? With proper education more people would recognize the role of the old mind's need for charismatic tribal figureheads. They would realize that, with the role television plays in American culture, there will be a continuing tendency to elect charming people with a sense of timing and public presence, even if they are sometimes nitwits. The public would understand the price of confusing the desire for such a comforting leader with the notion that such a person necessarily can master the problems of modern governance. Then a solution could be sought.

The obvious one is that America should have a monarchy, or something close to it. The United States could emulate those nations that have adaptively solved this problem (perhaps by historical accident) by separating the figurehead and functional aspects of government. In Great Britain there is a royal family upon which the population can lavish its emotions. Even in the United States everyone follows Lady Di's pregnancy, low-cut dresses, weight problems, and her relationship with her husband. It was front-page news in San Francisco when she fainted on tour in Australia. The adoration of those representing the country as figureheads allows for more real competence among those who actually run the government. Elections can be based more on party platforms, and the party that wins can select a Chief Executive to run the government.

In Britain the Prime Minister plays that role; the Prime Minister may or may not be charismatic, but the monarch is the center of national pride and the object of hero(ine) worship. The British system does not preclude the possibility that the Prime Minister could be an incompetent, as Neville Chamberlain, among others, convincingly demonstrated—or that the monarch cannot be brilliant. But at least when the time comes to find other leadership, there is no need to go against old-mind dedication to a charming figurehead. The tribal and administrative functions are not deeply intertwined in Britain and many other countries, as they are in the United States. We need a tall, optimistic, well-spoken man such as Ronald Reagan or a charming woman such as Corazon Aquino, as head of state because he or she would fill a certain need in us. But does charisma have much to do with ability to deal with the complex problems of modern society? We think not. America needs a king (or queen).

While this may not be the most serious problem we face, nor the most serious solution, there has been a steady deterioration of the ability of governments to cope with a world that is changing ever more rapidly, and that failure has probably been most publicized (if not necessarily most extreme) in the executive branch of the U.S. government. Neither the educational nor the political systems have mechanisms for training people with old minds to perceive and react appropriately to long-term change.

Nowhere is this clearer or more threatening than in the way politicians seem incapable of placing the confrontation between the United States and the U.S.S.R. into either a sensible historical perspective or the perspective of a resource-short world undergoing potentially catastrophic environmental deterioration. Distant regional conflicts did not carry the seeds of collapse of all of civilization until recently, and in the past ignoring faraway wars was of little consequence. But in the new world it matters; we can no longer afford xenophobia and chauvinism. The issue far transcends the rights and wrongs of Korea, Poland, Vietnam, Afghanistan, and Nicaragua. Most politicians cannot perceive that the stakes have drastically changed and the rules of the game also must be changed if civilization is to survive the accumulation of nuclear and thermonuclear weapons (to say nothing of environmental deterioration and growing vulnerability to epidemic diseases). Old-minded leaders still see security in terms of superpower balances and often act as if nuclear annihilation is a lesser risk than the risks associated with the other side gaining possible advantage.

The inability of cold warriors on both sides to recognize the insanity of their policies can be seen in a simple "thought experiment." Suppose the Romans and the Barbarians in the fifth century jointly had ten thousand megatons of nuclear explosives. The Romans faced a far more serious threat from the Barbarians back then than Americans do from the Russians today—by comparison with the tribesmen invading the Roman Empire, the minions of the "Evil Empire" are our kind of folks. As the walls of Rome were being breached, the advisers of the emperors of that time would doubtless have counseled to "nuke the bastards off the earth," and there would be no United States or U.S.S.R. to confront each other today.

As we have repeatedly seen, the old-mind assumption, built in by biological and cultural evolution, is that the way the international political system works is basically stable and unchanging. The opponent's military strength, the old mind tells us, is the key measure of threat to national survival, just as it was in the days of the Caesars. Before the nuclear revolution, that attitude threatened only lives and dynasties, not the life-support capability of the earth itself.

Unhappily the ability to greatly reduce the earth's carrying capacity for humanity will remain, even if we manage to avoid a large-scale nuclear war. If civilization doesn't end with a bang, it can still end with a whimper. That humanity is on a slow-motion march to catastrophe is indicated by the current extinction crisis. Earth is ever more rapidly losing its biological riches—its stock of species and distinct populations of plants and animals. We are now entering an episode of extinctions that promises to be even more severe than the one in which the dinosaurs disappeared.

It is being caused primarily by a gradual but inexorable destruction of habitat by human activities and by our escalating appropriation of the basic food supply of all animals—the green plants that grow by capturing the sun's energy in the process of photosynthesis. Roughly 10 to 30 million species of land animals exist on earth today. One of those species, humanity, now coopts almost 40 percent of the energy available for all—and it is "planning" to double its numbers in the next century.

Everyone should be vitally concerned about the impending loss of biological diversity, because other organisms are working parts of ecosystems, and ecosystems provide society with indispensable services—services that support our economic system. If the extinction process goes too far, civilization itself will be threatened.

It is not just that the loss of organic diversity is gradual, it is also that people have lost contact with that diversity. Cultural and biological evolution once made it necessary for all individuals to be highly knowledgeable about the natural world, with which they were in constant and intimate contact. But later, cultural evolution deleted much of that knowledge in most of the human population. Concern about cave bears, lions, and other beasts went when the threat of being killed became negligible.

No familiarity with the habitats and habits of plants and animals that can serve as food is necessary at the supermarket; that knowledge has been supplanted by understanding of the market layout, packaging, and the credit system. The properties of plant chemicals need not be considered in filling a doctor's prescription, though knowing what a drugstore is does count. Rare indeed is the person in a developed country who draws food, shelter, clothing, or medicine directly from other organisms.

The divorce of citizens of industrial societies from the need to interact directly with other organisms is nearly complete. Many people, perhaps responding to a half-erased genetic message as well as a portion of our culture, still maintain an interest in our fellow passengers on Spaceship Earth, but they don't connect survival of those organisms with their own. The extinction crisis is another slow-motion environmental catastrophe that is difficult for those surrounded by the easily grasped signs of humanity's technological triumphs to take seriously. It is signaled to birdwatchers by the decline of migrant songbirds in eastern North America, to fishermen trying to catch long-gone trout in acidic Adirondak lakes, and to viewers of TV nature specials, but it is hard for most people to grasp. No branch cracks; no hulking form looms at the cave door.

Responding to our environmental dilemmas is discouraged by the continued efforts of industry and government to minimize their seriousness and to avoid taking action. The industries that produce and use chlorofluorocarbons insist on "proof" that the ozone layer is being harmed before those chemicals are banned. The United States government has long argued that more research is needed before taking steps to clean up the sources of pollution that are causing acid precipitation. In both cases, the message basically is "don't interfere in today's economy just possibly to reap some future benefit." Old minds do not believe one should pay an economic cost today just to lessen the chance of a total collapse of the world's economy tomorrow.

Nowhere is this more clearly seen than in the almost universal denial of the environmental implications of economic growthmanship. It is crystal clear that if civilization is to persist, the physical scale of human activities *must be diminished* in some way. Yet political leaders in both capitalist and socialist nations, businessmen, economists, and media analysts all pray at the altar of perpetual economic growth without regard for its ultimate consequences. Just like frogs in a pan of water, we all sit still while our "leaders" struggle to keep turning up the heat.

Section Three

NEW WORLD NEW MIND

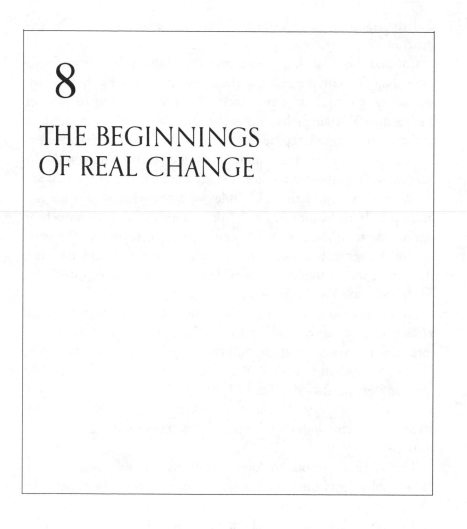

8
THE BEGINNINGS
OF REAL CHANGE

W E HAVE MADE two observations over and over again in this book. The first is that the world is an increasingly dangerous place, and many of its new dangers are not instantaneously obvious. The second is that our reactions to the modern world are often inappropriate because of the nature of our minds and the training we give them. This mismatch threatens the destruction of civilization.

Cultural evolution has always modified human default positions to fit changing environments, and cultural evolution has been keeping up rather well in many areas. But now the *overall* rate of environmental change has outpaced the ability of even cultural evolution to respond appropriately across the board. It has, for example, undermined the validity of the classic statement by Santayana that "those who do not study the mistakes of the past are condemned to repeat them." While we can obviously still learn a great deal from history, it can be dangerous to focus too much of our attention on the past. Increasingly we are getting into the position of the generals who are always preparing to fight the last war. As a consequence our society may well suffer the fate of those who depended upon the Maginot Line.

For example, it is now clear that science and technology make up *at least* half of our culture, and from the point of view of making informed decisions about the future, considerably more than that. Yet in the interesting book *Cultural Literacy* by E. D. Hirsch, the summary of the shared culture of "literate" Americans shows only about one quarter or less of that culture to be concerned with science and technology—and much of that in areas irrelevant to our future.

The average person no longer feels comfortably fitted into a rather stable environment. Rather he or she feels inundated by change, tends to adjust in areas where the need is seen as greatest, and simply fails to perceive change in others. Joe may adapt to his wife's being an executive and being more highly paid than he is, but he "can't handle" thinking deeply about the nuclear arms race. Susan works for a local environmental group on problems caused by a toxic waste dump, but keeps going to singles' bars because she doesn't perceive AIDS to be a personal threat. Father O'Shea warns his flock repeatedly about the immorality of the nuclear arms race . . . and the immorality of artificial birth control. Congressman Smith realizes that the budget deficit can cause enormous difficulties, but thinks the problem can be cured by perpetual economic expansion.

But although the problems that humanity now faces are immense, at least they are of our own making. The mismatch of our brains with our environments has been produced by millennia of effort, by the skill, ingenuity, and drive of our species—by the very minds that are now out of step with the world they live in.

There are already signs that successful steps can be taken to remedy the situation, simply by taking advantage of the flexibility and trainability of human minds. Widespread conversion to new-mindedness *might* eventually come along in the normal course of cultural evolution, but we cannot now afford to wait. Too many signs indicate that our ability to change the world is rapidly outstripping our ability to understand it. Too many trends in the arms race, in the environment, and in other areas, are harbingers of the destruction of civilization.

Before large-scale action can be taken, however, there must be public awareness, public debate, and a decision to take action as a society. We are not naive enough to think that this can take place overnight, but we do know that major transformations have already come about rapidly. Consider some examples:

· Social scientists in the 1960s believed that it would take decades of consistent government pressure to persuade Americans to change their reproductive habits and have small families. These "habits"— having as many children as one could afford—were considered a fundamental part of human nature, and the prognosis for rapid change was bleak. The shift to small families actually took about three years in the early 1970s, without any government pressure whatsoever.

· Some scientists believe we can't convert to a sustainable economic system quickly enough to prevent an ecological collapse, and yet our entire economy was transformed to a wartime basis in a matter of a year or so at the beginning of World War II and changed back to a peacetime basis in a similar period at the end of the war.

· Most nations have recognized the seriousness of the population problem, and many are trying hard to encourage their citizens to do something about it.

· Many governments and corporations have recognized that humanity faces serious problems, ranging from the depletion of oil reserves to the destruction of tropical forests and the modification of global weather, and some have taken steps to conserve resources (especially energy) and protect the environment.

· Many millions of people realize that nuclear weapons threaten everyone, including their owners, and are trying to find ways of eliminating them.

· The winds of change are blowing through such bastions of old-think as the People's Republic of China, the Soviet Union, and the Roman Catholic church.

· Innovative education programs are teaching children in many parts of the world to increase their intelligence, to cooperate, and to think in new ways.

· More people are becoming sympathetic to the other organisms that also inhabit the earth and are trying to save endangered species from extinction and to protect domestic and laboratory animals from abuse.

· Many people have begun to recast our spiritual heritage and adapt its "perennial truths" to the modern world.

· Science is providing increasing knowledge of the universe, the human environment, and the human mind—but people (including many scientists) increasingly realize that scientific information alone will not solve human problems. It is beginning to dawn on some that a major factor in our problems is how we think about the world—as the deep ecology movement and attempts both to humanize medicine and to take diplomacy into the hands of ordinary citizens all indicate. It is possible, we believe, for the rational and the spiritual to support each other rather than to conflict.

· For the first time, large numbers of people are concerned about the state of all humanity, our planet, and its other life-forms. But it will take more than just new thoughts or new ideas to make the difference. It will take a revolution in the way we bring up children and in the way we teach and what we teach.

· Biological evolution probably has given us brains that, when exposed to certain cultural environments, have default positions on the roles of the sexes and on appropriate reactions to people perceived as belonging to different groups. The interaction between biological and cultural evolution has modified those attitudes in various ways in different groups—and when the environment is appropriate, the modification may be very rapid.

In a few decades people in the United States have changed fundamental attitudes toward women, blacks, and other minorities. We no longer hear news reports of the "first woman pilot . . . executive . . . telephone lineperson," and so on. Blacks as stars of movies and TV shows, as personalities featured in advertisements, as sports heroes, astronauts, entrepreneurs, and so on, rarely inspire comment.

It is difficult to remember that, at the end of World War II, blacks still went to segregated schools in the South, were regularly lynched, played only menial roles in movies, and were largely absent from big-league sports. The notion that everyone both needs and has a right to quality unsegregated schooling and higher education has become widespread, even though full access has not yet been provided. While the default prejudices still often show through, and a great deal still remains to be done, virtually all the roles once reserved to male WASPs are now open to all.

Perhaps more telling, all but the most marginal members of society understand that it is no longer *proper* to let those prejudices show. That has been made clear by revulsion against Ku Klux Klan activities in the southern United States, capped in 1987 by a multi-million-dollar judgment against the Klan by an all-white jury appalled at the Klan's role in the murder of a black youth. It has also been underscored by the sensible statements of many Georgians about the problems of desegregating one of the last bastions of pure white supremacy in that state.

· Cultural evolution has also produced transformations in areas other than the provision of social justice. Like people all over the world, Americans since World War II have changed attitudes to fit new phenomena such as TV, jet aircraft, computers, terrorism, AIDS, and thermonuclear war. Other adjustments have been even more rapid. In a mere quarter of a century, the entire issue of environmental deterioration has entered the public consciousness and been integrated into the structure of society. The proper size for the human population and the possibility of limiting it became, in the same period, a matter of public debate.

This is not an exhaustive list, but it is enough to show that rapid change in society is already a commonplace. In addition the very process of growing up—developing from infant to child to adult—produces enormous changes in the way we think, as well as in the physiology of our nervous system. The cerebral hemispheres, for instance, become "wired up" for language (in the left) and spatial abilities (in the right) between the ages of five and eight, producing a child who is a very different animal from the one of four years old.

Most people do not realize that schooling also changes the structure of children's minds significantly. Reading, writing, and arithmetic, so commonly taught, are *not* natural acts of the mind, but are radical transformations of the way the nervous system operates. The mind's default positions are for talking and listening, but new mental routines are developed in the child's brain by their schooling, creating a new mind capable of reading and writing.

Why not reprogram other defaults to create a new mind suited to the demands of the new world? Changes in attitude on topics as diverse as racial and sexual prejudices, nuclear power, and the importance of preserving the environment all indicate that *when the time is ripe,* social change can move with astonishing rapidity.

We believe the same thing can happen with education for new-mindedness, and we think the time is ripe right now. We are writing this book to try to hurry this "ripening" in the minds of others. Nowadays there is widespread dissatisfaction with the quality of schooling in the United States and with most of what is spewed at us through our television sets. Many people are also aware that things are seriously amiss in the world and are groping for ways to set them right. But contrary to many remedies suggested recently, knowing the dates of the Civil War or having some familiarity with titles of Aristotle's books won't really help us to comprehend an unprecedented new world; the past is no longer prologue. Getting "the basics" is important, but getting a new curriculum is even more so.

There are even signs that remedies are within our grasp—not simple ones, not just a few, but remedies nonetheless. Human beings have always been the most adaptable creatures on the planet, and they should be able to chart a new course for themselves. Some of that charting is already being done. The old mind is today being challenged and changed by many scattered efforts. *Can we bring these efforts together to produce a large-scale program for a rapid "change of mind"?* We know what the problem is. The "solution" is not simple—to generate the social and political will to move a program of conscious evolution to the top of the human agenda.

Since the problems have taken centuries to develop, any effort to "solve" them is not going to succeed in a few years with a few programs or the production of a slogan or two. It will take a major worldwide cultural effort, much more intensive than the current effort to educate people about AIDS or that which has gone into changing attitudes about women and sexual equality. Many of the individual steps toward amelioration may seem quite trivial, but taken together, they will, if well directed, snowball. We would like to, but we can't present here a simple "Paul and Bob's ten-point program for the saving of the world in the new millennium." No "Bob and Paul's Project Supermind 2000," although such programs will likely be suggested by fringe elements in the next few years.

So we think there is no *simple way out* of the human dilemma, but there may well be a simple, constructive way to *proceed.* We have to create a widespread understanding that in the foreseeable future, human beings will continually be adapting to increasing threats caused by their own inventions—threats that our "nature" will make difficult for us to perceive or act upon.

What we can do is to begin to call the attention of people to their own caricatures of reality and to the new world itself. People may then be able to assess correctly the consequences of their actions in the world. Our society must resolve to cultivate a different kind of educated person, one trained generally to understand what kind of an animal we are and trained specifically to meet the challenges of an ever more rapidly changing environment.

"You can't change human nature" is a standard excuse for not taking action on a wide range of social issues. In part, as our analysis shows, the statement is true: we need tribalistic relationships, we are more responsive to current information than to long-term trends, and we focus on the superficial appearances of everything from automobiles to presidents. Part of the insight people must incorporate into their consciousness is that some of the default positions are firmly lodged in the mind and must be worked *around* rather than transformed. A need for tribal leaders probably *cannot* be refashioned completely and certainly cannot be genuinely changed within our lifetime.

Changing the built-in defaults of the mind can only come about at the snail's pace of biological evolution. Unhappily, in order to solve problems such as runaway population growth, the collapse of ecological systems, and the approach of a thermonuclear Armageddon we can't wait for the necessary tens of thousands of years until natural selection does its thing.

But we change human nature daily in schools and in a few years in society. We need, now, to consciously manage that change.

9

A CURRICULUM
ABOUT HUMANITY

I N THE LATE PART of the twentieth century, humanity
has run up against a fundamental barrier to its advancement
—itself. We are a more dangerous animal than we would like to
think, but we can also change more than we might have dreamed,
by calling on some of the very many diverse mental abilities within
ourselves. If we learn how we think, how our mind is structured,

and how to overcome the innate limitations and biases of mind, can we then learn to act on that knowledge?

Perhaps we can't change human nature completely, but we certainly can guard against that nature destroying us. Humanity's built-in default programs cannot easily be erased, but we can try to channel the output of those programs in safe and sensible directions. In this chapter we give a sampling of ways in which we think this might be accomplished. Our suggestions are not intended to be either categorical or comprehensive, but rather (we hope) a starting point for investigation and discussion. We need, most of all, to take a fresh look at how we are educating our young—especially how we are educating them before they get to college.

Knowledge in our society is specialized to a degree unknown in any previous time. Many businessmen know little beyond the "bottom line" world of p & l statements. Entertainers hire financial consultants and others to keep them from having to know anything beyond their immediate specialties. Many people's horizons are limited to family concerns, home repairs, and the pap of the latest soap opera. Things are not much better in the "intellectual" community. Many philosophers and classicists seem almost proud that they can't do calculus and never heard of the laws of thermodynamics.

Things are no better in our own ken, the world of science and technology. Indeed technical scientific training produces an extreme form of specialized caricature of the world that is designed to exclude everything irrelevant in order to produce a "clean" result.

And this is as it must be, for without continual training and narrowing of focus no one would be able to understand bubble-chamber physics, make a silicon circuit 0.1 micron (a tenth of a *millionth* of a meter) thick to form a gigabit memory chip, overfly Jupiter, look into the inner organs of the body with magnetic resonance, or unravel the complexities of ecosystems. But should the narrowing of scientific and academic specialists determine how information is transmitted to students, especially in the early years?

Because of the way knowledge has developed in separate disciplines, children come to learn about themselves and their worlds piecemeal. If they get through college, most are introduced to mathematics, chemistry, physics, biology, geography, history, sociology, anthropology, economics, psychology, art, music, literature, languages, and more. But they rarely learn to relate one area to another. They don't find out that internal body chemistry is affected profoundly by being out of work, that economics depends on ecology, or that people from different cultural backgrounds may see the same picture differently.

Knowledge is sliced up into departments, lessons, and what can fit on machine-scored multiple-choice texts. Some physicians may see only the liver, or the heart, or the brain; such specialists rarely make appointments with the whole person anymore. Indeed, a major problem in medical schools today is attracting people into family medicine or general practice; yet these are the very "nonspecialties" that are most likely to deliver health. Hacked-up knowledge makes it impossible for most people to decode their world, and yet we encourage the hacking.

The changes in the world, as well as increasing scientific understanding, have made it necessary as well as possible to take a fresh look at all aspects of education. Most importantly the divisions of scientific and intellectual inquiry, whether they remain useful or not for channeling research productivity, should *not* be the divisions for teaching and learning. A basic education should center not on memorizing Trivial Pursuit–like details of antiquated philosophies, nor a mass of cultural details, but on understanding the nature of humanity itself: our nervous system; our physiology; our evolutionary, as well as our recorded, history; our relationships with the environment; our society; our moral judgments; our possibilities.

And, most important, we have to shift our understanding of ourselves as separate individuals, each seeking our own welfare, to an understanding of how we fit into social, biological, and physical environments. It is not that increasing scientific knowledge makes learning morals obsolete, but that the new world we've created makes the nature of moral choices unprecedented.

We need to understand our nature clearly, and we need to teach it to children right at the beginning of their education. One way to introduce young children to a new view of humanity might be through a cleverly crafted series of Saturday morning cartoons. The first might present humanity, metaphorically, as one single animal. We could show that if humanity were one animal, that "creature" would now weigh more than 100,000 times its original weight. Think about an animal growing until it is now 10 million times more powerful than it was at birth. Wouldn't that creature have to behave differently at the time of its great power than in its weak infancy?

If we imagined humanity this way, we and our children could begin to think differently. Instead of pondering the local problems of our own life, we need to think about the collective life of our species. If, instead of thinking in terms of decades, centuries, or even the millennia of recorded history, we contemplated our history for many *millions* of years, then the problems we now face would take on a vastly different perspective.

Think about the life record of humanity as one "animal." Like an individual person, developing from infancy to adulthood, humanity gradually widened its world, increased its power and its control. It originally lived, like all animals, in its natural ecological niche. And then something special happened; it moved farther and farther from its home and began to create an artificial world, the world of civilizations.

It began to take control of all life, and its actions had overwhelming consequences. It created, then had to adapt to, medical wonders, the synthesis of pesticides, the existence of nuclear weapons. As humanity grew, its ability to dominate challenged its ability to adapt. And in the twentieth century its size and power, at least for a time, have overwhelmed it. If we can teach this understanding of our history and capabilities, both students and adults might begin to channel the development of humanity in new directions.

Unfortunately, though, society is faced with a chicken-or-egg problem. Until adults are really convinced of the need for change, curricula are unlikely to be altered much, and teachers will not be trained who can satisfactorily handle the new material.

You can hear the litany from the parents: Teach my kid about evolution? Never. . . . How dare you tell them that all cultures are equally valid? . . . Who the hell is this Franz Boas character anyway? Children can learn about how their minds work in college. . . . My child doesn't need to waste his time learning about farming; I want him to be a lawyer. . . . Ecology is a communist plot. . . . Concentrate on the basics. . . . Youngsters need to learn *our* values, not those of other peoples. . . . Teaching cultural relativity is what brought on our current troubles; kids don't even know what the Bill of Rights is or who was President during the Civil War.

Teachers will chime in too: I can teach Roman history, but I don't know Lucy from Neanderthal. . . . Probability? I have enough trouble explaining geometry! . . . Anthropology should wait until college.

The problems of teachers are myriad. Just a few of them include poor pay, lack of appreciation for their importance in society, poor training (thanks to mindless curricula in education schools with much too much emphasis on pedagogy and too little on content), and harassment from routine-happy administrators.

Nothing seems to get the juices of controversy flowing quite so freely as what is taught in the schools—and rightly so, since nothing should be more important to a society than the education of its children. But that is clearly not the top priority of a society that pays entertainers as much as a thousand times more than a teacher. When we say change the curriculum, therefore, it is really a code for saying change the whole society (since curricula are determined largely at the local level) and changing the entire educational system. It is a big order, our survival depends on it, and it is a task for grown-ups.

So the key to getting the curriculum changed seems to be changing the minds of adults, and the key to getting new-minded adults seems to be training them early. Clearly one can't be done without the other, which means that both must be attempted at once. We must try to generate discussion in society about the mismatch between our minds and the world they must contend with; we must also try to generate concern about the inadequacy of present child-training programs to correct the situation. We can challenge the default positions of adults in the hope that, in learning to recognize them, adults will begin to think that it would be easier if children were taught such things early—just as many adults who try to learn foreign languages recognize that it would have been easier if they had been exposed to them as children.

We'll consider some of the important changes in society as a whole in the next chapter, but here we consider some of the elements of a new school curriculum.

The potential exists for a new kind of educated evolution, which we call conscious cultural evolution, or *conscious evolution,* to supplement unconscious cultural evolution. There is nothing magical or bizarre about conscious evolution, it is a step that is already being taken by some. But we need to teach children about what is "natural" in our evolution and what now needs to be changed.

When a Neolithic man taught his son to make stone tools, a pioneer woman taught her daughter to cook, or a broker in the 1920s told a client how to get rich by investing in the stock market, they were "doing what comes naturally." The passage of nongenetic information from person to person and generation to generation went on, and goes on, without the participants in cultural evolution thinking about it.

That perceptions can be adjusted by conscious training is abundantly clear. A trained musician clearly perceives Beethoven's Third Symphony differently from someone whose exposure to classical music is casual. Biology students must be trained to see properly through a microscope. Good detectives and good scientists can be trained to build complex perceptions from scattered subtle clues. People who have never seen a black-and-white photograph have to be trained to perceive it properly (at first its dominant features are a rectangular shape with a white border surrounding an area of shades of gray). In fact only a very limited set of default perceptions are known to be completely wired into the nervous system. Remember that people who were blind at birth but had their sight restored in adulthood have to learn the difference between a black square and a black circle on a yellow sheet of paper, but not the difference between the figures and the background. The figure-ground relationship is "hard wired."

Important material for a new curriculum should be extracted from the extensive body of literature on illusions and perception. Let's take a little tour of what *could* be taught in an area that is unfamiliar to most people.

Recall that people from different cultures may not be "fooled" by the same optical tricks, because they do not share the same experiences growing up in the world. The effectiveness of illusions such as the Muller-Lyer depend to a certain extent on the kind of world one lives in. People from "carpentered" cultures are more readily "fooled" by the Muller-Lyer illusions than people who were not raised in such cultures. We are susceptible to this illusion because we come from a carpentered world. By contrast, some African tribes, such as the Zulus, live in round huts with round doors and plough their fields in circles; they do not experience the Muller-Lyer illusion as strongly as we do.

There is a wealth of material on cross-cultural perceptual differences that can be introduced to schoolchildren. For example, look at the figure of the hunter on the next page. Is the hunter closer to the baboon or to the rhinoceros? It is obvious that he is closer to the baboon. However, studying the responses to this figure of people from various cultures can make it clear that the automatic inferences of the mind are not the same everywhere. For instance, many Africans, who do not share the conventional Western "perspective" in drawing, do not make the same assumptions we do regarding the representation of three dimensions. They always answer that the rhinoceros is closer. At first this will seem odd to the students. However, they can be encouraged to look at the drawing as it is, in two dimensions on a sheet of paper. Then they may see that the rhinoceros *is* closer to the hunter.

They can be shown that Western conventions for representing three dimensions on a two-dimensional surface can lead to some interesting confusions. Students can be shown the "impossible" object sometimes called the Devil's tuning fork and told to draw it

from memory. The figure itself is obviously not impossible—after all, it's there on the page. But most of them will not be able to reproduce the drawing, because they interpret the drawing as an object that could not exist in three dimensions. They can then learn that it is their *interpretation* of the figure, not the figure itself, that *is* impossible. Our cultural rules for translating two-dimensional drawings into three-dimensional figures prevent us from seeing the figure as it is. Finally, they can then learn that Africans who do not share these conventions have little difficulty in reproducing this figure.

A new curriculum can include stories and experiments about perception that students can relate to easily and try for themselves. They can learn that their minds are subtly biased not only toward making the simplest meaningful interpretations of stimuli, but also toward immediate needs. Psychologist Jerome Bruner and colleagues conducted an experiment in which they compared the perceptual experiences of children from poor and well-to-do families. When shown a nickel, children from poor homes experienced it as larger than did the richer children. This same effect has been found in other cultures.

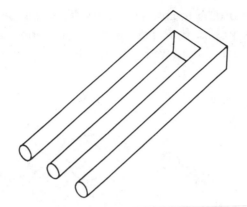

Simple experiments could demonstrate to children of almost any age the tendency of our perceptual systems to keep size, color, and brightness constant. Try some of the demonstrations yourself. For instance, hold your hand close to your face, then hold it at arm's length. Even though the image on the retina is very different in each case, the hand seems to be the same size. Size constancy is maintained. What color is your hand? Now hold your hand under a lamp, then turn the lamp out. You experience the hand as having the same color and brightness, even though the information is different. This page looks white both in sunlight and in an unlit room at twilight.

Perceptual mechanisms work so quickly and so well that we are unaware of the operations involved. Illusions are prized by psychologists not only because they are fun but also because they reveal the normal processes of perception. Many illusions are examples, in another context, of the mismatch in the mind. The converging lines in the figures on page 32 automatically signal perspective to the Western mind, so that a circle looks larger where the lines are closer together than it does where they are farther apart.

The central circle on the left of the figure on the next page looks larger than the central circle on the right, although they are the same size. They are perceived "incorrectly" because the central circle surrounded by larger circles is smaller relative to its context than the other central circle. We ordinarily perceive in a comparative way rather than according to absolute values. This is a basic principle of all thought processes, from perception to decision making.

How and when should we introduce these important attributes of

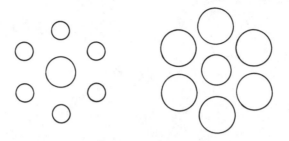

human perceptual systems into the curriculum? In grade school, children can study visual illusions ranging from the Muller-Lyer diagrams to M. C. Escher etchings, and the idea of the interaction between the brain and the sensory receptors can be taught in a simple manner. By the sixth grade the notion that people's worldviews are strongly shaped by their physical environments and cultures can be grasped by every student.

They could learn all about carpentered worlds and optical illusions. They can know that coins look larger to poor children than they do to rich children. They can see for themselves that the color of an object is perceived differently in different kinds of light and against different backgrounds. They can play games that teach them that their opinion of persons will be partly shaped by the situation in which they first met them, independent of their new acquaintances' actual attributes.

Such topics can be introduced throughout the curriculum in ways that are both interesting and fun for the students—especially through a series of experiments in perception and sensation that can demonstrate that we experience a world that is to a great degree shaped by our nervous systems. And variations of the basic examples can be repeated, year after year, so that the understanding of our mind as a very limited, specialized instrument becomes part of the basic knowledge of our culture.

Students can also be shown that we do not look directly at the outside world, but see through a thicket of blood vessels lying be-tween the retina and the eye's lens. They can learn that, because we are structured to respond to changes, we never see these vessels, since they are always there. It is also possible to show even young children that their experience of something in the external world depends on the activation of certain nerves that can be stimulated in many ways.

Anything that causes the retinal cells to fire, anything that stimu-lates the visual cortex (a blow to the head or a probing electrode), can give rise to a visual experience even though there is nothing "out there" to see. Children can be told to close their eyes and press their palms gently and repeatedly to their eyelids (contact lenses should be taken off first). They should perceive a phosphorescent green "light" triggered by the firing of retinal photoreceptors.

A classic demonstration of afterimages, too, can be very instruc-tive. Students can be told to stare at a red square against a white background for a minute. If they then take the square away and look at the background, they will see an afterimage of its comple-mentary color, green. Staring at a black square produces white. Blue produces a yellow afterimage. The color of these afterimages results from the way the ganglion cells of the retina code color informa-tion. The afterimages are not, obviously, present in the world, they are a product of our mind. What is important about this is not the colors themselves, but the fundamental understanding: there is no color in nature, no sound, but what we experience is in truth like the afterimages—a product of the nervous system picking and choosing to construct its caricature of the world.

There is a simple way to show students how they can experience the same information very differently. Fill three bowls with water, one hot, one cold, and one tepid. Have each student put one hand in the hot water and the other in the cold water, wait a few min-utes, then place both hands in the tepid bowl. They should notice that the hand that was in the hot water feels cold, while the hand that was in the cold water feels warm. Both hands *adapted* to their relative temperatures. Then, when the hands were in the tepid bowl, each hand signaled a *change*. Although both hands were in the same bowl of water, each responded differently to it. From this simple demonstration, students should be encouraged to remember that the particular message of change each hand signaled to the brain is based on a *comparison* of two events.

It is important to emphasize the basic import of the hands-in-the-water and three-way bulb experiments—to show that people respond to the *relative* differences between stimuli. The three-way lamp should be part of the equipment in every science classroom. The same lesson can be taught with nothing more than a candle. Its flame emits a fixed amount of physical energy, but it will be experienced differently depending on the surrounding circumstances. In a darkened room, it provides enormous illumination; in a bright room, it is hardly noticed. The relationship between the inner world and the external world is not a simple one. With equipment to vary the wattage of a lamp continuously, a class can be shown that if a 4-watt jump from 60 to 64 watts is required to produce a noticeable change in illumination, then one of 8 watts, from 120 to 128 watts would be needed to detect a change at double the level of illumination. If we could place a light bulb on the sun that used the entire electrical output of our planet, it would not make a change in the sun's brightness that we could perceive.

Indeed, these perceptions are such a standard part of being human that society should establish museums in all major cities where we could all go during our schooling, and in later years with our kids and grandchildren, to become aware of how we are seeing the world. It wouldn't be expensive, and our illusions are hardly likely to change. A recent exhibit at the British Museum exposed museum goers to distorted rooms, perspective and distance illusions, and auditory illusions. One simple exhibit had museum goers lift two objects of equal weight, one larger in volume than the other. The larger one *feels* lighter.

In San Francisco, in a fine old building, is the Exploratorium, which contains rooms where students can see and feel sensory distortions. And why not, as Robert Ornstein and Dick Thompson discussed in *The Amazing Brain* (and as David Macaulay magnificently illustrated), have a standard museum about the human brain in every city, one in which many of the basic characteristics of the nervous system could be experienced? It would cost much less than an MX missile, and we are sure society would get its money's worth out of it!

But what has this to do with a new mind? Why should we be making such a big deal about such simple sensory demonstrations, demonstrations that are sometimes done in schools anyway? The reason is that although they may be presented once or twice in an education, their import is most often ignored. They are vital to our knowledge of ourselves, because these characteristics of the nervous system underlie many of the judgments of the old mind. Illusions may be fun in school, but they are not fun at all when they could lead to thermonuclear destruction or the collapse of the planet's ecological systems.

Students ought to learn that they do not judge events by objective standards; that their mental system reduces its load by using relativistic processes, and that this applies to much more than perceptions of temperature and light. The consistent proportional relationship is also true of judgments of height, weight, income, and more. Comparative misjudgments, as we have seen, not only lead to errors in our purchases, our marriages, and our lives in general, but they also influence the way our government spends billions on medicine and defense.

Connections must, of course, be constantly made for students between these very basic lessons about perception and how those perceptions affect us personally. It is extremely damaging to society for people not to understand the working of their basic "instrument" for gathering information, their perceptual system. The same kinds of relativistic perceptions as are demonstrated by the three-way light bulb costs us billions. If the government announces that a new housing project for the homeless will cost a billion dollars, it seems a shocking amount. But when cost overruns add 2 percent to the cost of a $50 billion defense boondoggle, it doesn't seem all that bad. After all, they're bringing the project in at close to the estimated cost. But it's the same billion dollars.

Let's look more clearly at the nature of caricatures of thought.

Suppose you have decided that your new car will be an Italian "Provolone." You have read the automobile magazines; kept track of frequency-of-repair, recall, and resale-value statistics; and looked up the latest *Consumer Reports,* which cites statistics that the Provolone is a safe, reliable, good-handling, and adequately powered car. On these well-researched facts, you are on your way out the door to the Provolone dealership when your next-door neighbor drops by. He tells you in vivid detail about his new Provolone, saying, "It's a lemon!" You immediately change your mind about the Provolone and buy another car instead. Have you made a reasonable decision? Your decision not to buy the car is clearly not based on the real evidence. You make an immediate vivid caricature of reality and accept it in contrast to other reports with data from a large sample (the frequency-of-repair and other statistics).

This caricature of mind violates any reasonable approach to decision making. Since one default is to focus on the small world around us, we ignore the fact that large amounts of information summarized in statistics are more reliable than single personal experiences. The neighbor's story is the most recent and most available one in memory, and it is more emphatic than a published report, but this is not a good reason to give it more weight.

We often encounter problems where we must make decisions under conditions of uncertainty. We do not have full information, and there may be no single, correct answer, but the information that we have is probabilistic. How good are we at making such decisions? Not very, because the same kind of illusions that fool the visual system also fool the judgment system.

Psychologists Daniel Kahneman and Amos Tversky were among the first to study these "cognitive illusions" that demonstrate how easily we are misled. These effects can be particularly pronounced when decisions involve serious risks. One of their problems is this:

Imagine that the government is preparing for an outbreak of a rare disease that is expected to kill six hundred people. Two programs are available. If Program A is adopted, then two hundred people will be saved. If Program B is adopted, then there is a one-third chance that six hundred people will be saved, and a two-thirds chance that nobody will be saved. Which program should be adopted?

When the issue is framed this way, most people prefer Program A over Program B. They want to avoid the two-thirds risk that nobody will be saved. Now consider a similar problem involving the same disease and the same expectation that if nothing is done, six hundred people will die:

Two programs are available. If Program C is adopted, then four hundred people will die. If Program D is adopted, then there is a one-third chance that nobody will die, and a two-thirds chance that six hundred people will die.

When the issue is framed this way, most people prefer Program D over Program C, avoiding the certain consequence that four hundred people will die. This might seem reasonable to you until you realize that *Programs A and C have the same outcomes.* In both, of the six hundred people at risk, two hundred will live and four hundred will die. Programs B and D are also precisely the same; a one-third chance of six hundred people being saved is the same as a one-third chance of nobody dying. Illusions originate from just the wording of problems!

Decisions are often based on our beliefs about the relative likelihood of things happening—the price of real estate next year, the availability of jobs for engineers in the year you expect to graduate, whether the romance of the moment will last through marriage, and so on. People estimate the likelihood of such things by relying on oversimplified caricatures of reality.

Every student needs to be taught how they cut mental corners to make decisions. These "shortcuts" probably result in more efficient decision making overall, but they also lead to systematic caricatures that prevent us from being objective in certain kinds of judgments. Knowing about these common biases may help students to keep them from distorting their judgments.

They should learn that when people are asked to judge the relative frequency of different causes of death, they overestimate the frequency of well-publicized causes such as homicide, tornadoes, and cancer, and they underestimate the frequency of such less exceptional causes as diabetes, asthma, and emphysema. And they should know that this tendency causes disproportionate funds to go to the dramatic highly visible causes and relative neglect of the search for solutions to chronic problems.

In an important experiment that should be demonstrated in the curriculum, Tversky and Kahneman read to students lists of names of well-known people of both sexes. In each list the people of one sex were more famous than those of the other sex. When the subjects were asked to estimate the proportion of men and women on the lists, they overestimated the proportion of the sex with more famous people on the list. For example, if the list contained very famous women (such as Elizabeth Taylor) and only moderately well-known men (such as Alan Ladd), then subjects overestimated the proportion of women on the list. In both these cases, people's judgments were biased by *how easily they could recall specific examples.*

Students can learn how easily they caricature other people. Kahneman and Tversky told subjects to read the following passage. "This description of Tom W. was written by a psychologist when Tom was in his senior year of high school":

Tom W. is of high intelligence, although lacking in true creativity. He has a need for order and clarity, and for neat and tidy systems in which every detail finds its appropriate place. His writing is rather dull and mechanical, occasionally enlivened by somewhat corny puns and by flashes of imagination of the sci-fi type. He has a strong drive for competence. He seems to have little feel and little sympathy for other people and does not enjoy interacting with others. Self-centered, he nonetheless has a deep moral sense.

The subjects were then told that Tom W. is now a graduate student. Rank the following categories in order of the likelihood that they are Tom's area of graduate specialization:

> Business administration
> Computer science

> Engineering
> Humanities and education
> Law library science
> Medicine and physical and life sciences
> Social science and social work

Most students probably will choose computer science or engineering as Tom's most likely area of specialization, as did the subjects in the experiment, who thought that humanities and education and social science and social work were least likely. The character description probably fits the caricature of what "typical" computer science or engineering students are like. Using this kind of caricature to simplify judgments leads you to think these are likely categories for his field of study. But there are many more graduate students in humanities, education, social science, and social work than there are in computer science or engineering. Even people who know this fact, and who have very little faith in the predictive value of character sketches disregard such proportions in making their predictions. Everybody, including experts, is strongly influenced by his or her caricatures.

An imaginary coin is all that is needed to teach students that caricaturing things on the basis of their representativeness is also responsible for another common type of error. Ask them if they tossed a coin six times in a row, which of the following sequences would be more likely to occur, A or B:

> A: Head, Head, Head, Tail, Tail, Tail.
> B: Head, Tail, Tail, Head, Tail, Head.

Most will choose B because it looks more like our caricature of a random sequence than does A. They can easily be shown, however, that A and B are equally likely. With any given proportion of heads and tails, any one sequence is just as likely as any other.

This caricature is partly responsible for another common error. Suppose that you and a friend are tossing coins and you can bet on each coin toss. Assume that the coin is fair, and so over the long run will come down 50 percent heads, 50 percent tails. During one run of tosses, the coin has come down heads twenty times in a row. What's your bet on the twenty-first toss: Is it more likely to come down heads or tails? Most people feel strongly that tails are far more likely because of the "law of averages": Because the chances of heads and tails in the long run are equal, we expect a shift after a long run so that things will balance out. But the long-run averages have nothing to do with any one particular event. Just because heads came up twenty times in a row, the twenty-first toss is still an independent event, with a fifty-fifty chance of being heads or tails. This error is known as the gambler's fallacy—the belief that a forthcoming event will turn out a particular way because it's "past due."

Teachers can demonstrate another critical feature of the mind's caricatures—insensitivity to sample size. Students can be presented with a problem like this one:

A town has two hospitals, a large one and a small one. About fifty babies are born every day in the large hospital, and ten babies every day in the small hospital. As everyone knows, about 50 percent of all babies born are boys, but of course the exact percentage will fluctuate from day to day, sometimes being higher than 50 percent, sometimes lower. In one particular year both hospitals kept a record of the days on which more than 60 percent of the babies born were boys. Which hospital was more likely to record such days?

About half of the college students who were actually given this problem by Tversky and Kahneman judged that the likelihood was the same for both hospitals, while the other half split evenly between choosing the larger and the smaller hospitals. The correct judgment is that the smaller hospital is much more likely to have such deviant days. This becomes explicit in the extreme case of a really small hospital that records just one birth a day. If half the babies born in a year are boys, then on half of the days of the year this hospital would record 100 percent boys! If a hospital had two babies born a day, then (assuming the odds on each birth were exactly fifty-fifty) on one quarter of the days of a year it would record 100 percent boys (on half of the days of the year, on average, one boy and one girl would be born; on the other half, two boys or two girls).

Indeed, the problem with the comparative nature of our perceptions is most easily seen by our lack of reaction to small percentage increases, even increases that are small percentages of gigantic numbers. Citizens would be much more likely to be concerned about the "mere 2 percent overrun" in that $50 billion cost of a new weapons system, if the increase were expressed in absolute terms. An additional expenditure of $1 billion would not seem so minor. Similarly, a "mere 1.7 percent annual increase" in the world's population seems tiny compared with the actual number of people being added —over 80 million each year, roughly the equivalent of the population of the United States every three years.

At a more mundane level, students can be taught to calculate the consequences of the "just one more" syndrome. "Just one more beer can thrown out of the car window can't make that much difference." Millions of people with that attitude have turned much of the United States into a vast garbage dump. "Just one more child won't add significantly to our overpopulation problems." Think of the number of people gridlocked with you on the freeway who may have uttered those very words. "Just one more bet" has led many to bankruptcy. "Just one more drink won't do any harm before I drive home" has killed thousands. "Just one more potato chip" can be seen on almost everyone's waistline. People can't change the way their nervous systems work, but if they were more constantly aware of that system's comparative proclivities, a great deal of trouble could be saved.

The default tendency to judge rapidly on a few instances can be retrained if people simply get a chance to see the consequences of their decisions. One practical way to reprogram would be to have groups of young students make initial judgments about many problems, such as how to deal with terrorism or provide medical care to the aged. They could then test these judgments by simulating situations on computers, building models by consensus and agreeing on assumptions and the way different factors relate to one another. Running the models will then gradually teach them that initial judgments are likely to be inappropriate, largely because at first the mind automatically ignores relevant data. Field trips to nursing homes and interviews with the elderly could be used to help keep the assumptions of the medical care models realistic.

This would have two results: it would promote the development of decision aids that could be employed in crises, and it would give everyone firsthand experiences with the problems of the old mind in the new world. Luckily inexpensive computers are becoming increasingly powerful and are already capable of doing some realistic simulations. In addition, many of the simulation exercises could even be made into games with no loss of usefulness. Simulations that could serve as prototypes are already used extensively in various types of planning.

Critical thinking, based on understanding the nature of the mind and probability theory, needs to be a part of the curriculum, for as we have seen, most decisions are not made on a rational basis. So even decision making can be taught, along with critical thinking.

It is crazy to ignore these basic and important exercises in teaching elementary mathematics, because people continually make decisions about life and death on mistaken assumptions of probability. Why, instead of probability, is there so much focus on complex algebra problems, when algebra is one of the least-used kinds of mathematics in everyday life? *Everyone* makes probabilistic decisions daily; few people ever need to know how to calculate at what point two trains, traveling at different speeds and starting toward each other simultaneously from opposite ends of a hundred-mile-long track, actually crash.

In the stable "old world" of most animals, and of most of humanity until the Industrial Revolution, the nervous system had the needed probabilities hard wired. A loud noise of a certain frequency was responded to by flight. The mind calculated a high probability that the sound signaled the approach of a predator. A sound of a slightly different tone was ignored—chances are that was just Thang snoring.

But the brain is not hard wired for the new world. People have to learn to calculate the probabilities. A boy who sees fifteen thousand murders on television while growing up needs to know how to compute whether the world is really that violent a place. When he grows up, will that person purchase a gun for protection against murderers? Or will he be dissuaded from arming himself by the higher probability of being killed by the weapon rather than having it save his life? Low-probability events, such as terrorism, have enormous influence because of mistakes in probabilistic analysis, leading the President of the United States to miscalculate global strategy because of a few hostages.

Understanding the nature of the human nervous system and how it deals with probabilities is something to which we believe all people should be exposed repeatedly as they mature—making them more aware of the way they perceive the world and make decisions. The most important place, we believe, the road to new-mindedness should start is in the early grades of educational systems.

Since the world now changes more in a decade than it once did in millennia, the most important concept to get across in schools is that much of *whatever* is taught will soon probably become obsolete. That rate of change is, if anything, increasing; therefore *adapting to change must be the center of any new kind of teaching.* The idea of emphasizing "eternal truths," providing primarily a fixed curriculum of reading, writing, mathematics, history, the classics, and the like, ought to give way to a dual emphasis: more teaching of "fleeting truths" and the understanding that the *only thing constant in life is change itself.*

This is just as true of higher specialized education, in which physicians find drugs and therapies entirely different from what they learned in medical school. New research even changes what they learned about basic anatomy and physiology. Scientists must struggle constantly to keep up as their fields rapidly evolve. And while the law may not change as much as science, the society in which the law operates does.

In addition to decision making and learning how their caricatures distort decisions, students need a full background in how human culture develops and changes, and why many things they consider to be permanent, correct, or inevitable may be just part of their own particular cultural adaptation. For instance, they could read Marvin Harris's *Cows, Pigs, Wars, and Witches: The Riddles of Culture* (Random House, 1974) which proposes explanations for such diverse phenomena as the Jewish taboo against eating pork and the establishment of cargo cults among New Guinea natives.

They could read "Mother Cow," one essay in this book, in which Harris shows the value of going beyond the surface appearance of different people's beliefs and practices—avoiding quick, easy caricatures and producing a holistic understanding. Let's consider this analysis as if it were one of a series of like examples taught early in schools. He shows that the love of cows of the Hindus is "an active element in a complex, finely articulated material and cultural order."

It is often asserted that the taboo against cow slaughter is keeping 100 million "useless" animals alive. Students can learn that if they restrict themselves to this kind of superficial analysis they inhibit their ability to understand why such patterns survive within a culture. They will not realize that the patterns often survive because there are practical reasons for them to do so, reasons based on "ordinary, banal, one might say 'vulgar' conditions, needs, and activities . . . built up of guts, sex, energy, wind, rain, and other palpable and ordinary phenomena."

For the Hindu, Harris points out, "cows are the symbol of everything that is alive," and therefore "there is no greater sacrilege for a Hindu than killing a cow." People may die in the streets, but "Government agencies maintain old age homes for cows" free of charge. The cow is portrayed fat and milk-laden with the head of a beautiful woman on Hindu wall calendars. Though in actual fact "the average yield of whole milk from the typical hump-backed breed of zebu cow in India amounts to less than 500 pounds a year" as compared with the dairy cows familiar to us, which may yield 20,000 pounds of milk annually.

Investigating the agricultural life-style of the majority of the Hindu population, Harris realized the immense survival value inherent in cow worship. India is already suffering intolerable unemployment and homelessness in her cities. Therefore maintaining labor-intensive farms and avoiding mechanization makes it possible for more people to earn their living from agriculture. Indian farmers cannot afford to buy tractors. "To convert from animals and manure to tractors and petrochemicals would require the investment of incredible amounts of capital" and the result would be that farms would expand and no longer support as many individuals, creating further unemployment and homelessness.

Cows are an integral part of the country's equivalent of the petrochemical industry, producing fertilizer and providing fuel for cooking. India has little reserves of oil or coal and is already suffering from deforestation, whereas "the annual quantity of heat liberated by this dung, the Indian housewife's main cooking fuel, is the thermal equivalent of 27 million tons of kerosene, 35 million tons of coal, or 68 million tons of wood" and is ideal for their domestic routines. In addition to this, it is mixed with water to provide flooring material that keeps the dust down.

So the Indian farmer would rather starve than eat his cow, but he is *sure to starve* if he does eat it because cattle convert items of little direct human value into products of immediate use. "Cow love" works when you understand it. Similarly other cultures' seemingly bizarre behaviors can be well understood as adaptive.

Another anthropologist, Colin Turnbull, should be widely read in our schools. His *The Mountain People* (Simon and Schuster, 1972) shows a possible foretaste of the breakdown of a civilization. The story of an African tribe, Ik, that lost control of its environment and was forced out to starve, shows the perils of losing touch with nature. The people began to lose their courtesy and civility and then to steal and maim for food. Their society degenerated. Turnbull comments, in a way that presages our own analysis:

> The sorry state of society in the civilized world today, which contrasts so strongly with the still social society of the "primitive," is in large measure due to the simple fact that social change has not kept up with technological change, which has not only been almost inconceivably rapid but has been accelerating with even greater rapidity, carrying us with it in an unknown direction, leaving our old form of society behind but, the signs seem to indicate, holding in store for us the future already tasted by

the Ik. It is this mad, senseless, unthinking commitment to technological change that we call progress, despite the grim trail of disaster it is wreaking all around us, including overpopulation and pollution, either of which may be sufficient to exterminate the human race in a very short time even without the assistance of other technological benefits such as nuclear warfare. But since we have already become individualized and desocialized we say to ourselves that extermination will not come in our time, which shows about as much sense of family devotion as one might expect from the Ik, and as little sense of social responsibility.

Even supposing we can avert the disaster of nuclear holocaust or that of the almost universal famine that may be expected by the middle of the next century if population keeps expanding and pollution remains unchecked, what will be the cost, if not the same already paid by the Ik? They too were driven by the need to survive against seemingly invincible odds, and they succeeded, at the cost of their humanity. We are already beginning to pay the same price, but the difference is that we not only still have the choice (though we may not have the will or courage to make it), we also have the intellectual and technological ability to avert an Icien end. Many will say, are already saying, that it is too late—by which they mean it is too late for the change to benefit them. Any change as radical as that likely to be necessary, certainly, is not likely to bring material benefits to the present generation, though for those with a belief in the future, and an interest in it, there will be ample compensation, for only then *will* there be a future. . . . It is also difficult to say how long the choice will be open to us before we are irrevocably committed.

The Ik teach us that our much vaunted human values are not inherent in humanity at all, but are associated only with a particular form of survival called society, and that all, even society itself, are luxuries that can be dispensed with. . . . The Ik have relinquished all luxury in the name of individual survival, and the result is that they live on as a people without life, without passion, beyond humanity. We pursue those trivial, idiotic technological encumbrances and imagine *them* to be the luxuries that make life worth living, and all the time we are losing our potential for social rather than individual survival, for hating as well as loving, losing perhaps our last chance to enjoy life with all the passion that is our nature and being.

We strongly believe that students need to get the message of how fragile our modern world is and how easily it can change through unconscious cultural evolution, or conscious evolution. And they need to see this same message of fragility in ecology, anthropology, literature, psychology, history, and all around them, from all sources.

The analysis of cultural evolution, considered by Harris as the root of many significant changes, is well presented by Edward T. Hall in *The Silent Language, Beyond Culture,* and other books (Doubleday). Students have to understand the special nature of culture. At the biological level, cells band together to form tissues and organisms, and organisms form populations. Within populations most kinds of animals form recognizable patterns of association—if only that of males with females. In birds and mammals, groups are often involved in survival: in both subsistence and procreation. People form groups we call societies; these societies adapt to best deal with their subsistence and continuance. Even simple hunter-gatherer societies develop shared ideas, beliefs, and behavior that ensure that the group survives where a single family unit might not.

Thus a culture emerges. It emerges and grows in the group's selection of ways to deal with fundamental drives and needs, and in the way each group defines its own shared symbols. With the beginning of language our ancestors developed the ability to communicate far more efficiently with one another. We can talk of what might happen in the abstract and thus are warned of dangers and can plan for the future. Ideas and a concept of time develop, and once we know each other and share in each other's survival, we can ask and find answers to ontological questions such as "I wonder how it was before I came . . . and before my father came?"

Hall shows how unconscious codes are embedded in cultural traits and patterns. To many Westerners, Middle Eastern music sounds very strange. A delicacy to be savored for its taste and smell in one culture is hard to stomach in another: eating insects is common in many cultures but hardly to us. Middle Easterners would find eating a lobster as disgusting as we would find eating a cockroach. In *The Forest People* Colin Turnbull tells of eating bee grubs along with the honeycomb the Pygmies offered him—no doubt this took some getting used to! The colors selected by an African for her special wrap—gold, pink, red, and green, for example—would not be those chosen by high fashion in the West, nor would our fashionable Paris model scar her face, put a ring through her nose or lip, and consider it an enhancement of her beauty. Then again, a Pygmy woman would consider going to psychotherapy truly crazy. But all these are transient signs in any culture, our culture as well. We think that the work of Harris, Hall, and Turnbull, as well as that of many other anthropologists, if incorporated into the curriculum about humanity, would provide a genuine and fundamental insight into how society works, changes, and influences us.

All these illustrations, and those from the rest of the book, point to one central fact: in schools much more needs to be taught about the ways in which human evolutionary and social history has shaped the human mind. Special training to understand the human predilection for depending on simple caricatures instead of analyzing statistics, understanding different cultures as adaptive, or thinking probabilistically is a must.

Teachings about how perceptions are caricatured within oneself, how they are caricatured differently in other cultures, and about better ways of evaluating information and communication should be major elements in a new curriculum, but these are just a few of many changes in schooling needed to prepare people for the new world. Another important change is that much more attention should be paid to the areas of the human enterprise that are critical to the perpetuation of society. One of those is agriculture.

"Where we get our food" should be a major topic in grade school, dealt with frequently. Agriculture is mostly slighted in curricula today, and mishandled when it is included. But it is an ideal area in which to introduce the kinds of long-term analysis and what-if thinking that are often ignored as a result of old-mind defaults. The very first introduction of "Farmer Brown," even in kindergarten, should include the notion that Farmer Brown is really harvesting a gift from the sun when he harvests his crops. The study should emphasize how Farmer Brown has to *plan* the timing of his crops, calculating how much fertilizer and pesticide to use in different situations. And it should focus the what-if and long-term aspects of his situation around the topics of soil conservation and water use. How must he treat his soil if his great-grandchildren are to have a farm of equal or higher productivity? What will happen if the aquifer irrigating Farmer Brown's crops is pumped out too fast?

Along with agriculture the basics of how the climatic system functions should be taught, and the connection between the two carefully drawn. Students should know that the sun is not only directly essential to the growth of crops, but that it also delivers rain to them. Learning about the cycling of water and the role of plants in that cycling can be used as a stepping-stone to learning about the cycling of nutrients and then to the dynamics of ecosystems. Gradually the basic notion that human beings everywhere are dependent on services from natural ecosystems could become part of everyone's understanding of the world, and humanity would be spared politicians and pundits who rave about putting economics above ecology.

Another key topic in teaching students how the world works is the importance of that very-difficult-to-perceive but crucial part of our world—energy. The new-minded must have some background in what energy is and the rules that govern its use; among other things they will then become much more receptive to messages about its proper use. The connection between work and energy can be made in an elementary way early: kids with energy jump up and down and run and play; adults use energy to do their jobs. Automobiles, television sets, and all kinds of machinery also need energy to operate. Energy, which can be thought of as stored work, is found in different forms all around us. There is a lot in gasoline, there is a lot in electricity, there is a lot in a roller coaster at the high point of its run, and there is a lot in the food we eat.

At a technical level energy can be a complex topic, but it becomes much less daunting if it is introduced gradually throughout the curriculum. By the sixth grade the laws of thermodynamics should have been taught to the students in a simple form, even without naming them. Children should know that energy can neither be created nor destroyed, that matter is really a form of energy, and that nuclear weapons and nuclear power plants involve the conversion of a minute amount of matter into a huge amount of energy.

And the students should understand various manifestations of the second law—especially that spontaneous processes tend to move from order to disorder. They should know that this law is not based on high-flown theory but on the billions of observations that students and everyone else make day in and day out. Ice cubes always melt in Koolaid, and they never spontaneously form in it; dead cats never reassemble and run off; automobiles wear out, they never repair themselves. Students should know why each person gives off about as much heat as a 60-watt light bulb. A solid background in energy will go a long way toward arming students against claims such as those that say that manufacturing without environmental impact is possible.

One important topic should be much more strongly represented in the new curriculum than it is in the old: evolutionary biology, with special emphasis on human origins. People who do not understand the origins of their old minds will be handicapped in developing new ones, and evolutionary thinking is essential to understanding long-term trends, such as the growing threat from AIDS, and to evaluating claims, such as that people of one race are genetically superior to others. Teaching of evolution will, of course, be opposed by lunatic-fringe groups, but allowing them to deny children crucial elements in their education is a luxury society can no longer afford. Society would not tolerate legislation declaring that the theory that the sun circles the earth be given equal time with the theory of a heliocentric solar system; it should not pay attention to the equally preposterous notions of "scientific creationism."

Evolutionary thought could be introduced at many points. Human history should start not with classical civilizations but with paleontology and prehistory. Biological aspects of their backgrounds should be presented to students, even in early grades, as easily and naturally as the cultural and historic ones are. When farming is discussed, the idea that humanity has created new and better crops by evolutionary processes should be made clear just as, eventually, should problems of resistance to pesticides (and the connection of that resistance to antibiotic resistance). Dinosaurs, a subject that always fascinates children, can be used to acquaint students with the massive extinctions of the past, and the parallel can be drawn to the current extinction crisis. By high school, students should be ready to study more advanced topics, such as evolutionary aspects of the relationships between people and viruses.

Cultural evolution should, of course, be introduced along with biological evolution. One of the best ways of providing background for this is by teaching students to understand and value the great diversity of human cultures. Throughout the early years of schooling, that diversity should be explored. Then questions of the adaptive value of different cultural norms can be explored: Why should herdsmen on the southern edge of the Sahara traditionally have multiple wives? Why do Tongan men favor fat women? Why are Americans ignorant of their blood relationships while Australian aborigines are well informed? Why do the Soviets question American intentions when we know they are entirely honorable? Gradually the notion that cultural evolution has, to a large degree, shaped societies to survive in their environments will become thoroughly familiar. It is then but a small step to questioning how well cultural evolution has adapted us for the new world we now find ourselves in and to learning to look beneath the surface of human behavior in our own and other societies. The need to look beyond the immediate and ask "What then?" also needs to be emphasized early on. The story of King Midas is an excellent vehicle for teaching younger children to examine the consequences of their acts carefully, *if* it is followed with a discussion of ways of thinking, not just with the conclusion that Midas was silly or stupid. It can be integrated with thinking about such things as the consequences of taking up smoking or drugs and the entire philosophy of "fly now and pay later."

Similar points about the critical importance of foresight can be made quantitatively. Relatively minor changes in the examples used in math classes can be very important in promoting new-mindedness. By the time students are in junior high school, they should be accustomed to thinking about the long-term consequences of short-range decisions. They should have read of the king who promised to give a poor man one grain of rice for the first square of his checkerboard, two grains on the second square, four grains on the third square, eight grains on the fourth square, and so on, doubling the number of rice grains each time until all sixty-four squares were filled. When they do the necessary calculations, they will discover that the amount of rice needed to fill the sixty-fourth square would weigh more than all the grain harvested on the entire planet in a year—a very impressive result. Once the concepts of exponential growth and doubling times are introduced, the students will be able to figure out for themselves the consequences of the human population continuing to double every half century.

Mathematical exercises in the new curriculum can be used to demonstrate the silliness of one of the most pernicious and widespread ideas in our society—that economic growth can go on essentially forever. A version of the Parsons exercise could be used to accomplish this. The old-mind view on this topic was expressed by British economist Wilfred Beckerman, who stated that since economic growth had gone on since the time of Pericles, "there is no reason to assume it cannot continue for another 2,500 years."

A social scientist, Jack Parsons, did a new-minded analysis of Beckerman's assertion. With a simple calculation, Parsons showed that if economic growth had indeed gone on since Pericles at (by economists' standards) the very low rate of 1 percent annually, the average English family of Periclean time would have had much less buying power than a millionth of a penny has in England today.

Making a projection of growth at 1 percent a year into the future, Parsons showed that Beckerman's notion led to an equally absurd result. In 2,500 years the *average* Englishman would have an annual income of £400 trillion (about $700 trillion). In other words the average Englishman then would have about two hundred times as much buying power as all Americans have collectively today. It is a little difficult to figure out who would be willing to wait on the "rich" of that era, since presumably everyone would be immensely wealthier than the richest tycoons today.

If taught in junior high school or high school, and reinforced in college, the Parsons exercise could transform the way professional economists view the world. It could change the discipline of economics from one that promotes mindless growth to one that adds to the security of society by showing how to constrain economic activities so that they do not endanger critical ecosystem services.

At about the same level, students should begin to understand the constraints that the natural world puts on the functioning of human social and economic systems. They should know that perpetual growth of any physical quantity, be it the amount of steel or wheat produced in the United States or the number of human bodies in the universe, is impossible. They should understand the difference between humanity living on its capital and living on its income. And the source of that income would be clarified by tying in with discussions of agriculture, natural cycles, and ecosystems. All of this would not necessarily take significant time away from reading, writing, arithmetic, literature, and so on. But it would require new-minded teachers who are willing to reorganize the science and social science parts of the curriculum and to work pertinent materials into the classic subjects. Students can learn to read, "See the plant grow in the sun," as easily as they can, "See Dick and Spot run."

From junior high school on, students should continuously be exposed to the real dilemmas facing society. Programs to do this already exist in some schools. An excellent example is the "Science Symposium" series of the A. C. Davis Senior High School in Yakima, Washington. It illustrates what can be done with a dedicated, new-minded faculty, support of school administrators, and the backing of a traditional American community.

Davis is about as close to an inner-city school as one can find in a small Washington city. It has almost all of Yakima's minority students. Each year, however, those students have their minds immersed for several days in the important (and thus usually controversial) issues of the moment. They are treated like adults and encouraged to think for themselves, find answers, and reexamine beliefs and values. In the words of the school's staff and students:

During the three-day symposium students and staff from Davis, and invited guests, will have the opportunity to:

· Begin to analyze our present world.
· Participate in a large community as an individual engaging in a technological society.
· Converse in an open, democratic society requiring tolerance for different points of view.

These are the goals of the symposium.
It is an opportunity for the staff to:

· Work together on an interdisciplinary and academic experience.
· Find new forums for conversation—and maybe ask questions about education.

We want students to:

· Learn how to question.
· Produce written critiques of ideas presented from speakers, teachers, students, and community resource persons.
· Practice—and experience—listening aggressively.
· Read.
· Listen.
· Respect each other in a new setting.
· Find a new way to go through a day in school.
· Practice tolerance and acceptance.

The school district makes available funds to bring in speakers with national reputations and backs them up with resource persons drawn from the local area. In the 1986 symposium the topics discussed included euthanasia, management of wastes produced in the course of the manufacture of nuclear weapons, chimpanzee behavior, the role of the humanities in the human predicament, science and human values, overpopulation, space travel, water quality, abortion, and nuclear winter. If the Davis High school program were imitated in every high school in the nation, new-mindedness would be more widespread and our future more secure. If such topics were integrated into all secondary-school curricula, we'd be even further ahead. The kids are ready and eager for it. On average, they haven't yet become as old-minded as parents, teachers, school administrators, members of school boards, and voters.

We can easily teach both kids and teachers that people are quite adaptable and can learn to change more than most of us think. The brain of *Homo sapiens,* like that of all other animals, has its default positions. However, more than all the others, it is a brain characterized by its ability to change—if only in certain directions. We are able to modify our perceptual world using the more recently evolved, more adaptable part of our brains.

We inherit a lot of physical characteristics, as do other animals, but our most important is *the ability to go far beyond our inheritance.* It is this component that can and has been called into play in adapting to the new world. Our adaptability makes it much easier to produce great change than we might think.

Students can be reminded of the basic nature of the mind all through school. If every teacher took only five minutes per day stimulating this kind of awareness and showing students how to get around the defaults of the old mind, we are sure a radical change would follow. A radical shift in thought does not necessarily need a radical program; minds can be reshaped by countless small exchanges. Such exchanges between mother and child have already been shown to shape a child's later life.

In one study psychiatrist Daniel Stern videotaped all the activity between a twenty-five-year-old mother and her twin sons, Mark and Fred, in three-hour sessions from early infancy up to fifteen months. At three and a half months there were repeated exchanges in which the mother and Fred would gaze at each other. Fred would avert his face, his mother would respond with eye contact, and Fred would respond with an exaggerated expression. When mother looked away, though, Fred looked back at her, and the cycle would begin all over, until Fred was in tears.

With Mark mother never tried to compel eye contact. Mark could end contact with his mother when he wanted. When the infants were seen at twelve to fifteen months, Fred was more fearful and dependent than Mark. Mark greeted people openly and looked them straight in the eye. By changing the interactions these children could have been made to develop differently.

How much can older children change when they need to? One important and overlooked source of evidence concerns the amazing resilience of people to recover from the injurious effects of their world. Children deprived of normal stimulation are profoundly affected. Children in radically deprived environments show a much slower physical growth rate and become mentally retarded as well. There are children who have been prevented, for some tragic reason, from learning a language in the early years of their life. For these children the longer they are deprived, the harder it is for them ever to learn to speak.

However, children can *recover* from deprivation to a remarkable extent. Psychologist Wayne Dennis observed a group of babies in a Lebanese orphanage. These children were given hardly any stimulation; they lay on their backs all day in bare rooms, in bare cribs. They were touched only when their diapers were changed. At the age of one year the children's development was about that of a six-month-old.

Some of these babies were later adopted, and Dennis was able to compare their development with that of the children still left in the orphanage. Those in the orphanage remained retarded, but those who were adopted caught up in many aspects of development. This and many other studies show that we are capable of overcoming early deprivations *if later experience compensates.* In a sense, our old minds are born retarded in the new world; a new curriculum would overcome that with later experience.

Let's look at some ways to overcome early disadvantage. For example, experiences affect the IQ differences between whites and blacks in the United States. The environment can change: improved nutrition and more stimulating environments consistently lead to increased IQ test scores in children. Preschools and Head Start programs in the United States, as well as an ambitious program in Israel, are examples of current national programs to increase IQ in disadvantaged children.

Orphanages can have a profound effect on a child's mind, since they are bleak places that offer little human contact and minimal external stimulation. In the Lebanese orphanage the average IQ of the orphans was 63. In a well-baby clinic the average was 101. The difference was, that in the clinic, the infant orphans were propped up in their cribs for an hour a day. They could see what was going on, and their IQs rose dramatically.

Howard Skeels decided to find out whether stimulation and attention (tender loving care) are important in the development of intelligence. He placed thirteen preschool-age orphanage children with an average IQ of 64 (range 35 to 85) in an institution for retarded adults. Each orphan was "adopted" by an older woman.

All the adoptees became favorites of and were doted on by the patients and staff. Children between one and a half and six years of age who remained in the same or in a similar orphanage *dropped* in IQ an average of 20 IQ points in three years. The "adopted" orphans *gained* an average of 28 points.

Skeels's results stimulated the development of various enrichment programs in the United States aimed at increasing IQ. Many parents now send their children to preschools in the hope that such early training will enhance intellectual development. Children in preschools typically show an initial increase in IQ and a decline to the norm at around the second grade.

Children in programs that emphasize academic skills *alone* are most likely to show a later decline. Those preschools that emphasize *curiosity* and *self-motivation,* such as the Montessori schools, produce the greatest long-term gains. While members of our society are not exactly like deprived children, we live in our own restricted world, the caricatured world that has profoundly restricted our minds. However, there is good evidence that, even as adults, we should be able to change.

Many new educational programs to improve the operation of the mind itself are in the works throughout the world. We focus here on one called instrumental enrichment, which attempts to develop *specific* techniques and assessments for increasing intelligence. It is an experimental approach developed in Israel and is being applied in Venezuela in a large project on enhancing the intelligence of deprived children.

Instrumental enrichment does not teach a mass of facts about the world, but rather how to adapt to new situations, to *change* one's mental structure and contents: "learning how to learn." This process is called *cognitive modifiability*. Learning involves a change in information content; thinking involves a change in the structure of information in consciousness.

Since the function of mental processes is adaptation to the environment, it should also be the focus of testing. This has not been so in most school systems. Tragically our current concept of IQ focuses on short-term achievements and ability to memorize facts. Reuven Feuerstein, an influential Israeli educational psychologist, points out that this "has conspired to produce a widespread belief that intelligence is something that one either has or does not have and that attempts to change the structure and course of intellectual development are futile, if not impossible."

For our purposes, the roots of new-mindedness may be found in the way a child learns about his world and how well he or she understands it. One illustration is the difference in the phrasing of the same simple request "Please buy three bottles of milk" versus "Please buy three bottles of milk so that we'll have enough for tomorrow when the shops are closed." The second request provides a much greater opportunity for learning about planning one's life, although the same action is required in both cases.

We have to avoid the short-term caricature of intelligence as a fixed, inherited component of a person's brain. Instead a new-minded view is that intelligence has to do with making adaptive responses in new situations. So a new kind of intelligence test ought to be one in which the testee is scored on how well he or she *learns* something during the test rather than recalling (regurgitating) information.

We might discover something about promoting new-mindedness in our schools from the experiences of Feuerstein in teaching children who were retarded. How well did it work? Among a sample of Israeli children the I.E. program showed significant improvement compared with normal IQ tests. An assessment of I.E. programs by the Israeli military revealed impressive gains. After I.E., formerly retarded service-age youths were equal in performance to the general population. These evaluations are quite tentative, since few people not involved in the training group have had a chance to make their own independent assessment.

While this is only one program, it and others like it can begin to show the direction that we might follow: the focus of future research should be on the role of teachers and the quality of educational environments. Although not all of the programs may survive, they may make it possible to define more carefully and more completely how and when someone can become new-minded.

There is now enough material from studies of human development; cognitive psychology; decision analysis, and the physical, biological, and social sciences in general to develop a new curriculum to deal with the problems of the new world. The basic tools are already available, albeit often buried in irrelevant material. The key goal of a new curriculum will be to encourage students to think about the nature of their own minds and the limitations on their own thinking, about underlying physical and biological principles that govern the world, and about long-term trends in that world, as early and as continuously as possible in their schooling. *By college every student should be required to take an intensive course in the sorts of things discussed in this book as part of their "liberal education."*

The reason these analyses and teachings are so important is that, as we've said, the same basic patterns hold whether we are judging flavors, brightness, and temperature or prices, politics, and prospects for saving civilization. So refashioning how people are educated could have enormous import for the future of our species.

10

CHANGING THE WORLD AROUND US

CHANGING SCHOOL CURRICULA and teaching methods may be the most fundamental change that's needed, but, of course, that change will not bear fruit for twenty years or more, even if we can overcome all the serious barriers. Furthermore, if we continue to miscalculate the importance of budget deficits, nuclear arsenals, medical costs, and acid rain, those

234

years may never come. Obviously, we need to make new kinds of thinking and new ways of handling our problems immediately available to society's decision makers. And while changing the form and content of education would be a major step toward conscious evolution, much has to be done outside of the schools as well.

How do we begin to do that? We must expose leaders of society to notions that are not now current. We must get debate going in governmental, media (especially television), and intellectual circles, among the people who have leverage in our society, that is among people who have the education and interest to read as far as page 235 in a book like this.

One such notion is that people's ideas are not as fixed as is commonly thought—that in fact much is known about how to change them systematically. Our chances of becoming new-minded would be much enhanced by making that knowledge widespread. Reducing prejudice is crucial in a world that is armed with nuclear weapons and where caricatures of other cultures are a major factor in generating international tensions. When prejudiced people join less prejudiced groups, they adopt more tolerant attitudes. Another way of reducing prejudice is to increase contact with the prejudged group. This increases the availability of positive thoughts and decreases the availability of negative ones.

The rule is this: *the more you know about someone, the less likely you are to make sweeping judgments about him or her.* This holds true for judgments about groups of people as well. Because society has become less segregated in the past forty years, we should expect less prejudice toward minorities. Indeed there is less prejudice among people in public housing, where black and white families live together, than among people who live in segregated areas.

Scarcity is important in judging everything from cookies to other people. When there is intense competition for limited resources, prejudice and discrimination are likely to flourish. Psychological studies have found that the strongest antiblack prejudice was in people who were one step above blacks on the socioeconomic scale. It was especially severe when the two groups were in close competition for scarce jobs.

One interesting study shows both how prejudice can develop and how we might change it. Muzafar Sherif and his colleagues studied twenty-two boys who came to summer camp at Robbers Grave, Oklahoma. They were divided into two different groups, the "eagles" and the "rattlers." The experimenters encouraged each group to cooperate and to work together as a team toward goals, for example, making improvements to the camp grounds. The first phase of the experiment was then to create a strong group affiliation and cohesion in a random grouping of individuals.

Once each group had become a cohesive unit, they were pitted against one another in competitive sports events. Initially, the boys showed good sportsmanship, but gradually there arose resentment, hostility, and discrimination between the teams.

In the second phase of the experiment, the goal was to decrease the ill will between the groups. Simply eliminating competition did not work. The experimenters found that when both groups worked together toward a common goal, hostility decreased, cooperation and fellowship increased. Once a truck broke down, and all the campers were needed to tow it up a hill (pulling on a large rope). The cooperative effort probably reduced the feelings of differences between the groups. It allowed the two groups to share a sense of accomplishment and to discover similarities in each other.

Another systematic attempt to reduce prejudice through cooperation is the jigsaw classroom technique, developed by Eliot Aronson. Classrooms often stress individual competition. Here the stress is not on competitiveness but on interdependence. Students are divided into groups, and each group is assigned a project. Each member of the group is given information about one part of the assignment, one puzzle piece. The only way the assignment can be completed is if each member teaches and shares his or her information with the others. Thus, each person becomes an invaluable resource. In addition, the teacher gives grades based on group cooperation rather than individual effort.

Stereotypes can thus be overcome by increasing the availability of information about other groups, by fostering associations between members of those groups, and by stimulating cooperation among them. All of these elements could easily be incorporated into the routine training of young people in our society. Many are made to order for adoption in classrooms. They can also be (and are being) applied among adults—one example is exchanges with Soviets, especially those involving joint projects, whether climbing a mountain, competing in a bike race, or writing a joint report on the medical consequences of nuclear war.

Another place where training for the new mind can take place is in the use of energy. Most people do not volunteer to adopt new methods of conservation, even when it is cost-effective. Two hundred million dollars per year are spent in California alone to promote conservation. Eliot Aronson and his colleagues considered the problem of resistance to conservation as primarily a psychological one. They showed that information about energy use must be registered in the old mind, then evaluated, understood, and remembered. They asked how to make it more likely that the information would be incorporated into a person's worldview and acted upon appropriately.

Most mass-media attempts to promote conservation have failed because general statistics do not register on the old mind. Aronson and colleagues showed that energy is understood only in a caricatured, personal way. Instead of a mass-media attack, simple "social diffusion" seems to work, because information delivered through normal social situations is more likely to have an effect. Horror stories about energy costs told to you by neighbors are more vivid and dramatic than a note from the power company that "energy use must be cut over the next peak period." Few people understand what that means. But if your neighbor pays a high bill for leaving his lights on for a two-week vacation, that is easily registered, and more important, easily remembered.

The tribal mind can be used as the relay point. People who own solar homes, not an impersonal agency, are the best communicators to other people about energy conservation. People can then make the correct social comparisons and evaluations. Personal, social information seems to be communicated most efficiently.

One area that has enormous potential for encouraging new-mindedness in children is in the design of toys. Manufacturers have shown enormous ingenuity in adapting new computer technologies to the production of toys with enormous appeal. They have even come up with devices that interact with children's television shows. Unhappily, a great deal of that ingenuity has gone into producing toys that simulate engines of mass destruction, present and future. Without getting into the argument of the impact of those toys on the attitudes of children, it should be remembered that computer chips could be used to produce toys that would alert children to their perceptual limitations and encourage them to look at long-term trends. Toys that focus on "magic," that take advantage of our perceptual limitations would, if appropriately packaged and explained, make children comfortable with the idea that "what you see is not necessarily what you are getting."

Monopoly-like games could be constructed that include environmental constraints. You build on Boardwalk, but you lose your building because you pulled a card that says "Warming caused by carbon dioxide melts ice caps. Rising sea level erodes beach and destroys your property." A Trivial Pursuit question could be, "In the 1970s, oil-company advertising implied that developing the Alaskan Prudhoe Bay oil field would produce enough petroleum to solve America's energy problems permanently. In what year did production from the field peak?" The answer is 1987.

Even war games can be constructed in a way that encourages children to look at trends and options, as one does in chess, rather than just attempting to avoid immediate threats. Consider a war game in which the highest score goes to the person who finds a way for both adversaries to benefit from avoiding a war. The claim will be, of course, that children don't want those sorts of games. The answer is that children want the sort of games they are sold—and if we want to have children in the future, we'd better start selling different kinds of games.

Television, of course, is one of the most important tools for developing new minds that society possesses. While a relatively small portion of society, unfortunately, reads books, practically everybody watches television. TV is, however, a medium that must be used with considerable care. The knee-jerk reaction to the prizewinning children's program *Sesame Street* was that a show so well done had to be good for children. But *Sesame Street* seems to have had at least one unexpected deleterious effect. Some *Sesame Street* kids turned out to have a dreadful time in school. Accustomed by the TV show to learning from beautifully programmed segments of a minute or two, they don't do at all well under the relatively unstructured tutelage of elementary school teachers. The real world is not broken into tightly programmed intervals designed to fit between commercials.

Similarly, children and adults in our society have been conditioned, especially by television, to think of "news" as being about drama and sudden death. The slow trends that are strangling society are not defined as news and can only be mentioned occasionally when some dramatic event highlights them. People had been starving in Africa in large numbers for almost a decade when, in the early 1980s, some horrifying film from a refugee camp suddenly made it "news." The inexorable increases in the size of the human population and in the size of the nuclear arsenals designed to destroy that population are unquestionably (along with the threat of AIDS) the most important developments of the second half of the twentieth century. Neither of the first two trends is considered to be "news" most of the time. They are only mentioned by the anchorperson when some individual or group makes a dramatic statement or protest about them. The immediate event (not the underlying problem) then becomes "news."

In its issue of October 6, 1983, *Time* magazine summarized "The Most Amazing 60 Years in History." Among the stories the magazine's editors considered the most important stories of the 1923–82 period to be were: 1927: Lindbergh reveals that a man alone can conquer an ocean, captivate a world; 1929: New York stock market crash kicks off the Depression; 1937: Publication of Ernest Hemingway's new novel, *To Have and Have Not;* 1939: Hitler attacks Poland, unleashing World War II; 1945: Atomic bomb attack at Hiroshima ends the fighting, opens nuclear age; 1947: The Marshall Plan rebuilds postwar Europe. 1955: Jonas Salk's vaccine promises to eliminate polio; 1956: Soviets crush Hungary's rebellion; 1962: Kennedy forces Khrushchev to remove missiles from Cuba; 1973: Arab oil embargo causes energy prices to rise; 1974: Watergate ends, Nixon resigns; 1982: The year of the computer.

(We should note that *Time* is not being singled out for criticism, but had merely provided us with a convenient review of stories that typify media coverage of the period.)

But during this time some events unprecedented in history transpired. During the period that began when "Inflation ravaged Germany" to the "Year of the computer," the world population more than doubled in size. During the same period the environment deteriorated more than at any other time, and in the United States, *Time*'s main focus of interest, the federal budget deficit increased tenfold, the most destructive war in history, World War II, occurred, and nuclear weapons appeared. Only the last two exciting and eventful stories caught the attention of *Time*.

Their attention, even in long-term retrospect, is focused almost exclusively on the immediately prominent. The media bring the Beatles to everyone's attention; the Beatles become an important story. If as much hype as went into promoting the Beatles had been expended on the *real* story of the late 1960s—that earth's population was growing out of control and the environment was deteriorating at a record pace—many more people might have had their old minds changed and the kind of interest that *was* generated around the first Earth Day in 1970 might have been better sustained.

Furthermore, the *Time* coverage of nuclear weapons, like that of all the standard media outlets, has been superficial. Worse yet, it has often been based on the lies in government press releases rather than on careful analysis. Among the truly important stories of the 1970s and early 1980s was the destabilization of the nuclear arms race by American and Soviet technological initiatives. Yet a most critical step toward Armageddon—the MIRVing of our missiles and the Soviet response of MIRVing theirs do not appear in the "Amazing 60 Years" list.

To understand the problems of "counterforce strategy" requires both a fair knowledge of the technology of nuclear weapons and the comparative deployment of American and Soviet nuclear forces, and a willingness and ability to do some rather simple analyses. But the educational systems in both countries supply little of either to politicians, military people, or citizens. So media coverage of nuclear weapons developments becomes a comedy of the ignorant trying to inform the public about the dangerous activities of the equally ignorant. Small wonder that informed citizens feel that all they can do about our nuclear predicament is be terrified.

Of course, it is no surprise that media coverage of issues related to population growth, resource depletion, and environmental deterioration is inadequate. The people who work for magazines and newspapers and determine what is broadcast have the same defaults of mind as the rest of us; they are more-or-less random samples of the college-educated portion of the population.

In addition, more than most of us, people in the media are subject to pressures to focus on the immediate, to concentrate on "fast-breaking" stories. Reporters and editors are also subjected to continual harangues about the media concentrating too much on "bad news." This reduces their incentive to dwell on ominous long-term trends. Instead they are pressured to tell the public that sooner or later everything will come out just fine—to hunt for a silver lining in every cloud. We are fortunate that many reporters overcome these problems and manage to get parts of the real news to the public.

There are ways in which the media, with minimal effort, could do a great deal to promote new-mindedness. The statistics presented on American television are usually limited to events within our boundaries: thirty thousand will die of heart disease this month, 2 million are homeless. It would take little to change these numbers into world statistics and would greatly help change awareness of the hundreds of millions, at least, who are hungry. Also, there could be one segment on a long-term problem—climatic change, growth of the American population, acid rain, the decline of science teaching in schools, the rise of the national debt, the deployment of American and Soviet nuclear weapons—at the end of each television news program. The segment should review the problem, give the current status of efforts to deal with it (if any), emphasize why people have trouble perceiving it, make editorial suggestions on what needs to be done, and challenge viewers to think about it and to present opposing views.

Each "new world" segment could end with a chart listing the ten most serious long-term problems, perhaps with stock-market-type arrows indicating whether they are getting worse or better. In a similar vein, a "world box score" could daily be placed in a box on the front page of every newspaper, giving population size, environmental-quality trends, size of nuclear arsenals, and so on, and indexing stories in the paper relating to them. "Mind-blind" fillers could be developed for both television and print journalism. Those on TV could be similar to the two-stage ones already in use as "punctuation" on the ABC morning news.

A great variety of material could be presented. For example, first break: "Do you think it is more sensible to live on capital or income?" Second break: "Most people believe it is most sensible to live within your income, but if that's the case, why is our species increasingly spending its capital? Fossil fuels, groundwater, rich agricultural soils, and the millions of plants, animals, and microorganisms that share the planet with us are essential to the persistence of civilization. And yet we are spending this irreplaceable capital of nonrenewable resources at an accelerating rate and, in the process, destroying the only systems that are able to supply our society with income—the energy of the sun made available to us as food through the photosynthetic activities of green plants."

Or, first break: "We've just told you that 252 people were killed today in an airplane crash. How many people do you suppose were killed last week in automobile accidents?" Second break: "The answer is that 1,112 were slaughtered on our roads last week, but that ongoing tragedy is not considered news."

Or even, first break: "Do you think you see the real world?" Next break: "Bats put together their picture of the world from the echoes of their squeaks; electric fishes by perceiving distortions in electrical fields that they themselves create. These worlds are just as real as ours. We, too, have a highly selective view of the world. Our sensory systems emphasize what's going on in a narrow band of the electromagnetic spectrum of energy—that is, we 'see' things. Always re-member that our view of the world is biased by many things, not the least of which are the limitations of the sense organs we have evolved."

Fillers for newspapers could have similar content and could be made much more interesting than the sort of information conveyed now. People could be informed that "One reason Soviet agriculture is so backward is that an excellent group of Russian geneticists and evolutionists was purged by Stalin's henchmen in the 1930s. Under-standing evolution is so important to the maintenance of high yields that the Russian people have suffered shortages and stood in line for food ever since."

Such fare should be a welcome relief from "Hendrik A. Lorentz of Holland won the Nobel prize for physics in 1902" or "The nation of Burkina Faso in West Africa had only 10,000 telephones for its 6.9 million people in 1985." At least weekly each television and radio station could carry a full "real news" program dedicated to examining the news events that take place on time scales of a decade or longer. They could be complemented by "real news" columns in each issue of every newspaper and newsmagazine, which discuss the gradual trends that are now largely ignored. Needless to say, such suggestions are unlikely to be greeted with great joy by the media at present. But they should be gradually persuaded to move in the right direction—and the persuasion pro-cess itself, done in public, could help the movement toward new-mindedness. It is more likely that, since it is in the long-term public interest, a constant reminder of major changes in the world will need, at first, public funds for support. Such changes in the media are essential if we are to comprehend the "invisible" changes, such as population growth.

To understand the population explosion, one has to feel comfort-able with new-mind tools, such as the analysis of statistics and dealing with probabilities. Most people easily perceive brute "crowding." They quickly register being trapped in a freeway gridlock or having the solitude of their favorite mountain trails disturbed by mobs of other hikers and trail bikers. Crowding is easily translated into overpopulation.

But crowding is the *least* significant aspect of overpopulation. The entire human population of earth could stand on one thousand square miles (a piece of land smaller than the Los Angeles metropolitan area—just one fifty-thousandth of Earth's ice-free land surface) with more than five square feet for each person to stand in. The amount of space per person is not, however, what determines earth's carrying capacity for *Homo sapiens.* It is, rather, the number of people relative to the resources needed to sustain them and to the capacity of environmental systems to absorb and recycle human wastes.

Calculating carrying capacity is difficult even for scientists. First of all, one must ask *for how long* our species is to be supported. Right now the human population appears to be far above the long-term carrying capacity, simply because we are rapidly destroying our stock of capital in order to support 5 billion people. When enough of the capital is gone, the population seems doomed to drop well below current levels.

Long-term carrying capacity will vary with a number of factors. One is the extent to which the systems that supply us with *income* will be damaged by the present population "overshoot." Once humanity's capital is gone, income is all we'll have to live on. Another critical factor is the *behavior* of the people. Earth can support many more people living at the subsistence level of the People's Republic of China than in the life-style of Beverly Hills.

The old-mind tendency to ignore gradual trends and concentrate on the situation of the moment frequently surfaces in demographic debates. It is often said that earth doesn't have a population problem, rather it has a problem of the *distribution* of wealth. Actually, it has both. The planet undoubtedly could support more saints, living frugally and sharing equally, than real people, most of whom strive to live as high on the hog as possible. Thus any projections of future carrying capacity must take into account how people are going to live and what kind of society they are going to live in.

This, of course, adds complications that require new-mind analysis. A major factor that makes projections difficult is the capacity of *Homo sapiens* for technological innovation. How much, say, might agricultural productivity be increased by genetic engineering (and what will the side effects of that technology be)? Will environmentally sound, politically acceptable new energy sources be found?

Future carrying capacities will certainly depend heavily on the energy options available to society, which in turn will depend on a mix of science and politics. Nuclear fission power plants could abate the problems caused by adding carbon dioxide and the precursors of acid rains to the atmosphere. It is not at all clear, however, whether the problems of nuclear technology can be solved. Today's reactors present, in our opinion, unacceptable risks of proliferation of nuclear weapons and catastrophic accident, as well as serious problems of waste disposal. The latter two problems are probably amenable to technological solution. The first could be ameliorated but probably not solved by technological steps.

The difficulties of calculating carrying capacity accurately do not mean, however, that nothing sensible can be said on the topic. Today's population at today's level of affluence and using today's technologies, is far above earth's long-term carrying capacity. For the foreseeable future (and quite likely permanently), the long-term carrying capacity will be below 5 billion people—probably far below. The only sensible course for our species is to do everything possible to stop its population growth rapidly and *humanely* and begin a slow population decline. The exact future carrying capacities need not concern us at all today. The humane way to end population growth and start population shrinkage is to maintain birth rates slightly below death rates for hundreds of years. There will be plenty of time for research and debate on what an optimal size, distribution, and life-style of the population should be.

It is certainly possible to make policy decisions about a threat—in this case, exceeding the carrying capacity—in the face of considerable uncertainty about its precise magnitude and consequences. But making those decisions involves recognition of trends that stretch not years into the future (the far time horizons of most businesses and governments) but centuries.

The size of the human population and its continuing growth are surely the most fundamental and pervasive environmental threats to society (excluding nuclear war), but they are far from the only ones. Virtually all such threats, however, tend to be imperceptible and therefore, to many, inconceivable. Let's look at some of the most important.

A paranoid visitor from outer space might assume that television was deliberately trying to keep Earthlings from discovering what is really transpiring on their planet. Every time John Kennedy or Ronald Reagan *said* that the United States was behind the Soviet Union militarily, that was "news." The fact that the United States was actually almost always ahead, leading the way in giving humanity the means to destroy itself, has never been considered news. Every time a surgeon general issues a statement about how cigarette smoking kills, that is "news." The deaths of 360 thousand Americans from lung cancer annually is not news. Phyllis Schlafly railing against the use of condoms to slow the spread of AIDS is "news"; that AIDS might bring down civilization in a few scant decades is not news.

We cannot and should not completely change the responsiveness of the human system to sudden change. But as we have just shown, we could develop a new kind of "news" report that first analyzes the slow dangers affecting humanity and then portrays them in a way that is understandable to the old mind. Dramatic television commercials in Britain did more to reduce smoking and increase the use of seat belts than the countless health warnings. One showed a lung from which a quart of motor oil was slowly poured, symbolizing the gunk deposited by a lifetime of smoking. That ad reportedly had a powerful impact. It showed how effective television can be in converting a statistical trend—the correlation between smoking and lung disease—into a threat that registers easily on the old mind.

The new mind needs to build such necessary bridges so that certain kinds of information can penetrate the old mind. New minds must find ways to create *demand* for continuous updates in TV, magazine, and radio news about the human predicament, as well as straightforward delivery of the information required to solve it. We think that this demand would best be sparked by a new school curriculum such as we have described. If people insisted that a substantial portion of every news program analyze the complex problems that face society, the media would respond. Furthermore, innovations such as computer graphics and satellite access to images of distant people and events could provide the means of making subjects that tend to bore old minds much more interesting.

Even scientific training itself doesn't always keep scientists from surrendering to the old-mind defaults. The scientific method produces, in essence, an even more extreme caricature of the world than is our normal one. Scientists like to simplify, and they crave systems that can be reduced to a few simple relationships with neat, short, causal pathways. Split the uranium nucleus, and a small amount of mass is converted into a huge amount of energy. Replace one amino acid with another, and normal hemoglobin is converted into the kind that produces sickle-cell anemia.

Both of us, trained in sciences that deal with extraordinarily complex systems, also find ourselves striving to design simple experiments that will yield insights into those systems. Paul Ehrlich takes special pleasure in having done a simple field experiment that demonstrated how small, plant-eating insects could greatly influence the evolution of plants. Robert Ornstein developed a simple technique using an electroencephalogram to allow psychophysiologists to measure the activity of both brain hemispheres in a living normal person. Although we're specialists in the complex, our old minds find a simple experiment somehow more satisfying than a complicated analysis.

Scientists' penchant for simplicity, though, can lead the unwary old mind to inappropriate caricatures when dealing with environmental problems. A classic example was provided by Sir Robert Robinson, a British Nobel Laureate in chemistry. In 1971 he wrote a letter to the London *Times,* claiming that there would be no problem for oceanic plankton from adding leaded compounds to the oceans. He wrote, "Neither our 'Prophets of Doom,' nor the legislators who are so easily frightened by them, are particularly fond of arithmetic" and then proceeded to do what he called some "simple arithmetic." He calculated what the dilution of lead would be in the vast volume of water in the oceans, showing that the lead would have no biological effect.

Unfortunately for Sir Robert, his arithmetic was just too "simple." Lead and other toxic substances are often not evenly diluted in the environment, because organisms have the power to concentrate them. The mechanisms are several, and need not concern us, but they can result in the poisons being tens of thousands of times more concentrated in animals' bodies than they are in the animals' environment. Sir Robert did a straightforward, obvious analysis of the sort that often leads to great discoveries in a reductionist science like chemistry. Such procedures frequently produce misleading results in sciences dealing with higher levels of complexity such as ecology and psychology.

With scientists so easily misled, small wonder that the untrained person cannot grasp that a thin, colorless, tasteless, odorless film of pesticide on an apple represents a much greater threat to health than a worm inside the apple. More difficult still is recognizing that virtually indestructible poisons can gradually accumulate in other organisms, be concentrated as they move up food chains, and threaten human lives not only directly but by assaulting the very fabric of our life-support systems.

The flaw lies in the simplistic way scientists are trained. Missing in the constant attempts to study smaller and smaller components of reality is any real concern in the scientific community with the *integration* of all the knowledge that is being produced. It is now easy, even desirable in terms of career advancement, for a young geneticist to know nothing about human development and behavior; for a physicist to know nothing about ecology; for a physician to know nothing about the lives and society of his patients. No Nobel prizes are given for understanding how the earth is being transformed, for knowing what the sum total of modern science means for society. No long-view, long-term understanding is prized when promotions are considered, and few appointments in universities exist for those whose knowledge does not fit a "slot" in an academic department. Small surprise that generations of students are trained to think in a narrow way that will lead to short-term personal success, but not advance civilization, except through minor technical improvements.

Governments should institutionalize the long view. The exact mechanisms, obviously, will vary from nation to nation. The United States government might establish a "foresight" institute, which (like the present National Science Foundation) is relatively insulated against political interference. The institute could be charged with examining and integrating long-term trends, evaluating their consequences, and making recommendations to the government on steps to be taken to adjust society to them. An annual report could be produced, somewhat like the valuable "State of the Environment" reports once available from the now nearly defunct President's Council on Environmental Quality, but aimed more at *forecasting* rather than the current situation.

The *Global 2000 Report,* released in 1980 by the Carter administration, was distinguished by its *integration* of projected trends. Government agencies routinely make projections of future trends in their areas: the U.S. Census Bureau makes population projections; the U.S. Department of Agriculture forecasts world agricultural production; the Forest Service projects trends in lumbering and reforestation; the Fisheries and Wildlife Agency projects fisheries yields, and so forth. But these projections are mostly extensions of the recent past and are conducted in a vacuum of information from other ongoing changes in the world (although population growth is usually taken into account).

Global 2000's unprecedented contribution was to harmonize these usually separated trends, account for how they affected each other, calculate possible conflicts over resources (such as in land use, freshwater supplies, or availability of investment capital), and produce new projections. It also examined some developing problems, such as acid rain and the rise in atmospheric concentrations of carbon dioxide and their potential effects on agricultural and forest production, which had not been monitored by the government.

In a real sense *Global 2000* laid the groundwork for a permanent "global foresight" entity within the United States government. If developed, such an agency could continue to combine information from all the various agencies and produce an increasingly realistic projection of the integrated trends, including the outcomes of alternative policies. In an evermore interdependent world, in which national policy changes can have extremely far-reaching effects in both space and time, such a forecasting ability is essential.

Remarkably enough, the trends predicted for 1975–2000 by *Global 2000* are, so far, quite close to reality. Where they differ, the changes can be readily traced to changes in policy *(Global 2000*'s projections assumed no major policy changes). Food production is a little higher than the projections; this is partly due to lower energy prices, which in turn result from an "energy glut" largely caused by a significant reduction of fossil fuel consumption by the champion consumer, the United States!

The amount of money required to establish a foresight institute would be small by governmental standards, and if it were done right, the institute could become society's "new mind." A key factor in doing it right would be to attract a permanent research staff of scholars from a wide range of disciplines and give them only the most general charges or paths of investigation to follow. To prevent the institute from drifting more and more into esoterica, a system of temporary positions, again well funded, could be established that could be filled by politicians, businessmen, labor leaders, social activists, and the like, on "sabbaticals" from their primary activities. This would both keep the pot stirred within the institute and help to disseminate its concerns and results.

Of course, existing governmental institutions could be made much more new-minded. The National Environmental Policy Act (NEPA) and similar state statutes could be amended so that every environmental-impact statement would have to consider possible global as well as local impacts of any proposed activity. Then the development of a new factory would not have to consider just the impact of the workers' automobiles on local traffic patterns and the impact of any emissions from the factory on local populations and ecosystems, but it would also have to consider the factory's contribution to the global carbon dioxide buildup and to regional acid-rain problems. Even paving a parking lot changes the earth's reflectivity and could contribute to climatic change. Though changing such a small area would have no discernible effect by itself, cumulatively, "development" activities are changing the climate. Having to consider global effects as each project is planned would help educate people to the long-term impacts of human activities.

Not all resources are governmental, however. Among the great assets that rich nations ignore is the minds and traditions of the people of the planet who do not participate in industrial society. It is a bit of Western vanity to think that the few groups of people who still hunt and gather are "primitive" and that simply introducing them to mechanized agriculture would solve their "food problems." In fact, hunters and gatherers and traditional farmers alike have superb, time-tested techniques for extracting food from hostile environments—to ignore their knowledge in trying to solve the world food problem is the height of hubris.

Hunting-and-gathering peoples, including our Cro-Magnon ancestors, have classically harvested a wide variety of the animals available in their habitats. Herders and farmers have based their activities on a continually narrowing resource base—a few species of domestic animals and plants. This specialization has both advantages and disadvantages. In Africa the dependence of herders on cattle—animals not native to Africa—has been a major factor in desertification. Cattle must have daily water in semiarid environments, so they must walk to wells or water holes. The daily trek uses energy that could be converted into beef, and the trampling damages already-sparse vegetation and compacts the soil, making it less able to absorb water and more subject to erosion. The moist cowpats produced by cattle harden into a "fecal pavement" that further limits plant growth by smothering it. The pats heat up in the sun, killing the bacteria and fungi that normally break them down and release fertilizing nutrients. As grazing intensifies, the grasses and herbs the cattle prefer become less common, and less nourishing ones become more common, and the capacity of the range to support cattle declines. Partly as a result of these factors, the Sahara Desert marches inexorably southward, and people starve to death.

In contrast, most native African grazing (grass-eating) and browsing (shrub-eating) antelopes and other hoofed animals are much more efficient in their water use than cattle. Some native animals seem to get all the moisture they need from the plants they eat and never need to drink at all; others drink only occasionally. In either case daily treks to water holes are not necessary. The native animals, conserving water by reabsorbing it in the hind end of their guts, produce dry fecal pellets, which drop through the vegetation and fertilize without smothering it. Furthermore, the different species of African grazers and browsers eat different kinds of plants; for example, giraffes can eat the tops of thorny acacia trees that cannot be used by other species.

As a consequence of these differences, a mix of native animal species does not degrade a range physically or chemically the way cattle do. Observing this, and taking a cue from more "primitive" peoples, some pioneers have been experimenting with ranching not cattle but antelopes, giraffes, and other native African plant eaters. On the Athi Plain of Kenya, David Hopcraft has a thriving twenty-thousand-acre game ranch where, since 1978, antelopes, zebras, and giraffes have been harvested along with cattle. The cattle, which are being phased out, may eventually be replaced with a native bovine, the Cape buffalo. At the moment, having some cattle gives better control over the grazing regime, since the cattle can be herded from place to place where the range is ready for grazing.

One night a week the game is harvested. Men in Land Rovers spotlight selected animals and kill them with a high-velocity rifle bullet in the brain. The carcass is then transported quickly to a modern, government-inspected packing plant and processed in sanitary conditions.

The ranch is more successful than the Hopcrafts had hoped. The range is *improving* steadily, and the yield of meat is higher than could be obtained from herding cattle alone. Furthermore, the game animals are more resistant to local diseases than cattle, and large amounts of money aren't needed for pumps, pipes, dams, and other devices to supply water. The main ranching "tool" is a thirty-mile-long perimeter fence specially designed to ensure that animals are not injured if they run into it. And the animals handle their own predator control—they have long evolutionary experience to help them avoid the depredations of lions, leopards, cheetahs, and wild dogs.

As a result of all this, the potential for profit is far above that of a cattle ranch, *if* some additional new-mindedness can be cultivated. First, a taste for game must be promoted in people long accustomed to beef, for without substantial markets, game ranching will fail. Second, people such as the Masai, to whom cattle are the traditional form of wealth and an important element in their religion, will have to be converted to game ranching. If such barriers can be overcome, game ranching could be a major factor in reversing the tide of desertification in much of Africa south of the Sahara.

The potential of such schemes need not be limited to Africa. For instance, much of the western United States is also being overgrazed and desertified—in no small part because of massive government subsidies to cattle ranching. Game ranching of native deer and antelope might help to reverse the trend. But an important obstacle to replacing cowboys with game harvesters is old-mindedness, and not only among beef eaters, the Masai, or American ranchers. Even professors of animal husbandry usually find the idea of game ranching too novel. Societies should even be willing to give short-term subsidies to game-ranching operations in order to overcome such barriers, since the long-term benefits in arresting desertification would be enormous.

In a few centuries cultural evolution has produced the most persistent and pernicious notion ever to afflict humanity. It is the belief that what we do today is always better than what we did yesterday, that all forms of "progress" are desirable, inevitable, and irreversible. If herding one species of animals replaced hunting many, that must have been progress, and we can't go back. This belief is especially strongly held about economic and scientific progress. The gross national product (GNP) must always continue to grow; a society cannot consciously decide that it has "enough" and enter an

economic steady-state or (perish the thought) *reduce* its GNP and
"de-develop." Many scientists believe that anything that can be done
technologically *should* be done—progress demands it. This makes
many other scientists nervous as the time approaches when biologists will have the capability of engineering viruses that can kill
everyone. Similarly people claim that weapons inevitably must become increasingly destructive as science advances—the road led inexorably from the sword to the musket to the machine gun and on
to the hydrogen bomb.

The inevitability of such military "progress" was made explicit by
Lord Dunsany, who wrote in 1938: "We can no more go back from
poison [gas] to the gun than we can go back from the gun to the
sword." But a little-known historical event demonstrates clearly that
a society can reverse a deleterious long-term trend and actually
move from the gun to the sword. And it happened in one of the
most happy and prosperous societies of which there is historical
record, one in which progress was gradual and carefully controlled
and which nonetheless earned the admiration of knowledgeable
foreign observers: Japan in the seventeenth century. In short there
were clear signs of new-mindedness centuries ago.

Modern guns of the sixteenth century, harquebuses, were first
brought to Japan by Chinese trader-pirates in 1543. These guns were
matchlocks, the powder being ignited by a continuously burning
fuse that the trigger brought into contact with the powder. Japan
was in a period of almost continual internal military conflict as
feudal lords battled for control of the nation.

With a characteristic alacrity, the Japanese adopted the new technology and improved on both the weapons and the techniques of
their use. Within a few decades the Japanese were slaughtering each
other much more efficiently than the Europeans, who had used
harquebuses much longer. But not everyone was pleased with this
example of progress. In *Giving Up the Gun: Japan's Reversion to
the Sword* 1543–1879 Dartmouth professor Noel Perrin, writes of
Japan's early affair with firearms, "Not to know how to use them
was not to be a soldier. But at the same time, the first resistance to

firearms was developing. It arose from the discovery that efficient weapons tend to overshadow the men who use them."

No longer was there much room for the heroism of individual combat; the skilled and armored samurai knight, carrying a blade never surpassed in the technology of cutting weapons, could be potted like a partridge at two hundred yards by a crude peasant. In short, the warlike Japanese gentry greeted the gun with all the enthusiasm that U.S. Air Force bomber generals greeted the advent of intercontinental ballistic missiles or that our battleship admirals gave to the development of the aerial and submarine weapons that made battleships completely obsolete.

Generals and admirals in the West have had some success in delaying "progress" in weapons. As we have seen, armies mounted men on horses long after it made any sense. American admirals even managed to persuade the Reagan administration to take old battleships out of mothballs in the 1980s, forty years after the sinking of the *Repulse* and *Prince of Wales* by Japanese land-based bombers sounded the death knell of those giant vessels armed with heavy artillery. One of the lumbering monsters actually hurled shells at Lebanon in 1985 before retreating ignominiously, having demonstrated its total impotence in late-twentieth-century warfare, even when the enemy was not equipped with nuclear-tipped cruise missiles and torpedoes. But neither cavalry buffs nor battleship admirals run Western nations; otherwise we might not have to live with machine guns and thermonuclear warheads.

The samurai, on the other hand, did run Japan. They managed to restrict the manufacture of guns, and the last battle in which they were extensively used occurred in 1637. By the early eighteenth century, guns were a curiosity. Subsequently, the Japanese advanced in agriculture, mathematics, hydrological engineering, marketing, and other fields. It was not a stagnant society that forgot how to make and use guns; it was a sophisticated society focused on quality of life (rather than progress for its own sake) that eschewed them. It did not take up guns again until intrusions by modern navies, especially of Commodore Perry's squadron in 1853, began to persuade the Japanese that their national security demanded firearms.

Their return to a highly skilled gun manufacturing/using nation occurred with lightninglike speed in the last decades of the nineteenth century.

The experience of Japan with guns shows that a progressive, cultured, and happy people living in a sustainable society can decide that a scientific development is undesirable, even though it is an "improvement" on previous technology. It gives hope that the culturally evolved notion of technological imperatives can be rather readily countered by conscious evolution. The Japanese, after all, showed that there is nothing whatever inevitable about the deployment of novel technologies. True, their circumstances were unique (their islands were isolated and easily defended, and the sword played a central role in Japanese culture), but so are ours today. Rather than assuming that population growth, environmental deterioration, arms races, and all the rest are "inevitable," we must make the opposite assumption—that the job of reversing those trends can be done.

Even the seemingly overwhelming problems of war and peace, we believe, could be solved by a conscious effort to change our ways of thinking about them. One substantial step could accompany a general effort to make people more aware of the kinds of comparisons the mind tends to make. One of the major barriers to disarmament agreements is the fear that the enemy will "cheat"—fail to dismantle systems it has agreed to relinquish or clandestinely build replacements. On the face of it, this concern is not unreasonable—no agreement could be so ironclad as to foreclose completely the possibility. The tendency of the old mind is to stick to the status quo: "We're safe now," it counsels, "why take a chance?"

But, of course, the old mind is not making the proper comparison. First of all, present safety is an illusion, created in part by the difficulty of continually imagining that those faraway missile fields and unseen submarines represent a danger infinitely more deadly than any enemy horde swarming over the horizon brandishing spears and clubs. To modify an old saying, "out of sight, out of old mind." Moreover, our feeling of safety is bolstered by history; despite the mounting arsenals, they haven't been used yet. We assume the preventative mechanisms of the past will continue to operate; we have the old-mind attitude that the future will be like the past.

A more realistic comparison, though, would be between our safety today and our safety several decades in the future if a comprehensive arms-reduction agreement were reached tomorrow. Presented with that choice, an American old-minded warrior is likely to say something such as, "We'll likely be dead or slaves in a couple of decades if we enter an arms-reduction agreement because, regardless of any system of verification, the Russians will find a way to cheat."

The proper comparison, in contrast, is a probabilistic one that recognizes that the future is unlikely to resemble the past and that we have some power to change that future. The American should ask, "Which gives us a greater chance of being alive and happy in a couple of decades—if we agree to start disarming now, with the best safeguards that can be invented, *or if the arms race continues?*"

That puts the whole thing in a different light. Because of technical developments in the delivery systems of nuclear weapons, especially "MIRVing" (the placing of multiple, independently targeted reentry vehicles on missiles), the arms race has already led to "crisis instability." Once launched, a MIRVed missile "multiplies" into three to ten or more bombs able to hit different targets. If two nations have equal numbers of ICBMs, one can attack all of the other's missiles by launching just a portion of its force. Two hundred missiles with ten warheads, each carry enough warheads to aim two at each of a thousand enemy missiles still in their silos.

That means that both American and Soviet military planners see great advantages to shooting first and, in times of crisis, will put pressure on the civilian heads of government to do just that. Should substantial antiballistic missile defense systems (such as "Star Wars") be deployed by either or both sides, that instability would greatly increase. Star Wars systems would be much more effective against a relatively small, uncoordinated return volley of missiles from a nation that had been attacked than against a massive, well-orchestrated surprise first strike. Deploying an antiballistic missile defense system of limited effectiveness is therefore all too easily interpreted by the enemy as implying an intention to attack *first*.

So the risks of a carefully planned, verified disarmament look very small indeed when compared with those of continuing an increasingly unstable arms race. At least theoretically, disarmament might eventually proceed to a rather stable end point, a world either lacking nuclear weapons or with just a few designed to provide a stable deterrent, with a system in place to prevent large numbers of such weapons from being produced again. It is difficult to hypothesize a stable end to the present arms race without reducing the stockpiles, so a new-minded comparison makes it clear that the only sane course for both the Americans and the Soviets is to agree on bilateral, mutually verifiable force reductions.

Fortunately, even though only a small amount of thought has gone into disarming compared with arming, some ingenious disarmament plans have been proposed. One of the most innovative is the "I cut, you choose" system, the essence of which is very simple. It is based on the principle sometimes employed when two children have to share a piece of cake. One child cuts it, the other chooses which of the two pieces it gets.

When dealing with nuclear arms, both sides would first agree on, say, a 10 percent cut in their overall nuclear arsenals. Each then lists all of its weapons and assigns a "military-value percentage" to each —the sum of those percentages to be 100. Each side is allowed to choose 10 percent of the other side's list of weapons to be dismantled. Each side is presumed not to care which of its weapons is selected, since it has already assigned them values so as to be indifferent to any selection, giving higher values to those it believes most enhance its security. Thus A can start B's disarmament by removing the weapons that A thinks are most threatening, and B can do the same with A's arsenal.

Such a system avoids the problems of disagreement over the value of a given weapon, a topic on which the two sides almost invariably disagree. For instance, the Soviets put a much higher value on Pershing II missiles than we did. They saw the Pershings as an extremely threatening first-strike weapon; we saw them as being much less important, since they were emplaced largely with political goals (reassuring NATO allies) in mind.

With pauses to reevaluate forces, the entire procedure could be repeated until, through a series of steps, substantial disarmament is achieved. Anxiety over cheating should be relieved since little could be gained by cheating at any one step, the costs of cheating (losing credibility, ending the process, or even having a war) would be high, and there would be plenty of time for verification. And the process would quickly reduce each side's perception of the other as being poised for a first strike, as those weapons each found most threatening would be the first to go.

We have given only the briefest outline of a possible program here, and, needless to say, many details would have to be hammered out if such a program were to be initiated. But you can see that innovative ideas are already available that could help humanity out of its nuclear dilemma, if only enough people began to change their minds. In the meantime, however, some new-minded Americans are acting on their own.

Such people have seen that the real problem isn't weapons, but the distrust and suspicion with which we and the Soviets have viewed each other for the last few generations. These people have attempted to penetrate the stereotypes and open genuine communication with Soviets as private citizens. Some, such as Armand Hammer, Norman Cousins, and Iowa farmer John Crystal, began their contacts in the Stalin era or soon after. More recently, contacts have begun to multiply, and ordinary Americans have visited the U.S.S.R. for exchanges of ideas on schooling or the arts or for joint activities such as bicycle tours or mountain climbing. Some of these "citizen diplomats" have played historically significant roles; some, such as young Samantha Smith, have focused public attention on the problem; others have just contributed to breaking down the communications and stereotype barriers between East and West. Soviet peace activists are now joining in. Little by little, partly due to their efforts, the Cold War is thawing out.

A new, younger, more globally oriented Soviet government is

now in place. As a result there might well be an opportunity to turn an enemy into, if not a friend, at least a mutually respected economic competitor. The reality that Americans and Russians have more in common with each other than with the peoples of many other parts of the globe may eventually guide superpower politics— and make the nuclear arms race obsolete.

There is a new understanding of the human mind, developed from modern brain research and studies of thought processes. The potential role of conscious evolution in overriding the defaults of the mind needs to be understood by everyone as easily as they now understand ordinary speech. The scientific knowledge that has helped to trigger our current difficulties has also produced an unparalleled amount of wisdom about how human beings perceive and understand the world. This understanding can allow people, for the first time, to alter many of their mind's default positions while permitting them to learn to live with other default positions.

What can be taught is, first, the awareness of the existence of these default positions, in much the same manner as history is taught. People can learn to observe their own tendency to overestimate the relevance and importance of single cases, their inability to shift modes of thought, and the problems they have with stereotypes and preferences for small-group processes. Most human beings can grow up examining the sources of the mistakes that they and society often make.

The time has come to think about it. The time has come for society to make an organized effort to train *all* minds to filter in, not filter out, the imperceptible but dangerous trends that now characterize the human environment. The default way of thought has to be overridden, especially in politics, for without overriding it, in the short run, to revise John Maynard Keynes, we are all dead. We believe that the framework of our lives, and especially of our schooling and scholarship, must change as well. It sounds like an impossible task, but it is not.

Indeed, some of the most well-regarded leaders of the Western world have moved along this path. Earlier we cited the experience of Robert McNamara, Secretary of Defense in the Kennedy administration, who was often vilified for his support of the Vietnam war. His soundness of judgment about United States–Soviet Union relations, however, was rarely appreciated in those days. He cites another example from the Cuban Missile crisis:

I should point to a second lesson that can be drawn from the Cuban experience. It is perhaps the most paradoxical tenet of the nuclear age. It was not enough that the United States was firmly deterred from initiating the use of nuclear weapons if the Soviets were uncertain of this fact. They were keenly aware of the seventeen-to-one advantage. It is probable that they feared the United States might try to use its numerical superiority. This Soviet insecurity put our country in great danger for one very simple reason: any indication that we were planning an attack would have placed severe pressures on Soviet leaders to launch a preemptive strike against us. If the Soviets had felt that a U.S. attack was imminent, they would have been tempted to move to destroy as large a portion of the American nuclear force as possible, rather than wait and allow its full strength of five thousand warheads to be launched against them. . . .

It is very much in the interest of both sides to move away from such extremely unstable situations. They can do so by reducing the perceptions of vulnerability. . . . This suggests that it is in the best interests of the United States to make its adversary feel more secure. Many argue precisely the opposite: it is important to keep the Soviet Union on the defensive and wary of American strength. But in the age of nuclear weapons, where one country holds the fate of another in its hands, old rules no longer apply. One story clearly illustrates this paradox.

In 1962 the columnist Stewart Alsop visited me in my Pentagon office. He had just learned, he said, that the CIA had evidence the Soviets were hardening their missile sites to make them more difficult to destroy. Wasn't I concerned? he asked. I said, "Stew, I never comment on information relating to the CIA. But let me say this: if the Soviets are hardening their missile sites, thank God." Alsop printed my views in the *Saturday Evening Post*. The Congress was outraged. Several congressmen literally asked for my resignation. What kind of Secretary of Defense, they asked, would be pleased that the Soviets were strengthening their forces?

My point was, of course, that the Soviets had only three hundred strategic warheads and their missiles and bombers were "soft," meaning they were vulnerable to attack. In a period of tension I wanted the Soviet leaders to have confidence that those forces would survive an American attack and would be capable of retaliating effectively. Then they would not feel a pressure to use them preemptively. I wanted to improve crisis stability.

Thinking of the security of one's enemy is not the sort of attitude we normally assume our military would have. Our caricatures would not allow it. But the "security" in this case is not a soft-headed weakness; rather it is directness—letting the Russians know exactly what we will do (and following it up when required) if they make a move that is stabilizing. Could we do more today to promote peace if we understood the mind's tendency to caricature? If we have three hundred times the missiles necessary to deter, what is the real cost, not the comparative cost, of beginning a graduated reduction? We need more thinking like McNamara's—now.

We close with one man, again, who seems to us to exemplify the transition between the eras. Dwight Eisenhower, for all of the hilarious malapropisms delivered at his press conferences, was, like Robert McNamara, a person who concluded through his own direct experience that he and others were living in a new world and had to change and change drastically. Would that we, among others who found his informal musings a bit scatterbrained, had not been blinded by his extemporaneous style. He wrote,

I have spent my life in the study of military strength as a deterrent to war, and in the character of military armaments necessary to win a war. The study of the first of these questions is still profitable, but we are rapidly getting to the point that no war can be won. War implies a contest; when you get to the point that contest is no longer involved and the outlook comes close to destruction of the enemy and suicide for ourselves —an outlook that neither side can ignore—then arguments as to the exact amount of available strength as compared to somebody else's are no longer the vital issues. When we get to the point, as we one day will, that both sides know that in any outbreak of general hostilities, regardless of the element of surprise, destruction will be both reciprocal and complete, possibly we will have sense enough to meet at the conference table with the understanding that the era of armaments has ended and the human race must conform its actions to this truth or die. The fullness of this potentiality has not yet been attained, and I do not, by any means, decry the need for strength. That strength must be spiritual, economic, and military. All three are important and they are not mutually exclusive. They are all part of and the product of the American genius, the American will. But already we have come to the point where safety cannot be assumed by arms alone. But I repeat that their usefulness becomes concentrated more and more in their characteristics as deterrents than as instruments with which to obtain victory over opponents as in 1945. In this regard, today we are further separated from the end of World War II than the beginning of the century was separated from the beginning of the sixteenth century.

—DWIGHT D. EISENHOWER, *letter of March 4, 1956*

This message now brings us full circle. Earlier in this book we described one of humanity's greatest technical triumphs, the intercontinental ballistic missile. And we end with a statement from a leader who, in the context of avoiding the use of such weapons, expresses a basic theme of our book, that the world is changing faster than people can adapt to it. Learning to live in such a transformed world is akin to learning to "fly blind" through clouds. A pilot must learn to trust the airplane's instruments in order to operate safely without being able to see the horizon. Our sensory system makes flying without visual references an impossible act without devices that give the pilot information on the attitude, altitude, and speed of the aircraft. The semicircular canals of the ear cannot differentiate between a steep climb and a steep turn, and in the clouds a pilot cannot see the real horizon to determine which is which. Unless the pilot trusts his or her artificial horizon, a crash is virtually certain. Learning to override gut feelings and trust the instruments is the critical first step in becoming an instrument-rated pilot.

Similarly we all must learn to depend on our "instruments" more than our gut feelings. Nuclear war can't really happen; cigarettes will give other people lung cancer, not me; there can't be a population problem because there is all that empty space out West; economic expansion can go on forever—all are gut feelings that go against what the "instruments" tell us.

Those instruments include careful analyses (especially statistical analysis) of ongoing trends that people must learn to weigh more heavily than superficial immediate reactions. We need also to incorporate into everyone's thought processes the findings of a diversity of scientific disciplines that make clear that other people and other societies have their own sets of limited truths and needs, not necessarily any "better" or "worse" than our own.

We need to make available to students in a straightforward way the conclusion by all the world's great religions (and by some social scientists) that people can be best seen as "one animal"—or all as brothers and sisters as it has previously been put. And we need to do much more than that; we need to produce a new kind of synthesis between the modern scientific understanding (which is different than it is often assumed to be) and the essence of religious or esoteric traditions (which is also different from that offered by many of the "religious").

Such new-mindedness could give an enormous boost to conservatism. After all, it is not conservative to destroy the riches of the earth for the sole benefit of a few people living in this generation. Nor is it conservative to build up armaments that, if used accidentally or purposefully, could annihilate civilization. It is not conservative to deny the full rights of large segments of society—people of the wrong color, sex, religion, or social class. Conservatives want to preserve society, a task that will now claim the cooperation of virtually everyone, cooperation that will not be forthcoming from those not permitted to participate in the fruits of success.

A new conservatism—true conservatism—would be dedicated to organizing a human society that can persist for millennia without degrading the life-support systems of its only home; that can avoid large-scale conflict; and that, we hope, can enjoy not only freedom from want but the political freedom that is necessary if the minds of all are to cooperate in maintaining society.

Our species is now at its most important turning point since the Agricultural Revolution. For the first time humanity has the knowledge to destroy itself quickly, and for the first time humanity also has the knowledge to take its own evolution into its hands and change now, change the way people comprehend and think. What we have tried to show is how humanity can change and where humanity can change. The rest is up to all of us. Can we learn to become conscious of the problems that face us collectively? Can humanity win through to a new conservatism and a better world? We think so.

If this book stimulates some more people to think about the roots of the human predicament, and how we might begin to adapt our society, then we will have accomplished our purpose. With luck, we will have started to change your mind.

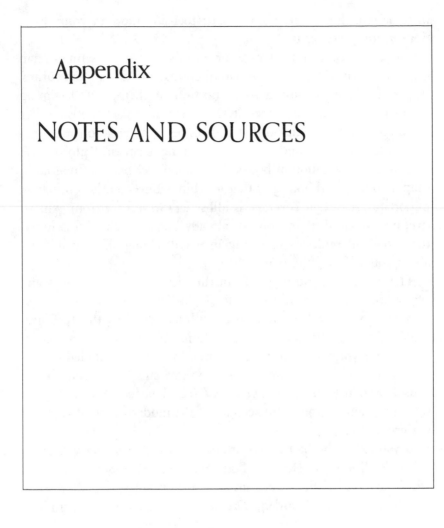

Appendix

NOTES AND SOURCES

PART OF BECOMING NEW-MINDED is becoming informed. It is not possible to change your way of thinking without having something to think about. This appendix serves three purposes: it gives you sources for many of the assertions we did not reference in the rest of the book, it expands on a few controversial points, and it provides a starting point for finding information, should you wish to start focusing more of your attention on long-term issues.

There are, of course, a gigantic number of sources on human origins, human history, the human dilemma, and the human future. A person can read only a small portion of them, but becoming familiar with a sample of this literature is essential if one is to alter the mind's natural focus so that it gives less emphasis to the immediate and parochial and more to the long term and global. We discuss here a selection of books that have either been influential in shaping our own thinking or that we think conveniently summarize important areas. Our coverage is idiosyncratic and far from exhaustive, but we think if you do not already know much of this literature, you will find that browsing in it will change how you think about yourself and the world.

The way the world works from the viewpoint of ecologists and evolutionists is summarized in Paul Ehrlich's *The Machinery of Nature* (Simon & Schuster, 1986), which discusses the technical rather than the political side of population biology in terms accessible to the layperson. If you are interested in a more detailed discussion of evolution than that found in Ehrlich's book, you should consult Richard Dawkins, *The Blind Watchmaker* (Norton, 1986), which contains a wonderful account of the modern view of Darwinian evolution.

Beyond that the best books are two texts: *Evolutionary Biology* (second edition) by Douglas Futuyma (Sinauer Associates, 1986), which focuses on the mechanisms of evolution; and Paul Ehrlich and Jonathan Roughgarden, *The Science of Ecology* (Macmillan, 1987), which includes much of modern evolutionary theory integrated with ecological thought and provides the technical background for understanding environmental problems. Futuyma's *Science on Trial* (Pantheon, 1983) is a simpler treatment designed to convince people that "scientific creationism" is neither science nor Christianity, but as Richard Leakey has said, "An insult to both."

Michael Ruse's *Darwinism Defended: A Guide to the Evolution Controversies* (Addison-Wesley, 1982) is also excellent in this regard. People unaware of their origins are out of touch with fundamental aspects of their humanity, which is why Ruse describes scientific creationism as "a betrayal of ourselves as human beings" (p. 327).

The physical aspects of human origins are summarized in Donald Johanson and Maitland Edey's vastly entertaining book *Lucy: The Beginnings of Mankind* (Simon & Schuster, 1981), which describes one of the most exciting fossil finds of the century in the context of the whole story of human evolution. Some paleontologists differ with the details of Johanson's views on human origins, but the sweep of the story is beautifully presented.

Perhaps the best exponent of evolution is Stephen Jay Gould, whose *Ever Since Darwin* (Norton, 1977) and *The Panda's Thumb* (Norton, 1980) should be part of everyone's basic education.

Some anthropologists doubt the binocular-vision-and-grasping-hands-for-tree-climbing view of primate anatomy; they think our ICBM-building capabilities had more complex roots. Anthropologist Matt Cartmill has argued (in *Science* 184[1974]:436) that living in the trees alone is unlikely to explain our close-set eyes and opposable thumbs. He thinks the existence of tree squirrels argues against the notions that such important characteristics evolved to keep our progenitors from falling out of trees on their heads.

Cartmill points out that tree squirrels are highly skilled arborealists with neither close-set eyes nor opposable thumbs, and that comparison of tree and ground squirrels shows no evidence of natural selection for eyes-front or independence of the thumbs in those that live in the trees. Squirrels have some binocular vision and can move their heads to help judge distance (from the different apparent motion of near and distant objects) and their claws tend to give them firm purchase, even on vertical tree trunks. And squirrels have never even started down the evolutionary road to the development of either heart transplants or nuclear weapons.

Cartmill looks to our ancestors' diet, instead of their jumping from branch to branch, to give them their start on that road. He points out that chameleons, certain small bush-dwelling marsupials, and tarsiers and their relatives all have grasping feet and differ in an important way from squirrels—rather than eating plant materials, they are all predators that hunt insects by sight and stealth. Our earliest primate ancestors, then, may have been selected for excellent binocular vision and fine hand-eye coordination because they spotted and grabbed the bugs that swarmed the trees and bushes of tropical forests. They, like cats, could judge the distance to an insect visually without having to move their head and thus alert their victim.

Like chameleons, they could maneuver through a fine tracery of twigs while maintaining a firm hold with grasping hands. And like small arboreal marsupials and tarsiers, they could use grasping hands to snatch up the insects they stalked and hold the squirming prey while it was devoured, while other hands held firmly onto the twigs. Thus not only did the hands acquire the grasping ability to keep our forebears from falling (something the squirrels do quite well with claws), but they gained great dexterity as well (far beyond the capacity of arboreal rodents). The fingers that are now on the violin bow and the button, in his view, first closed on bugs.

A balanced overview of human paleontology is presented in *A Field Guide to Early Man* by David Lambert and the Diagram Group (Facts on File, 1987). The book contains, among other things, a summary of brain development, evolution of prehuman primates, various versions of the human phylogenetic tree, and events up through the origin of cities. It also contains a good discussion of how fossils are formed, found, and interpreted. A more detailed description of human fossils, with many photographs of them, is contained in Michael Day, *Guide to Fossil Man,* 4th edition (University of Chicago Press, 1986). A more broad-brush approach to human evolution characterizes Bernard G. Campbell's *Humankind Emerging,* 4th edition (Little, Brown, 1985). It covers the gamut from human anatomy and genetics through human origins to modern society and is perhaps the best single source in this area.

The hominid fossils of 5 to 25 million years ago are known variously as *Dryopithecus, Ramapithecus,* and *Sivapithecus.* The most recent interpretation of these is that the latter two are related to the Asian orangutan, and *Dryopithecus* to the African branch of the hominoid family tree—chimps, gorillas, and us (Pilbeam, *Scientific American* 84[1984]).

An important book providing a new-minded look at the origins of our sexual behavior is Don Symons's *The Evolution of Human Sexuality* (Oxford University Press, 1978). He provides the beginnings for a contentious, but new-minded analysis of the real differences between the sexes. Also important to read is a recent collection of J. B. S. Haldane called *On Being the Right Size* (Oxford University Press, 1986). The great evolutionary biologist's essays, edited by Maynard Smith, allows the reader to begin to think like a biologist and look at common phenomena in a different way. Also see Brant Wenegrat's interesting *Sociobiology and Mental Disorder: A New View* (Addison-Wesley, 1984) for excellent source material for the ideas, drawn from evolutionary biology, that are now influencing psychology and psychotherapy.

The seminal work on sociobiology is Edward Wilson's book of that name. *Sociobiology: The New Synthesis* (Harvard University Press, 1975) was front-page news when it first appeared and still excites admiration and controversy. The book brings together an amazing amount of knowledge and does synthesize them admirably.

Stella Chess and Alexander Thomas's *Know Your Child* (Basic Books, 1987) is an important contribution to child rearing in that it presents the modern evidence on the inheritance of temperament and its importance in childhood. Jerome Kagan's *The Nature of the Child* (Basic Books, 1985), does too.

The origins of the human spirit are explored in John Pfeiffer, *The Creative Explosion: An Inquiry into the Origins of Art and Religion* (Harper & Row, 1982). The creativity of our ice-age ancestors can be appreciated emotionally by perusing the beautifully illustrated *Dark Caves, Bright Visions* by Randall White (Norton, 1986). Looking at the art and artifacts of our ancestors some 35,000 years ago provides evidence that there has been relatively little physical evolution of the human brain in the intervening 1400 generations.

The beginnings of the era of a human-shaped world are outlined in two richly illustrated books, John Gowlett, *Ascent to Civilization: The Archaeology of Early Man* (Knopf, 1984) and Ruth Whitehouse and John Wilkins, *The Making of Civilization: History Discovered Through Archaeology* (Knopf, 1986). The focus of the former is on the steps leading to civilization, the latter on early civilizations. More of the world we made can be explored in Ronald Clark, *The Works of Man: A History of Invention and Engineering from the Pyramids to the Space Shuttle* (Viking, 1985).

On the shaping of the modern world from a personal historical point of view, there are a spectacular set of books, Fernand Braudel's "Civilization and Capitalism Fifteenth to Eighteenth Century" series (Harper & Row, 1981–3). Braudel presents the origins of our daily lives in detail, the beginnings of the cities we live in, the food we eat, the way we dress—all as they actually developed during the beginnings of the changed world. This background is essential for an understanding of how we've created our surroundings.

A huge collection of books is available on issues relating to the nuclear arms race, military thinking, and so on. The Stockholm International Peace Research Institute produces an annual yearbook entitled *World Armaments and Disarmament: The SIPRI Yearbook* (Oelgeschlager, Gunn and Hain). It gives the most recent information on the deployment of weapon systems, military expenditures, systems under development, arms trade, and so on, and is a good source if you are *really* interested in military issues. Another one is the International Institute for Strategic Studies, *The Military Balance,* which is another annual production, this one more heavily weighted toward conventional forces than the *SIPRI Yearbook* and giving less detailed coverage of nuclear forces. Some grasp of the price we pay for useless and dangerous megatonnage can be found in Ruth Leger Sivard, *World Military and Social Expenditures, 1985* (World Priorities, Washington, D.C., 1985).

A fascinating overview of how the military-industrial complex operates in many cases to reduce military capability while wasting money is James Fallow's *National Defense* (Random House, 1981). If you want to understand the development of current nuclear strategy, see Lawrence Freedman's *The Evolution of Nuclear Strategy* (St. Martin's Press, 1981). If you would like to understand how close we are to blowing up the world, Dan Ford's *The Button* (Simon & Schuster, 1985) will scare the pants off you. He discusses the possibility of a U.S. first strike and concludes that it is primarily civilians that are sufficiently frightened of nuclear return fire to be deterred, but that the military's established outlook in the nuclear age is different. Ford states, "As George Orwell wrote, 'Traditions are not killed by facts,' and there is, in any event, enough narrow military logic behind the existing first-strike plans that it is unlikely they will ever be abandoned so long as weapons fit for this purpose are in military hands."

While we don't agree with Ford that the configuration of the American command and control system indicates the United States is planning a first strike on the Soviet Union, we believe it could certainly make the paranoid Soviets think that—which could be just as catastrophic. More detailed on this topic is Paul Bracken, *The Command and Control of Nuclear Forces* (Yale University Press, 1983). The history of plans for the use of those forces can be found in Peter Pringle and William Arkin, *S.I.O.P.—The Secret U.S. Plan for Nuclear War* (Norton, 1983). Some of the things that might be done to reduce the chance that a confrontation will lead to Armageddon are discussed in Desmond Ball, et al., *Crisis Stability and Nuclear War* (American Academy of Arts and Sciences and Cornell University Peace Studies Program, Ithaca, N.Y., 1987). Among other things, it urges expeditious movement to single-warhead ballistic missiles as a move away from the inherently destabilizing situation in which one missile with many warheads can threaten many missiles on the other side, adding to the pressure to "shoot first."

Descriptions of nuclear weapons systems can be found in Thomas B. Cochran, William M. Arkin, and Milton M. Hoenig, *Nuclear Weapons Data Book, Vol. I, U.S. Nuclear Forces and Capabilities* (Ballinger, 1984), which is loaded with pictures and statistics. Details of the manufacture of those weapons are given by Cochran, Arkin, Robert S. Norris, and Hoenig in the second volume of the series, *U.S. Nuclear Warhead Production* (Ballinger, 1987). If you want to read something about the impact of the use of those systems, some good sources are the report of the Greater London Area War Risk Study Commission (GLARWARS), *London Under Attack* by Robin Clarke (Basil Blackwell, 1986); the more technical Samuel Glasstone and Philip Dolan, *The Effects of Nuclear Weapons* (U.S. Government Printing Office, Washington, D.C., 1977); and the Institute of Medicine/National Academy of Sciences, *The Medical Implications of Nuclear War* (National Academy Press, 1986). In the introduction to the medical book, Lewis Thomas writes of the consequences of leaving the problem of nuclear war to others: "first thing you know some crafty statesman or some other crafty unbalanced military personage, one side or the other, is going to do something wrong, say something wrong, drop something, misread some printout, and there will go 30,000 years of trying since Lascaux right up to Bach and beyond into this benighted century—all civilization gone without a trace. Not even a thin layer of fossils left of us, no trace, no memory" (p. xi).

The original work on "nuclear winter" effects—the damage that will be done to environmental systems by atmospheric changes following a large-scale nuclear war—is covered in Paul Ehrlich, Carl Sagan, Donald Kennedy, and Walter Orr Roberts, *The Cold and the Dark: The World After Nuclear War* (Norton, 1984). Subsequent studies have suggested that temperature declines and obscuration of the sun are not likely to be as severe as indicated in the first computer models. They would still, however, in combination with other impacts on ecosystems, entrain an unprecedented biological catastrophe and probably kill as many people or more (largely through starvation) than the immediate effects of the attack. Recent pooh-poohing of nuclear-winter effects primarily reflect on the old-mindedness of commentators unfamiliar with basic biology.

An excellent collection of essays on various aspects of nuclear war is Abner Cohen and Stephen Lee (editors), *Nuclear Weapons and the Future of Humanity* (Rowman and Allenhead, 1986). See especially John Holdren's outstanding article "The Dynamics of the Nuclear Arms Race: History, Status, Prospects." To get a well-done, but deeply old-mind view of the nuclear situation, read the Harvard Nuclear Study Group's *Living with Nuclear Weapons* (Harvard University Press, 1983). The inability of this otherwise well-informed group to project trends is truly impressive.

Those who are frightened of the prospect of a Soviet invasion of Western Europe if the U.S. "nuclear umbrella" is lowered are advised to refer to Andrew Cockburn's readable *The Threat: Inside the Soviet Military Machine* (Random House, 1983) or the statistics-loaded *The Myth of Soviet Military Supremacy* by Tom Gervasi (Harper & Row, 1986). Cockburn comments on the Soviet's attempts to emulate America's bankrupt weapons acquisition policies: "Soviet adherence to the military fashions set in America has ensured that the Soviets too are following policies that steadily diminish the actual combat performance of their forces" (p. 282). He shows how NATO consistently overstates the capabilities of Soviet conventional forces. Victor Suvorov (a pen name) provides a Russian view of the Soviet military in *Inside the Soviet Army* (Macmillan, 1982). He claims that in a major conventional war Soviet troops would defect to the West by the millions, given the opportunity.

The development of the war system itself is described in Richard J. Barnett's *Roots of War* (Atheneum/Pelican, 1972–73), and Nazli Choucri and Robert C. North's *Nations in Conflict* (W. H. Freeman, 1975), the latter is especially interesting because it deals with the connection between resource demands and international conflict. An older, but still valuable source on how minds from different cultures look at the nuclear arms situation can be found in Jerome Frank's *Sanity and Survival: Psychological Aspects of War and Peace* (Random House, 1967). Another classic is Philip Green, *Deadly Logic: The Theory of Nuclear Deterrence* (Ohio State University Press, 1966). Green dissects the basic premise of deterrence: that we can count on national leaders to make sane decisions in times of stress and conflict. Green quotes Karl Deutsch, "The theory of deterrence . . . first proposes that we should frustrate our opponents by frightening them very badly and that we should then rely on their cool-headed rationality for our survival" (p. 144).

If you are interested in the details of why Star Wars is a terrible idea, John P. Holdren and Joseph Rotblat, *Strategic Defenses: Technological Aspects, Military and Political Applications* (Macmillan, 1987) provides a superb analysis. Also impressive on this topic is Sidney D. Drell, Philip J. Farley, and David Holloway, *The Reagan Strategic Defense Initiative: A Technical, Political, and Arms Control Assessment* (Ballinger, 1985). Plans for moving international relations from a system of threats to a network of positive relationships are outlined in the essays in Don Carlson and Craig Comstock, *Securing Our Planet* (Jeremy Tarcher, 1986). See especially Stephen Salter's chapter "I Cut, You Choose."

If you're interested in how arms-control negotiations have actually gone, there is Strobe Talbott's fascinating account of them in *Deadly Gambits* (Knopf, 1984). The most up-to-date coverage on negotiations between Ronald Reagan and Mikhail Gorbachev can be found in Michael Mandelbaum and Strobe Talbot, *Reagan and Gorbachev* (Vintage, 1987). For things that individuals can do about superpower relations, we recommend Gale Warner and Michael Schuman, *Citizen Diplomats* (Continuum, 1986), which describes the experiences of Americans who have gone on their own to learn about the Soviet Union.

For a fine journalist's view of Soviet society, see Hedrick Smith, *The Russians.* New-minded people will want to know all they can about our main competition. Those who want to understand the fine points of the relationship between the two superpowers should consult Raymond L. Garthoff, *Détente and Confrontation: American-Soviet Relations from Nixon to Reagan* (Brookings, Washington, D.C., 1985).

If you are interested in the dark side of the history of Soviet Russia, you should read Robert Conquest, *The Harvest of Sorrow* (Oxford University Press, 1986). It is a detailed history of one of the greatest social tragedies of our century—the collectivization by terror of the Soviet peasantry and the famine that it produced. Useful insights into military ethics are discussed in Michael Walzer, *Just and Unjust Wars: A Moral Argument with Historical Illustrations* (Basic Books, 1977). The hopeful view that military technology need not take on a life of its own is detailed in Noel Perrin, *Giving*

Up the Gun: Japan's Reversion to the Sword, 1543–1879 (Shambhala, 1980).

The standard reference on environmental problems is Paul Ehrlich, Anne Ehrlich, and John Holdren, *Ecoscience: Population, Resources, Environment* (Freeman and Co., 1977). Over one thousand pages long and with some three thousand references, it remains very useful, although it is now out of date in some details. The basic form of our environmental dilemma has not changed in the decade since it appeared. The Ehrlichs' *Earth* (Franklin Watts, 1987) is a photographically illustrated update of *Ecoscience*, designed for the general reader.

Note that our calculations in Chapter 2 of the increase in human numbers and impact were done as follows. First, we assumed that humanity became upright some 4 to 5 million years ago (around the time of the first australopithecines) and that the line then consisted of fifty thousand people—a conservative figure that could easily be too large by an order of magnitude or more. Accepting that figure means that today's population of some 5 billion is 100,000 times as large.

Second, we employed commercial energy use as a measure of environmental impact. Again *very* conservatively we assume that australopithecines had available to them commercial energy equivalent to that of the poorest people today, the equivalent of the energy in about forty pounds of coal annually. The average person in the 1980s uses the energy equivalent of about four thousand pounds of coal annually, 100 times as much. The product (100,000 × 100) gives us the 10-millionfold figure. Less conservatively we could have assumed that our earliest upright ancestors were a group of fifty "protohumans" that, like all nonhuman animals, used no energy outside of that obtained from their food. By assigning each such ancestor an arbitrarily inflated environmental impact of 1 pound of coal equivalent annually, we arrive at an estimated increase in impact of 400 billionfold.

Current information on the state of the environment can be found in the excellent annual "State of the World" series, edited by Lester R. Brown and his colleagues at the Worldwatch Institute and published by W. W. Norton. It deals with a variety of topics, such as African famines, global food production, sustainable agriculture, energy policies, economics, population growth, and so on. Abundant data on the size and growth of the human population can be found in the *Demographic Yearbook,* published annually by the United Nations. The most accessible source of basic information on population and related topics is the annual *World Population Data Sheet* and *Population Bulletin,* both issued by the Population Reference Bureau, Suite 800, 777 Fourteenth Street, NW, Washington, D.C. 20005. The intricacies of one of the most difficult and ethically complex demographic problems are explored in Paul and Anne Ehrlich, *The Golden Door: International Migration, Mexico, and the United States* (Ballantine, 1979).

Demographic data along with extensive statistics on agriculture, manufacturing, finance, education, and the like are in the United Nations' annual *Statistical Yearbook.* More extensive statistics on agricultural and fisheries production are published annually in the *Production Yearbook* and *Fisheries Yearbook* by the United Nations Food and Agriculture Organization (FAO) in Rome. The FAO also brings out the most informative annual *State of Food and Agriculture.* Economic aspects of development are covered in the World Bank's annual *World Development Report* (Oxford University Press, New York).

An overview of how the earth's environmental systems work and what is happening to them is presented in Norman Myers's fine *Gaia: An Atlas of Planet Management* (Anchor/Doubleday, 1984). By far the best discussion of climate and human affairs can be found in Stephen H. Schneider and Randi Londer, *The Coevolution of Climate and Life* (Sierra Club Books, 1984). Many of the most serious long-term problems faced by humanity are climatic or tied into climate: carbon dioxide increase, ozone depletion, drought in the Sahel, acid precipitation, tropical deforestation, and so on. This book puts them into understandable perspective.

Another of the most serious problems of humanity living on capital is discussed in Paul and Anne Ehrlich's *Extinction: The Causes and Consequences of the Disappearance of Species* (Random

House, 1981). See especially the discussion of the interruption of ecosystem services. Norman Myers's *Sinking Ark* (Pergamon Press, 1979) gives a fine account of the economic values that humanity is losing as life-forms disappear from the planet. The scientific response to the growing extinction crisis started with the volume edited by Michael Soulé and Bruce Wilcox, *Conservation Biology: An Evolutionary-Ecological Perspective* (Sinauer Associates, Sunderland, Mass., 1980). The biology, ethics, philosophy and economics of endangered organisms are examined in the volume edited by Bryan G. Norton, *The Preservation of Species* (Princeton University Press, 1986). Some of the philosophy is hard going, but worth it for the insights provided.

The critical issues at the environment-economics interface are dealt with in Herman Daly, *Steady-state Economics: The Economics of Biophysical Equilibrium and Moral Growth* (W. H. Freeman, 1977) and in the volume he edited, *Economics, Ecology, and Ethics: Essays Toward a Steady-state Economy* (W. H. Freeman, 1980).

Early attitudes toward the environment are described in J. D. Hughes, *Ecology in Ancient Civilizations* (University of New Mexico Press, 1975). A classic book by one of the most new-minded of modern scientists is the late Harrison Brown's *The Challenge of Man's Future* (Viking, 1954). Brown perceptively analyzed the interactions between population, resources, and technology, anticipating many of the concerns that ecologists and others brought to the forefront fifteen years later. A volume of essays by people who provided early warning of humanity's building population-resource-environment problems is Paul Ehrlich and John Holdren, *The Cassandra Conference: Resources and the Human Predicament* (Texas A & M University Press, 1988). A volume of essays giving a biologist's views on the human predicament—views that will start you thinking, whether or not you agree with the essay's conclusions—is Garrett Hardin, *Filters Against Folly* (Viking, 1985). Another fine collection, this one by a resource geographer, is Daniel B. Luten, *Progress Against Growth* (Guilford Press, 1986).

One excellent source that can guide you toward developing a

new-minded approach to analyzing environmental problems is John Harte, *Consider a Spherical Cow: A Course in Environmental Problem Solving* (William Kaufmann, 1985). Don't let the math deter you—many of the exercises require only arithmetic and a novel approach.

All well-informed analysts realize that overpopulation is a central factor in the human predicament. But old minds have an especially difficult time realizing that the message, inculcated by 4 billion years of biological evolution and millions of years of cultural evolution, that more people is better, no longer holds. There seems to be a desperate search among some to find some way of not facing the population situation, to find some way of arguing that population growth is still desirable.

A recent example of this is a book by journalist Ben J. Wattenberg, *The Birth Dearth* (Pharos Books, 1987), a volume that combines utter neglect of how the physical-biological world works with the misuse of statistics to urge larger families on Americans. In a nation that properly tolerates lunatic-fringe viewpoints, such works deserve to see print; but particularly instructive was the number of reviewers, often writing in prestigious journals, who were unable to see that the book could serve as a text on how *not* to analyze difficult problems.

It's not just that the book does not consider the environmental and resource components of overpopulation; it is flawed even when dealing with relatively simple demographic issues. Wattenberg, for instance, makes much of the aging of the American population, an *inevitable* consequence of the slowing of population growth. He focuses on the increase in economically dependent old people, not on the fact that more and more old people are remaining economically active, not on the much larger decrease in numbers of economically dependent young people, and not on the decline in crime rates that can be expected in an aging population. Above all, he does not explain that there is no way that aging of the population can be avoided eventually, except to keep the population growing *forever.* Presumably Wattenberg thinks either that that is possible or that any problems of dealing with an aging population should be passed on to be solved by future generations in a much more polluted, resource-short world.

In Wattenberg's defense we must note that many of the population notions he espouses are part and parcel of the view of standard economists, recently championed by one professor of mail-order marketing. This simply indicates that John Maynard Keynes underestimated the number of ears defunct economists whisper in.

For a controversial look at our inability to make projections into the future, see Charles Murray, *Losing Ground: American Social Policy 1950–1980.* This book claims that programs started in the 1960s to help the poor often had exactly the opposite effect. It became a bible of the Reagan administration and deserves thoughtful consideration by all those concerned with improving the lot of our population. It also contains excellent examples of how the old mind often defeats careful analysis in dealing with these problems. For an in-depth look at Ronald Reagan, see *Reagan's America: Innocents at Home* by Garry Wills (Doubleday, 1987). Wills shows how Reagan plays to some of the deepest needs of the American people.

Thomas McKeown offers the most thorough analysis of the reasons for the remarkable improvements in health in the past few centuries. He argues that the declines in infectious-disease mortality for the most part occurred before the introduction of specific medical interventions and are better explained by improvements in nutrition, sanitation, and behavior. For example, see Thomas McKeown: *The Role of Medicine: Dream, Mirage or Nemesis?* (Princeton, University Press, 1982). For a critique of the reductionism of biomedicine and argument for a broader view of the determinants of health and disease, see George Engel, "The Need for a New Medical Model: A Challenge for Biomedicine," *Science* 196 (1977): 129–36. Probably the best standard works are René Dubos, *Man Adapting* (Yale University Press, 1965) and *Mirage of Health* (Doubleday, 1959).

In *Persuasion and Healing,* (Johns Hopkins Press, 1973) Jerome Frank investigates such diverse therapeutic approaches as shamanism, faith healing, religious revivalism, placebo effect, and the modern psychotherapies. He finds some striking commonalities, including the ability of the healer to mobilize expectant faith, restore morale, and alter the beliefs of the patient. For a discussion of how superficial characteristics are linked to imaginary racial differences, see Paul Ehrlich and Shirley Feldman, *The Race Bomb* (Quadrangle, 1977).

Robert Ornstein, Richard Thompson, and David Macaulay, in *The Amazing Brain* (Houghton Mifflin, 1984), describe in drawings how the brain was "built" and the functional architecture of the cortex. It includes a description of the brain museum referred to in Chapter 10.

Stanley Coren, Clare Porac, and Edward Ward's *Sensation and Perception* (Academic Press,) is the best textbook on the sensory processing of the mind, while Irwin Rock's *Perception* (Scientific American, 1985) is a good treatment of perception as traditionally understood, well-illustrated and compelling. Carol Michaels and Carol Carello's *Direct Perception* (Prentice-Hall, 1981) is the most recent outline of the emerging ecological viewpoint in perception. Robert Ornstein's *The Psychology of Consciousness* (Penguin Books,) attempts to bring together much of the diverse literature on consciousness.

Everyone should have some familiarity with Idries Shah's books, since Shah has been able to make the essential contributions of spiritual thought available to a modern Western audience. He uses traditional stories that, if read over and over again, begin to change the patterns of thinking. Indeed a study of Robert Ornstein's showed that reading these stories stimulates the right hemisphere of the brain. Recommended are *Seeker After Truth* (Harper & Row, 1982), *Tales of the Dervishes* (E. P. Dutton, 1972), and *The Exploits and Subtleties of Mulla Nasrudin* (Octagon Press, 1985) for the beginnings of a short course on changing your mind.

For a course on judgment, read Michael Arkes and Kenneth Hammond's *Judgment and Decision Making* (Cambridge University Press, 1986) for an up-to-date summary of research in the field with articles on rationality, expert judgment, decisions in clinical practice, and the like.

Most seminal in this area is the collection edited by Daniel Kahneman, Paul Slovic, and Amos Tversky, called *Judgment Under Uncertainty* (Cambridge University Press, 1982). A compilation of much of the classic work on how we use "heuristics" in judgment, how we make mistakes, and the nature of the mental system that underlies these processes. Technical, but interesting and worthwhile.

Richard Nisbett and Lee Ross's book *Human Inference: Strategies and Shortcomings of Social Judgment* (Prentice-Hall, 1981) gathers together many of the mistakes we make in judging the world. For instance, they give great examples of how vivid information is very influential in judgment. The tendency to disregard statistical information and to overemphasize vivid examples extends even to some of society's most important decision makers. Nisbett and Ross describe an acquaintance of theirs

who often testifies at congressional committees on behalf of the Environmental Protection Agency. . . . She reported that the bane of her professional existence is the frequency with which she reports test data such as EPA mileage estimates based on samples of ten or more cars, only to be contradicted by a congressman who retorts with information about a single case: "What do you mean, the Blatzmobile gets twenty miles per gallon on the road?" he say. "My neighbor has one, and he only gets fifteen." His fellow legislators then usually respond as if matters were at a stand-off—one EPA estimate versus one colleague's estimate obtained from his neighbor.

Robert Cialdini's *Influence* (Scott, Foresman, 1984) is an excellent book about how social caricatures *influence* our decisions; it is well worth reading and important. Elaine Hatfield and Susan Sprecher, in their *Mirror, Mirror: The Importance of Looks in Everyday Life* (State University of New York Press, 1986), show how overwhelming surface appearance is.

Feuerstein's work is summarized in *Instrumental Enrichment* (University Park Press, 1980). Other views of the multiple mental processes within people are found in Howard Gardner's *Frames of Mind* (Basic Books, 1984) and Robert Ornstein's *Multimind.*

(Houghton Mifflin, 1986). Also see Sandra Scarr's *Race, Social Class, and Individual Differences in IQ* (Lawrence Erlbaum, 1982) for an overview and presentation of the genetic evidence for the inheritance of some individual differences. Daniel Goleman's *Vital Lies, Simple Truths* (Simon & Schuster, 1985) is a popular and well-thought-out book about how emotions and the nervous system by their design deny feelings.

Finally Allan Bloom's *The Closing of the American Mind* (Simon & Schuster, 1987) and E. D. Hirsch's *Cultural Literacy* (Houghton Mifflin, 1987) decry the current state of American education. Their prescription, if we can lump the two books together, is to have students learn more about the traditional knowledge base of our culture. We agree, as far as they go, that our students today lack much of the basic knowledge of our culture. But we are also worried, because it is not clear to us that very much of our "historical culture" is truly prologue to today. Learning about the past—the knowledge, the ideas, the concerns—is useful only insofar as the past perseveres into the present.

Note: We have made many suggestions for possible changes in our and others' societies, but we are all too aware of the difficulty of making these changes. For instance, our analysis about trying to modernize the way Africans farm may well prove to have many complexities and difficulties. For instance, the Masai herders live on the East African plains. They believe that God gave them their cattle to look after, so for centuries they have lived a seminomadic pastoral life and have structured their society around the need to maintain the herds of cattle put in their trust. They separate all males into three distinct groups based on age. Each male lives and works with his peers, first as a herder, then as a warrior, and lastly as an elder when he will provide leadership for the group, making its important decisions.

Male bonding is important for the maintenance of these groups, and boys are separated from their families between the ages of six and eight. They live together as herdsmen of the tribe, looking after the cows, often traveling on foot more than twenty miles a day in

search for water. "In all of their activities there is an air of unspo-
ken camaraderie and cooperation that will last a lifetime."

At the ages of twelve to fourteen the group will be circumcised
and become warriors, or *moran,* whose duties are to protect their
people and camp, competing in ritualized battles with the *moran* of
a neighboring camp. At this stage they live apart in *opuu,* or hidden
training camps. There they do everything together, including domestic work, for a period of seven years. Thus, in a society where
women's mortality rate is probably high, the women are preserved
for the elders in the camp. The warriors are magnificent, tall and
graceful, ornamented with braided hair—a mark of distinction and
bravery for the *moran* alone. When they are ready and have been
purified by drinking the blood of a cow, they will become elders,
and their mothers will shave their heads: a rite of passage that
symbolizes their new status in the tribe and further reinforces the
group. And these are only a few of the elements connected with
cattle herding!

Index

287

ROBERT ORNSTEIN is president of the Institute for the Study of Human Knowledge. He teaches at the University of California Medical Center in San Francisco, and at Stanford University. He has done extensive research on the human brain and is the author of *The Psychology of Consciousness* and *Multimind*, and coauthor of *The Amazing Brain* and *The Healing Brain*, among many other books.

PAUL EHRLICH is Professor of Biological Sciences and Bing Professor of Population Studies at Stanford University. His previous books include *The Machinery of Nature, Earth*, and *Science of Ecology*.